filling the glass

The Skeptic's Guide to Positive Thinking in
BUSINESS

Barry Maher

DEARBORN™
TRADE
A **Kaplan Professional** Company

This publication is designed to provide accurate and authoritative information in regard to the subject matter covered. It is sold with the understanding that the publisher is not engaged in rendering legal, accounting, or other professional service. If legal advice or other expert assistance is required, the services of a competent professional person should be sought.

Senior Acquisitions Editor: Jean Iversen Cook
Senior Managing Editor: Jack Kiburz
Interior Design: Lucy Jenkins
Cover Design: Design Alliance, Inc.
Typesetting: Elizabeth Pitts

Published by Dearborn Trade, a Kaplan Professional Company

Printed in the United States of America

01 02 03 10 9 8 7 6 5 4 3 2 1

Library of Congress Cataloging-in-Publication Data

Maher, Barry.
  Filling the glass : the skeptic's guide to positive thinking in business / Barry Maher.
      p.   cm.
  ISBN 0-7931-3865-5
  1. Success in business.   I. Title.
  HF5386 .M246   2001
  650.1—dc21

                                        00-011147

Dearborn Trade books are available at special quantity discounts to use as premiums and sales promotions, or for use in corporate training programs. For more information, please call the Special Sales Manager at 800-621-9621, ext. 4514, or write to Dearborn Trade, 155 North Wacker Drive, Chicago, IL 60606-1719.

D e d i c a t i o n

To Jeanne Maher, who always fills my glass—
though I stay away from her coffee.

Contents

Acknowledgments

More people have helped create this book than I can possibly thank. But let me start with those who have shared their observations and their stories with me over the years, sometimes even at risk to their careers.

I'd also have to thank Andrew Stuart and Frank Weimann of the Literary Group International. I wasn't planning on doing another book when Frank first contacted me. (So if you hate *Filling the Glass,* he was the first mover.) And Andrew was not only instrumental in developing the concept and the proposal, but also fought for the book far above and beyond the call of duty. If you're a best-selling author looking for a skilled, dedicated, loyal, and responsive agent, call Andrew.

As temperamental as I am, you'd think I'd be a lot more talented. Jean Iversen, my editor at Dearborn, has put up with me anyway. This book would not exist without her. I hope it's successful enough to make Dearborn appreciate her judgment and her talents. I'd like to thank the rest of the Dearborn team as well.

And if you have a great filling-the-glass story you'd like to share, contact me:

Barry Maher
P.O. Box 2126
Santa Barbara, CA 93120
barrymaher@aol.com

CHAPTER 1

To Build a
Better Buzzword

Ron Campbell tested high in intelligence and even higher in sales skills. His positive, high-energy outlook impressed the interviewers at Industrial Solutions, and both his former employers raved about his ambition and his honesty. Bright, talented, upbeat, ambitious, and ethical—those were the qualities that won Ron his dream job. And those were the qualities that caused him to quit in disgust less than a year later.

I met Ron while I was consulting with Industrial Solutions, immediately after he'd been hired. Twenty-eight years old, he'd moved from a $33,000 per year sales rep position with a mom-and-pop operation to a professional sales career with a Fortune 500 giant, where average first-year earnings were $67,000. And, someone with Ron's potential could make well over $100,000. Then, there were the company car, expenses, and a benefits package tempting enough to make me or anyone else question the joys of self-employment. As a result, Ron's infectious grin became a near-permanent fixture on his face.

When I arrived each morning at 7:30 AM, he was already in the training room, studying hard. When I left, sometimes as late as 7:30 or 8:00 in the evening, he'd still be around, usually picking the brain of anyone who had anything to teach him. In his second month on the job, the division manager asked him to deliver a motivational presentation at a key sales meeting. Even the veterans were impressed.

I figured he'd be a memory in 18 months. Cynicism was practically a job requirement at Industrial Solutions. I'd seen too many of those who should have become the best and the brightest crushed by the realities of selling for such a demanding company. Ron seemed particularly vulnerable.

The day I finished my contract with the company, Ron volunteered to drive me to the airport; he wanted a chance to pick *my* brain. I gave him my card.

"Everyone around here has been raving about your potential," I said. "But if things ever get too rough, please give me a call before you do anything that can't be undone."

He thanked me, but assured me that he considered this job the chance of a lifetime. "I'm lashing myself to the saddle on this bronco," he said, reminding me that while Ron was from New Jersey, his sales manager was from Texas. "It can buck, it can even bite, but there's no way it's going to throw me."

The call came eight months later. He told me he was quitting the next day.

"Their prices are just too high," he explained. "I just can't sell their machines."

"Ron, you can sell anything you choose to sell."

"I can't sell this stuff. Not in amounts large enough to meet their ridiculous quotas."

"How many of the others are making their quotas?"

"Some of them. Most of them, I suppose. But the company puts so much pressure on the reps to make their numbers, who knows what they're telling the customers? I sell clean, and I don't sell enough. And I don't feel good about what I do sell. I get prospects to trust me, then use that trust to talk them into buying something they wouldn't have bought on their own. That's what selling is all about—and that may be fine if you've got the best product in the marketplace . . ." His voice trailed off.

"But," I said, finishing the thought, "not everybody can have the best product in the marketplace."

"That's the problem."

"That *is* a problem, Ron. But aren't you the guy that told a division meeting that in Chinese the word for *problem* is the same as the word for *opportunity?*"

"*Crisis.* The word for *crisis* is the same as the word for *opportunity.*"

"You're quitting your job tomorrow, Ron—the job you told me was your chance of a lifetime. If this isn't a crisis, it will certainly do until one arrives."

"Which means?"

"Let me tell you about filling the glass . . ."

Norma Landry was on the side of the angels; an administrator in a small religious denomination, and anything but a salesperson.

"I couldn't sell ice water in Hell," Norma told me when she called my office. "Neither could most of our ministers. That's why the bishop wanted to book you for our yearly colloquium—to *edify* them with your sales workshop." Her tone made it clear that she did not approve of this particular brand of edification.

"I've heard it said that Jesus was a master salesman," I tried, filching from some televangelist I'd stumbled across while channel-surfing. I always check out the televangelists. As a professional speaker, I'm impressed by their fervor. As a bald guy, I'm amazed by their hair.

"So's Satan."

"Salespeople do cover a broad spectrum," I admitted.

But Norma's problem wasn't really with salespeople or even balding consultants. Her problem was with her new bishop.

"Suddenly, everything is measured in money," she confided to me when I arrived on the day before my workshop. "And I'm the one who's supposed to do the measuring. I'm constantly dunning the ministers to improve their collections, and then improve upon the improvement. That's hardly what I took this job to do. The old bishop measured our success in souls."

She handed me a sheet of paper.

"What's this?" I asked.

"I'm thinking of inserting it into the bishop's speech welcoming the ministers tonight."

I read:

Please inform your parishioners that—while our churches have minimal financial needs that must be met—God, himself, does not need their money. I spoke to him this morning, and he says that one of the best parts about being God is that you don't have to rely on contributions to do whatever it is you want done. He mentioned the creation of the universe with virtually no capital expenditure. And he asked me to tell all those who've been so nice as to be collecting money for him for so long that it might be more fitting for them to be *giving* money to those they keep saying they're trying to help, rather than taking money from them. He'd like this to start immediately. Otherwise he's coming for his money. And it had better be all there.

I looked up smiling, but Norma didn't smile back. Rather than serving as a release, sharing the joke seemed to make her angrier.

"Norma," I asked, "why don't you come to my workshop tomorrow?"

"Why?"

Why indeed? Ron Campbell was a salesperson, so it's probably not surprising that a person like myself, who started out as a sales consultant, could help him deal with his crisis. I don't know if the word for *crisis* really is the same as the word for *opportunity* in Chinese. People keep telling me it is. They also keep telling me that in Chinese *Coca-Cola* means, "bite the wax tadpole." I'll give you the details in a moment, but right now let me just say that we managed to work through Ron's near-terminal opportunity. Today, he's one of Industrial Solutions' most successful salespeople. And though, in his words, he's "grayer and wiser, and a touch rounder," he's still one of their least cynical. He's generous enough to give me much of the credit, though unquestionably, Ron has heeded my advice and become his own guru.

But what could a workshop by someone who made his mark as a sales consultant offer a Norma Landry? "It's made all the difference in the world," she says. "It showed me how to turn the job I had into the job I wanted. It gave me an honest, open-hearted enthusiasm for everything I do."

Her bishop says, "Nowadays, Norma is so good she makes me a better boss."

As I say, I started out as a sales consultant. A good portion of my business continues to be sales consulting. But this is not a book about selling, it's a book about succeeding. The strategies we'll be discussing are aimed not at salespeople but at anyone in the world of business.

A recent article on me in *Selling Power* magazine said, "To his powerful and famous clients, Barry Maher is simply the best sales trainer in the business." I'm not. But now that I've worked in that shameless brag, let me set aside the false modesty and admit that I'm damn good at what I do—if a bit overpriced. But why do I find myself working more and more with executives, managers, and workers—people like Norma Landry—who have nothing to do with sales? And what could a book by a sales consultant offer anyone who isn't a salesperson?

How about integrity?

Integrity?

Integrity. Not integrity as some vaguely reassuring concept in a mission statement in the company manual. Not even integrity in the sense of honesty or ethics. I'm a big fan of honesty and ethics, but that's not what this book is about. I'm not going to be preaching or moralizing. I intend to irritate you in other ways. (No matter who you are, I hope there's something in this book that you vehemently disagree with.)

No, by integrity I mean integrity in the sense of wholeness, oneness, relief from the dichotomy between what we believe we should be doing in our careers and our lives, and what we actually find ourselves doing.

And what if the book could provide an effective, practical method for getting wherever you might want to go in life, for achieving whatever you might want to achieve, without sacrificing who you really are and who you would like to be?

That would certainly be worth the price of the book, wouldn't it—even if you can't rely on my pronouncements about Chinese?

TWO SAD AND SIMPLE TRUTHS

As practiced by the best, selling is about integrity—not about cynical manipulation. And the qualities that make a truly great salesperson are qualities that can help anyone to reach his or her goals.

But here's a sad and simple truth about salespeople: Most salespeople are not as sold on their product as they believe they have to appear to be in order to make the sale.

Far too frequently, what they'd like to believe about the product, what they say or at least imply about it, fails to match up with what they've discovered to be true.

Here's a sad and simple truth about the population in general: Many of us, perhaps most of us, believe our careers and our business lives should be one thing, while the untidy facts keep insisting that those careers and those lives are something else—usually something considerably less.

And when we're honest with ourselves, we often have trouble selling those lives and those careers to ourselves and to those around us.

Salespeople and non-salespeople both suffer from the same fundamental disconnects. And the strategies that have been so effective for me in helping salespeople make peace with their negatives and regain their sense of integrity work every bit as well with the disconnects that non-salespeople face.

These ten, easily understood techniques enable salespeople to sell—and to sell a great deal—with an integrity that leaves both themselves and their customers feeling positive about the transaction. If applied correctly, these techniques can make all of us—salespeople and non-salespeople alike—more successful, regardless of what our individual definition of success might be.

As I said, this is not a book about selling; it's a book about succeeding. And it's not about morality. It's about strategies that work.

ATTILA AND ME

So, what does a sales consultant know about helping non-salespeople to succeed?

Before discovering *Leadership Secrets of Attila the Hun,* what would you have said Attila knew about management? A great salesperson is every bit as much an expert on seat-of-the-pants psychology as Attila was on rape, pillage, and—I guess—20th-century management technique. Anyone who doubts that there are important psychological truths at the heart of the most effective sales techniques must have difficulty explaining the thousands of new cars on the streets, the billions of dollars in life insurance policies gathering dust in safe deposit boxes, and the trillions of Ginzu knives, Veg-O-Matics, and Pocket Fishermen that fill the closets of America and the world. You can argue about how those truths have been used: Norma Landry and I were both right, Jesus and Satan were both great salespeople. But you cannot deny these truths exist.

In fact, if you and I are ever simultaneously held hostage by two separate groups of heavily armed, distraught postal workers, you can have

Dr. Joyce Brothers, Dr. Carl Rogers, or any other human behavior guru negotiate with your pack of dementos. I'll take Zig Ziglar, Ron Popeil, or for that matter, master salesman and attorney Gerry Spence to help me get out alive.

Filling the Glass should arm you with the kind of power these experts wield.

A BETTER BUZZWORD

There are two types of people in the world: those who divide the world into two types of people and those who don't. Those who divide the world into two types tell us that one of those types of people can look at a glass and see it as half full, while the other looks at the same glass and sees it as half empty.

It's common knowledge that seeing the glass as half full is a more successful mind-set. Like much of what passes for common knowledge in business, this idea is more common than it is genuine knowledge. It's time for a new metaphor. The person I want to be, the person I want to hire, and the person who ultimately will be more successful and more valuable to his company, his family, his society, and himself is the one who takes a look at that glass and is concerned, not with whether it's half empty or half full, but with figuring out how to fill it up.

And that's what the strategies in this book are all about: taking that half full or half empty glass and filling it—ideally, until your cup runneth over.

REMEMBERING TRUTH

When used properly, these strategies can help anyone:

- Achieve peak performance for realizing their dreams—without sacrificing their personal integrity.
- Take control of their own accomplishments and their own destiny.
- Motivate themselves and those around them.
- Come to terms with the negatives in their life.
- Gain perspective and match their life to their values.
- Relate to others with increased empathy.
- Overcome adversity—capturing the value in every failure as well as every success.

Many of the strategies are novel, some even counterintuitive (*brag about the negatives?*). A few will sound familiar, reflecting things you may already believe to be true, but probably haven't gotten around to making a part of your life. With case studies, examples, brief tips, detailed tactics, and even a few parables, maybe we can find a way to get you started.

Plato said that all learning is actually remembering. If that's the case, I think there are a few truths here I can help you remember.

TRANSFORMATION MADE DIFFICULT

Filling the Glass has been called "a book that can transform your life," but if you think the process will be easy, you'd better put the book down right now. I'm not going to tell you that all you need is a little positive thinking and a touch of pixie dust and—poof!—all your dreams will come true.

Filling the Glass has also been called inspirational. I hope it is. But if so, it's a hardheaded, reality-based inspiration. If there are any pixies flying around here, they've got calluses on their hands and a slightly skeptical tilt to their smiles. They aren't going to be working at Disney.

I've been a consultant as well as a professional speaker since 1986, and my client list includes many of the largest companies in the world. As a consultant, I'm far more interested in reality than theory—in dealing with what actually works rather than what sounds good, or what should work, or what I wish worked because it's what the client wants to hear. "Filling the glass" is a great catchphrase, and it gives me a unique marketing hook. But as a consultant, I'm hired to produce concrete, verifiable results. The only marketing hook that keeps clients coming back for more and keeps the phone ringing in my Santa Barbara office is a program that delivers.

And though following these strategies isn't always easy, it isn't so difficult that it can't be done by anyone who chooses to do so. Being all too human, I have to admit that I have been known to stray from them myself from time to time. Preaching has always been easier than practicing. But when I do follow them, my career, my business relationships, and my life all go far more smoothly for myself and for those around me.

THE TEN STRATEGIES

The ten strategies of *Filling the Glass* are:

1. *Make peace with the negatives.* Every situation has its negatives; make them work *for* you.
2. *Fill the glass.* Attitude is important, but reality rules.
3. *Become your own guru.* You're your own best guide. The most important decisions take place when Stephen Covey can't be with you.
4. *Add water.* Far too often we keep our strongest selling points hidden. Learn ways to promote your ideas, your projects and proposals, and ultimately, yourself.
5. *Bring out the prospect in yourself.* Look inside and outside for empathy and understanding.
6. *Become an expert witness.* Let the other side make its points— and make yours convincingly.
7. *Fail toward success.* Become a master craftsman, a master craftsman being someone who's already made every possible mistake.
8. *Brag about the negatives.* Make your biggest liabilities your strongest assets.
9. *Change the scale to make the sale.* Size may count, but it's not how big it is, it's how big it seems.
10. *Never settle for success.* Keep your goals from getting in your way; make the journey even more enjoyable than the destination.

As the saying goes, all generalizations are false, including this one. You can't capture reality in a case study or an example or a speech or a book. The complexity of the simplest situation guarantees that the best a writer can ever do is to give his or her impression of reality. *Filling the Glass* is my best impression. But all the strategies, all the tactics, all the tips have been tested time after time against the realities of the business world.

Beyond that, some of the names in the pages that follow have been changed, some of the situations disguised: to protect the innocent, and to protect the confidences of those who have confided in me. Once or twice it's been done to protect the guilty. Some stupid mistakes are recorded in this book. We can learn from stupid mistakes, but there's nothing to be gained from subjecting real people to ridicule. We all make stupid mistakes.

I would never claim that the path outlined in *Filling the Glass* is the only route to success. Obviously, it isn't. But these ten strategies can turn around unsuccessful careers—and reconcile the disconnects between what we believe and what we often find ourselves doing—faster and more completely than any other techniques I've ever encountered.

That's what happened to Ron Campbell and Norma Landry.

The prices on the machinery Ron had to sell were too high in comparison to the competition. So—as we often teach salespeople to do—Ron turned himself into the ultimate value-added feature, the final benefit that lifted his products above the competition.

He's become a major resource, developing an expertise his customers no longer feel they can do without. "His machines may not be quite as reliable as his competition's," one of them admits. "But he knows more about that type of milling than anyone in the industry. The free information we get from him more than offsets the cost of the occasional problem we may encounter with his products. He's indispensable. Besides, when there is a problem, Ron's on it—practically before the machine stops humming."

I recently spoke with Bill Swetland, a customer service rep with Industrial Solutions, Ron's company. "When one of Ron's accounts has a problem," Bill said, "he fights for them harder than they'd ever fight for themselves. . . . Sometimes I wonder who he's working for."

"But that's part of what they're buying," Ron explains. "They're buying me. That's what they are paying for and that's what they get. I make sure I'm worth the extra money our products cost and then some."

Because he's free from doubt about the value his clients will be receiving, Ron can sell honestly. He can tell the truth to his customers and to himself and still close any deal. He sells to more customers and he sells more to each customer.

And Norma Landry, the church administrator who was so concerned about her bishop's constant focus on fund-raising? How did Norma fill the glass? Among other things, on her own time she created a breakdown of how the money they raised was being used. Then she made it a matter of church pride that they become more efficient than comparable nonprofit groups—so every penny did the most possible good. She reported the results to the ministers to share with their congregations, and to the press, earning the church some impressive PR. Contributions increased, and Norma felt much better about her job. She wasn't dunning people for money; she was feeding the hungry, tending to the sick.

Her bishop was so impressed he made monitoring distributions a permanent part of Norma's job, making sure the church became even more efficient and got even more value for every dollar spent.

The world is full of decent people like Ron Campbell and Norma Landry, people who want, need, and deserve to be able to feel good about the way they're occupying their time on this planet. *Filling the Glass* can help.

I've seen it work.

CHAPTER 2

Reality and the Manoogian Death Spiral

A SKEPTIC'S GUIDE TO POSITIVE THINKING

It was the last day of a training class for new hires. I'd been flown in to give them a motivational sendoff. They didn't need me nearly as much now as they would in a couple of months. They all knew what kind of income they could expect if they were successful. They all still had visions of sugarplums dancing in their heads.

Selma, the lead trainer, was a former elementary school teacher with little actual sales experience. She explained who I was, then offered a few inspirational words of her own.

"Believe!" she implored them as she concluded, scrawling the word in huge blue letters with three exclamation points across the white board behind her. "J.M. Barrie, the author of *Peter Pan,* said, 'To have faith is to have wings!'"

Barry Maher, author of several far less popular books, got up and walked to the podium.

"Selma and J.M. Barrie are right," I said. "To have faith is to have wings. But for a long flight, you can't count on pixie dust."

I'm not a big believer in motivation by fairy tale.

Most of the men and women in that room were fresh out of college. And they were as eager to believe in the product they'd be selling and the company that was going to be rewarding them so richly as Ron

Campbell ever was. Few converts embrace a new faith with as much enthusiasm.

As a motivator, I know that you can motivate people for the short term by pumping them up with happy illusion and wishful thinking, by sugarcoating the facts, even by out-and-out lying. We've all seen it done; we've all had it done to us. But if you want to motivate people for the long haul—to get them where they want to be, to get the company where it needs to be—you'd better start by dealing with reality.

Someone once called my approach "a skeptic's guide to positive thinking." That's exactly what it's intended to be.

RON CAMPBELL WASN'T UNIQUE

Like those new hires, most of us started out enthusiastic, eager, and excited about our career and our business lives. Excited about the potential, excited about where we were going to go. Like Ron Campbell, we often discover that the reality of those careers and those lives is very different from what we'd like to believe it is.

It's a reality that comes in a wide variety of forms.

David Bonney dreamed of being a photographer. But his pictures didn't sell and his portrait shop folded. After that, he was never sure what he wanted to do with his life. Whatever it was, it certainly wasn't getting up a 5:30 in the morning and stumbling onto the factory floor to supervise 23 people who'd rather be anywhere else on the planet, working for any company other than JaspCot, Inc.

"What we've got here is classic rubber-band management," David explains. "The company stretches employees until they break then tosses them away and picks up some more. A few months back, the president must have read some article about helping employees improve the quality of their lives. He circulated a memo gushing about his recent photo safari to Kenya. He quoted Thoreau or somebody about how we should all get more in touch with nature. Then he advised us to spend some time every day *looking out the window*. During our breaks of course."

Not only did that sound like the rich man's perennial caution to the poor to be frugal with their money, but it showed the employees just how much time their president had spent in any of his factories.

"We're lucky if we even *have* a window in the break room. And even luckier if it overlooks anything more than the beauty of an alley, complete with scenic dumpsters, graffiti, and the occasional bloodstain."

Charles O'Neil got an MBA from a prestigious school and a starting salary that was even larger than he'd hoped. Nine years and a number of promotions later, he's on the fast track to success with a legitimate shot at the very highest levels of management.

Charles works 65-hour weeks, has money in the bank and rental property, and whenever he gets enough time off for a thought of his own he can't help wondering why such a promising future looks "so goddamn empty and boring I sometimes feel like setting the company headquarters on fire. I can't help thinking that I'm living my life for the long run but, as somebody once said, 'In the long run, we're all dead.'"

On a business trip several months ago, he'd sensed something slightly off in the last phone message or two that he'd gotten from his wife. On his return he went straight to the office, but he hoped to leave early and spend a rare evening at home. He did manage to drag himself away from his desk eventually—shortly after 7:00 PM.

The note from his wife was nailed to the mahogany door of the master bedroom of his recently remodeled "mini-estate." She'd used a six-inch spike one of the workers must have left behind. She was leaving him. Along with her jewelry and her Mercedes, she'd taken the kids and the family dog whose name Charles couldn't remember.

DeAnna Harris loves being a doctor, a family practitioner. She loves curing people. And her boss at the clinic is a wonderful woman. But pressure to squeeze in more and more patients, "assembly-line medicine," along with mountains of paperwork and red tape, have taken so much of the joy out of the work that she frequently thinks about leaving the profession altogether. One former colleague has actually given up medicine for multilevel marketing.

DeAnna smiles ruefully. "He says his only regret is that he didn't attend that Amway meeting 15 years ago instead of wasting his time with medical school."

Ellen Sutter got her law degree at night, cleaning houses during the day to support her two little girls. At home, Ellen recycles and scrubs the fruit and vegetables she serves her daughters with a special pesticide-removing cleanser. At work, she helps the company skirt environmental regulations.

"Nothing illegal," she explains shaking her head, "just what my boss calls 'using the law to our best advantage.' It puts bread on the table; I only hope the company hasn't contaminated the wheat that was used to bake it."

Leroy McDaniels built up his own tool-and-die shop from nothing. He's tremendously proud of the achievement, and of the fact that he provides employment for 28 people. He's less proud of the fact that he pays considerably less than some of his competition and that he's going to have to cut wages and benefits once again this year. He's even less proud of the corners he's had to cut on the parts he turns out; he hopes that most of his customers won't notice.

Helen Terrance is a professional liar.

"At least that's what I feel like," she insists. Actually, Helen manages the regional office of a national charity. "I feel like I'm constantly lying to my contributors. The only promotion pieces I'm authorized to use are those produced by the national office. And every single one features a picture of at least one PSK—pathetic suffering kid—and stresses the agony of afflicted children."

"Sell the kids!" she's been told repeatedly. The reality is that few kids ever contract the disease, and little of the money raised is used to help anyone under 35. Helen feels like she's exploiting children, lying to contributors, and lying to herself whenever she tries to justify her job.

"This is not the way I wanted to live my life," she insists. "I know we do some good, but it's not the good the people who give us the money believe we're doing. Beyond that, we're supporting a heavy bureaucracy. Sometimes it seems that anything we accomplish comes in spite of the people above me—in spite of even myself, perhaps. Because the truth is, I'm not as good at this as I thought I would be. But how can I admit that to anyone? I've got kids of my own to support."

THE MANOOGIAN DEATH SPIRAL

Too often what we believe we should be doing in our jobs doesn't match up well with what we actually find ourselves doing. Obviously I could easily fill the entire book—or an entire library—with examples.

In *Creating You & Co.,* William Bridges claims that the word *job* is derived from a Celtic word for "mouth or something in the mouth." Gradually it came to denote "a hunk, a bunch, or a *job* of something in the mouth." Then, "whatever one did with that pile of stuff." And finally, "any task or undertaking."

Which may explain why our jobs so often leave a bad taste in our mouths. Few of us are completely sold on our jobs.

Even though a salesperson may want to do the best job possible, even though his paycheck depends on it, the less sold he becomes on the product, the less he sells.

Even though the rest of us may want to do the best job we possibly can, the less sold we are on our careers and our lives, the worse we perform.

And the worse we perform on the job, the worse we feel about it and the less sold we are on it. The less sold we are, the worse we perform, taking our career even further downhill. In sales this vicious circle is sometimes called the "Manoogian death spiral." (Salespeople love to overdramatize. We're not selling toilet paper, we're on an epic quest, a life or death struggle for self-realization.) Avak Manoogian was a mythic Armenian carpet salesperson who allegedly worked for 207 different companies in a 47-year career.

Sometimes the Manoogian death spiral leads to alienation and cynicism. Often it leads to leaving the company, even to giving up a profession altogether—quitting medicine for multilevel marketing.

Then we try to make a fresh start somewhere else—in another job we can be excited about. Until the same thing starts happening all over again.

CHAPTER 3

Pixie Dust, Pollyanna, and Making Peace with the Negatives

THE TOUGHEST CUSTOMER

Though every product, every company, every career has its negative aspects, many of us are never confronted by the negatives associated with our jobs quite as aggressively as salespeople are. After all, on a daily basis, they have to face the most sophisticated and skeptical purchasers the world has ever known and try to generate trust, enthusiasm—even excitement. They have to try to prove value.

That doesn't mean that the negatives the rest of us have to deal with do less damage. It simply means the death spiral takes longer.

The negatives are going to be there. You've got to sell yourself—and keep yourself sold—on your job, on your career, on your business life, in spite of them. If a salesperson wants to be honest, before he can sell anything to a customer he first has to sell it to himself. That's the toughest customer an ethical salesperson will ever have to face.

Like the salesperson, if you don't make this particular sale with complete honestly, if you fudge, you will be less committed to whatever you are doing than you could have been. Than you should have been. You will be less successful. And you will find far less satisfaction in the work. And sooner or later that fudging will probably come back and bite you in the butt.

To paraphrase Lincoln, you can fool part of yourself all of the time and all of yourself part of the time, but you can't fool all of yourself all of the time.

You've got to deal with the negatives.

POLLYANNA AND PIXIE DUST

"What the hell kind of motivator are you?" a low-level manager once demanded of me. He'd walked in on my presentation ten minutes late then had listened to less than five minutes before interrupting. "You're focusing on what's wrong with our jobs, our careers, our business lives; what's wrong with the product; what's wrong with our company." He glanced nervously around the room as if he wanted to cover the ears of his charges and shut out this heresy. "What's wrong with you?!? What kind of a positive attitude is this? We've got all the griping and complaining we need around here without you encouraging it."

Isn't there a certain amount of truth to what he said? Aren't I back to seeing the glass as half empty? What about positive thinking? What about enthusiasm? How can you sell something, even to yourself, without enthusiasm?

Positive thinking is a powerful concept. And enthusiasm does more than just sell. There's a story of Frank Sinatra chastising his son, Frank, Jr., for just going through the motions on a song. "Don't ever let me catch you singing like that again," he supposedly said. "You're nothing if you aren't excited by what you're doing."

As a motivator and a consultant, one of my main goals is to help people generate enthusiasm about what they're doing. But here's what happens too frequently in a sales situation: The salesperson knows that if he isn't excited about his product, he can hardly expect his potential customers to be. So he tries to be overwhelmingly positive and enthusiastic when talking to his prospects. But since he can't avoid seeing the negatives that exist in every product and in every company, he feels two-faced. He feels dissonance and he feels stress. Or he simply becomes cynical.

Positive thinking that isn't firmly rooted on reality shouldn't be called thinking at all. It's nothing but Pollyannaism—pixie dust.

There's a joke about two cowpunchers, Slim and Tex, who couldn't find a cow that needed punching anywhere. Then the local Navajos jumped the reservation. The government announced they'd pay a bounty of ten dollars for each Navajo rounded up and brought in. So Slim and Tex signed on, and rode off in search of Indians. Three days went by and they hadn't seen anything but rattlesnakes and scorpions.

Then that night, Tex was awakened by noises outside the tent. He peered through the flap. And there in the moonlight, he saw a thousand heavily armed Navajo warriors, surrounding the tent and advancing toward them.

He leaped back inside and shook his partner awake. "Wake up, Slim! Wake up! We're rich!"

Pollyanna positive thinking strategies often make the problem worse. You want to be positive so you try to block out the negatives. You refuse to acknowledge them or worse, ignore them. Unfortunately, like the Navajos around Tex and Slim, reality has a way of refusing to stay blocked.

In *How to Succeed in Business by Breaking All the Rules,* Dan S. Kennedy talks about a group of life insurance agents in his hometown of Akron, Ohio. Every morning, they'd have their meetings and "repeat positive affirmations, sing the company songs, march around the table, listen to motivational tapes, watch motivational videos, and get pumped up." Afterward, "ten feet tall and bulletproof" they'd grab a final jolt of caffeine at a breakfast place called The Egg Castle before charging out to conquer the world.

What Kennedy found so fascinating though, was that in the same shopping mall as The Egg Castle was a bar called The Dry Dock. Happy hour started promptly at 4:00 PM and that's when the same people would reappear. Only instead of being on top of the world, now they were on the bottom, motivation evaporated, bullet-ridden rather than bulletproof, thoroughly disheartened by the reality of the marketplace they never seemed to be prepared for.

We've all known this type of Pollyanna. They run around desperately trying to convince themselves that everything is wonderful. They read all the self-help books, listen to all the tapes, and mouth the latest company line. When things don't work out just the way the tapes tell them, they either become cynical or they slide into the steepest of death spirals—the Pollyanna spiral of death—leading to a quick crash and burn. At that point, they do more griping than any ten other people, and blame everything on the company or the job or whatever it is that failed to live up to their "everything is wonderful" standards. Which is usually everything. Then they go off searching for some other company where the best of all possible worlds actually exists. Personally, I've never known a Pollyanna who ever accomplished much.

HIDING BEHIND HOPE

Far too many companies encourage, even demand, this type of shallow positive thinking. They hide behind it to avoid confronting problems. Everything *is* wonderful, think happy thoughts, the glass is half full, not half empty, and anybody who even hints that anything is wrong anywhere in the known universe is suffering from a negative attitude and ought to stop bringing himself and everybody else down.

To management "he has a positive attitude" often means, "he doesn't bitch about our stupidity, and he says all the right things." No matter how blatant and ludicrous the insincerity. Critical voices are dismissed with, "Oh, he's just being negative." Well, maybe there's a reason for the negativity—a vital reason that the company can't afford to ignore.

According to *Business Week,* when Daniel P. Burnham took over Raytheon, he found himself repeatedly blindsided by bad news. The company's senior executives were, he said, "almost institutionally incapable" of backing away from a projection or a forecast no matter how much it differed from reality.

"Goddamn it," he finally told them, "tell us what's going on here. Don't hide behind hope."

To Burnham, "One of the attractive aspects of this company is the can-do attitude. But it fundamentally blinded people."

At one point, discovery of such overly optimistic assumptions forced Burnham to cut profit projections in half. Raytheon's shares plunged 40 percent. Such is the power of Pollyanna positive thinking.

TIP: It's amazing how quickly "can do" becomes "can't do" when it's not based on reality.

POLLYANNA FACT-FINDING

Hank Engholm was an "experienced, level-headed veteran," according to his boss, and a first-rate accountant. He was respected and trusted by his peers. Then he was promoted. It was immediately made clear to him that as a manager his duty was to toe the Pollyanna company line. Within weeks, he'd lost all credibility with those he was supposed to lead. He felt two-faced, he felt dissonance, and he felt stress.

"What's more," Hank adds, "by trying to be perpetually upbeat and positive, I was denying the company part of what I was supposedly being paid for, which was my honest assessment of the situation. The reality, of course, was that nobody wanted to hear it."

In other words, the company was denying itself the benefits of the very experience that had gotten Hank promoted in the first place.

In *Unconventional Wisdom,* organizational development expert Thomas L. Quick tells of being asked to sit in on what was supposed to be a discussion of a proposed new project. After listening for a while, he thought he detected a few flaws in the proposal, so he suggested a couple of changes.

"There was an embarrassed silence; then one of the plan's proponents angrily declared that *he* thought it was quite acceptable and would we please vote on it. I was a pariah—I had introduced uncertainty. There were further discussions . . . but I was conspicuously excluded from them. Implementation of the plan, as I recall, was an expensive failure."

Too many of us who have been in management have had similar experiences.

Often this type of avoidance of negatives shouldn't really be called Pollyanna positive thinking. Often it might more accurately be called Pollyanna fact-finding—though those who practice it call it diplomacy or office politics or playing along to get along. Whatever you call it, if I could collect for myself all the time the average corporation spends lying to itself—trying to avoid one negative or another—I'd be immortal.

HOW TO LIVE FOREVER

Think about the company you work for. How often are things said in meetings or official pronouncements that everyone knows are not true but no one is allowed to challenge?

How much time do you spend listening to platitudes and corporate lip service that not only have no relation to the reality but that actually attempt to cover up the reality? Often these come in the cloak of the latest buzzwords, key phrases from the latest management fads. Fads that were frequently excellent ideas to begin with—sometimes revolutionary ideas—until they were misused, misunderstood, or just plain co-opted in the service of something very different from what the experts who developed them intended.

If I were collecting minutes to add to my life from any particular company, I'd probably start looking wherever people were talking about customer service and customer orientation. I called one business the other day that had just been involved in a massive merger. They'd recently changed their corporate motto from "100 percent customer satisfaction" to "The easiest company to do business with."

"Our number-one core competency is customer service," management bragged. "That's the prime reason we were so attractive as a merger partner."

Having worked with this particular company and having dealt with any number of its customers—as well as having been a customer myself—I knew that its "number-one core competency" was *talking* about customer service. No one inside the company seemed to realize that there was a distinction between talking about it and actually having it.

When I called that day, I was of course thrown into voice mail Hell where for the next 28 minutes—on the clock—I was repeatedly played the following mind-boggling message: "Because we value your business, please continue to hold."

I still can't believe it. *Because we value your business, please continue to hold.* In other words, "Your business is so important to us that we are perfectly willing to increase our productivity by decreasing yours—to cut our costs by spending your time." If they didn't value my business, I guess I would have gotten through immediately.

After the 28 minutes, I hung up. If I'm going to be robbed of time or money I prefer to have it done without the hypocrisy. I'd like the thief to stick a gun in my belly and say, "Because I value your money, please give me your wallet."

I know of one company where I could probably live forever just by gathering the time wasted on the single empty phrase, "customer-driven." And if I could collect all the time they squandered on empty blathering about "employees being our most valuable assets" and how they've got to treat them as such, I could keep several friends alive for companionship.

Pixie dust.

HOW TO KILL A CAREER

The president of a large telecommunications company went on a fact-finding tour of regional offices. When he got to Illinois, the local management carefully handpicked several veterans and a couple of promising new recruits to attend the fact-finding dinner. The new recruits were the most gung-ho in the office. The veterans could be counted on to behave with discretion; they understood company proto-col. Jim Aronson, the most knowledgeable, if the most cynical, veteran in the division, was deliberately not invited. Jim understood his value to the company, and wasn't interested in being promoted. No telling what he might say to the president.

But Aronson being Aronson, before the dinner he sought out one of the new recruits and took her aside. Shelly Channing was young, ambitious, and intelligent. She was a sincere, dedicated, hardworking Pollyanna, a likeable woman in her late 20s. She wanted to be a manager, and everyone knew that in time she would be.

Shelly had been around just long enough to realize that Aronson was absolutely right when he said that the regional offices had one problem that overwhelmed all the rest. That problem was the yearly evaluation program that based pay increases on activity rather than genuine achievement. Overspending, empire-building, procedures for the sake of procedures, and reports for the sake of reports were rewarded at the expense of true productivity.

"Then there's the hard feelings these things generate," Aronson added. "All these vague personality issues: *Not a team player; lacking in loyalty; no initiative.* You've seen them. A lot of times, they're more accusations than assessments—a chance for management to get even with those they don't like. How do they measure that stuff? How can anybody refute it? How can you work on improvement if your SOB manager still doesn't like you next year?"

Shelly nodded. Aronson even armed her with an article that he'd clipped from an old magazine. Among other things, it mentioned a study showing that performance evaluations were usually followed by a drop in performance of upward of three months.

"Around here it's longer than three months," he insisted. "Around here it probably lasts right up until time for the next evaluation. This company is 15 years behind the times. They need to be focusing on behaviors—productive behaviors, not personalities: *Met 83 percent of on-time goals; reduced consulting costs by 11 percent.* That's something I can do something about. What they're measuring now is who's doing the most busywork and how well they suck up. No wonder we lose so many of our best people."

So Shelly was ready that evening, if a bit nervous. At the lead table on a dais sat the president, along with the regional vice president and all the local management. The invitees were at floor level at two smaller tables.

After the dinner, the president stood up. "As you know," he said, "We're here tonight because I want—I need—your frank and open feedback. Your comments, your suggestions and, yes, if it's warranted, your criticism. This, of course, is a safe environment. A completely safe environment. You have my word on that. You can say anything you feel has to be said without fear of retribution." He smiled. "No matter how many of your bosses might be sitting up here beside me."

Everyone laughed. Shelly laughed. But unfortunately she didn't catch the edge of nervousness in the other laughter.

Then, one by one, all the invitees had their chance to get up and say their piece. About how wonderful it was to have a president who cared enough to come out and ask for their opinion. About how this kind of openness was what separated this company from the competition and made it such a fantastic place to work and build a career. About how this kind of thinking was why the company was a true industry leader.

No one mentioned the company's industry-leading turnover or why it trailed the industry in virtually every other major benchmark. The problems that were mentioned were small, usually process-related. The president would assign either the regional VP or the division manager to "check into the situation and see if we can improve on our systems and procedures." No one anywhere took any notes on these "assignments." No one even recorded that they'd been made.

Shelly's turn came near the end. She stood up. Respectfully, she thanked the president for coming. Then she said, "The problem I'm concerned with is a little more basic." She didn't notice the sudden concern on the face of her immediate boss at the lead table. "Have we looked into whether our current evaluation and compensation system is rewarding the wrong type of behavior?"

Nobody actually gasped out loud. But the psychic gasp was nearly loud enough to be heard. To an outsider, the question might seem harmless, but every single person at that dinner—everyone but Shelly—knew just how *verboten* the topic was. Six years previously, before his promotion, the president had been the prime mover behind the development of the standardized system she was questioning. It had been his crowning achievement.

"We've looked at all types of compensation strategies," the president said coolly and dismissively. "We know what the competition is doing. After studying all the alternatives I think I can safely say that we've got one of the finest compensation systems in the industry." He pointed to the man seated beside Shelly. "Next."

"But, sir," Shelly insisted, compounding her mistake exponentially. "It's everybody's major gripe—how unfair the assessments are. And how counterproductive. Instead of rewarding people for cultivating more beans and cultivating them as efficiently as possible, we reward those who find more and more elaborate ways of bean counting and recounting."

This last was a virtual Aronson quote, and all the local managers knew it. But Aronson was untouchable.

"Everybody's major gripe?" The president's voice was cold. "Then why didn't anyone else here even mention it? Not one single person. Anybody else here agree with Ms.—Ms., what was your name?"

"Channing, sir" she said, tensely. "Shelly Channing."

"Anybody else agree with Ms. Channing here?" His tone made it plain that nobody in that room could possibly agree with such an absurd proposition. Not surprisingly, nobody did. "But I think I see your problem, Ms. Channing. Your problem is that you're in the wrong line of work. We aren't even in the bean business."

He smiled. Everyone else laughed nervously and he called on the next invitee.

Without knowing it, Shelly Channing had just destroyed her chances of ever being promoted to management within that company. Within six months she was gone.

And afterward when local management told the story, it was always as an object lesson on how not to behave in front of upper management, and on the danger of not properly selecting and briefing your people before such a meeting. The next time a VIP came to town, the regional vice president personally instructed the local managers that this type of incident was not to be allowed to happen again.

In other words, they were to make sure that, in their fact-finding, upper management would find no embarrassing facts they didn't want to find.

So it didn't happen again. But it should have. It should have happened in every meeting—until the company realized and acknowledged they had a problem. Even if for some reason there really was nothing they could do about the problem. At least properly acknowledging it would give them a chance to explain why there was nothing they could do.

CUSTOMER AND EMPLOYEE NEGATIVITY

TIP: Nobody wants to hear criticism. But not hearing criticism is not the same as not needing it.

We don't want customers to raise problems but we've all come to realize that we're better off hearing about those problems if they're there, because we can't control customers. We'd never think of telling an irate customer that they should work on their attitude or that they're just being negative. Companies can control employees—or think they can. And far too many companies still seem to believe that the best way to deal with the issues employees raise is with Pollyannaism, lip service, and pixie dust.

Team playing does not mean mindless acceptance. You aren't really part of the team if you aren't allowed to have an opinion. And you aren't much of a team manager if you don't avail yourself of all the resources that the different members bring to the team.

Often management has a good reason for what people on another level perceive as a problem. Great; if so, bring out the justification. Honestly. In those extremely rare instances when you can't confide the reasons for a questioned policy, explain that as well. If you need to investigate, tell people that. Then do it; don't just use it as a way to put the people off.

THE LESSONS OF VIETNAM

Pollyanna fact-finding can be extremely tempting, particularly when things are going poorly. As a manager, when you insist on getting the news you want, that's the news you get. When you insist on getting the numbers you want, you get those numbers—only far too often the numbers aren't real.

As a consultant, I sometimes mystery shop: I go undercover as a customer or a new hire or a new manager. When I see how some of these numbers are produced and forced to add up, when I see how much mid-level management time is wasted providing upper management with the news they insist on getting, all I can think of is Vietnam and the daily body counts we were all subjected to. Numbers so ludicrous they soon became an extremely unfunny national joke—a joke that the Army brass seemed to be the last to catch on to.

And we wonder why studies show that though most young workers start out with great hope for their working futures, they quickly grow alienated and cynical. And that the longer they're with a company, the more alienated and cynical they become.

One high-level corporate executive told me that, outside of playing the bagpipes, the worst waste of breath he could imagine was trying to explain to his CEO what was really happening "down in the bowels of the company with the employees."

Are your veteran employees all cynical? Are you afraid to expose potential new hires to them and afraid to let them have anything to do with new-hire training? If you're worried about the effects of their alienation and cynicism on productivity, you should ask yourself why they're so cynical in the first place.

DISCOVERING DISAGREEMENT

When Alfred J. Sloan was chairman of General Motors, he once asked a committee, "Are you all agreed we should go ahead on this?" They all nodded. "All right, then we'll adjourn this meeting until someone can come up with a reason why we shouldn't."

Paul Corrigan is the author of *Shakespeare on Management,* a book I always wish I'd thought of first. Corrigan points out that management needs to cultivate sources outside the power grid, sources that will tell them the truth and provide unvarnished and direct advice. In Shakespeare, "Jesters do often prove prophets" and the king's fool was frequently more trustworthy—more honest and unbiased—than many of his ministers. This is a concept not totally alien to American business. At least that's the only explanation I've ever been able to come up with for the careers of several corporate vice presidents I know.

> **TIP:** Protect and nurture those who tell you the truth; no matter how disagreeable it or they might be.

I'd develop an entire network of out-of-the-loop advisors, capable of providing a number of varied perspectives throughout the company.

Pollyanna thinking and Pollyanna fact-finding are deadly to business. As business expert Dan Kennedy notes, "The idea that raising questions, doubt, skepticism, reasons why something may not work, marks you as a 'negative thinker,' a cancer to be cut out, a dangerous voice to be ignored is sick and stupid." Kennedy isn't a man who minces words.

Make no mistake: Positive thinking is a wonderful and a powerful thing—if it's based in reality. Research has repeatedly demonstrated the benefits of a positive outlook. In one study of women who'd been recently diagnosed with breast cancer, optimists not only experienced less distress, they were more likely to face up to the seriousness of the disease and to be more active in trying to cope with it. Pessimists were more likely to experience denial or to simply give up.

But as one researcher explains, "What you want is to teach children to be realistic, not unrealistically optimistic."

STATUES FOR CRITICS

Unrealistic Pollyanna positive thinking is counterproductive. It masks real problems. It breeds cynicism and alienation in both those who practice it and those they practice it upon. It destroys the biodiversity of thought.

> **TIP:** Harvest the biodiversity of thought.

If you're a manager and you've got 100 people and they all agree, instead of 100 perspectives, which could generate a number of possible solutions, you're only getting one. Obviously, you want your people to buy in, but never demand complete agreement.

"The plaque on the president's desk says, *'None of us is as smart as all of us'*," one senior executive explains. "But everything he does makes it clear that the rest of us had better be smart enough agree with him on anything of any importance."

> **TIP:** A subordinate who agrees with everything you say and do is a person who is not doing his or her job. If you insist on or encourage or even allow that kind of relationship, you are not doing yours.

Did you ever wonder how much respect Rush Limbaugh could have for his fans if he refers to them as "ditto heads"? *Ditto heads?* To me the phrase implies people who not only are incapable of independent thought, but who are incapable even of expressing whatever it is they supposedly believe in.

> **TIP:** As an individual, if you don't have any ideas that are out of step with the majority, you don't have any ideas.

Art Hammer is a principal of QualPro, Inc., of Knoxville, Tennessee. QualPro helps companies generate, refine, and test ideas for improving their processes. Art has empirically tested hundreds of thousands of ideas. "What we have consistently discovered is that whenever everyone involved unanimously agrees an idea is going to help, a quarter of the time it will improve results, half the time it will have no effect, and a quarter of the time it will actually hurt."

More than once I've heard a Pollyanna manager dismiss someone with a legitimate problem by quoting composer Jean Sibelius: "A statue has never been set up in honor of a critic."

The best response I ever heard came from a new librarian who was being upbraided by her boss. "Really?" she asked, pointing to a bust in a nook behind her boss's desk. "Voltaire over there was a pretty fair critic. So were Thomas Jefferson, Tom Paine, and Jean-Jacques Rousseau. Lots and lots of statues. Still, when Upton Sinclair was exposing the horrors of child labor back in the early 1900s, I guess someone should have told him to just stop being so damn negative. And that Frederick Douglass. He couldn't find one single positive thing to say about slavery—what a naysayer."

US VERSUS THEM

Obviously neither a company nor an individual benefits by focusing on the negatives as a way of life. You don't want to drown in them; you want to understand them. And yes, it is necessary to keep everything in context. No business wants or needs an employee who does nothing but gripe and spread negativity, who ferrets out the worst in every possible situation. That's why it's so important for companies to provide a mechanism for allowing employees to be heard. The employees get to vent; the company gets the input and gets a chance to address the issues.

Employees who believe their voices are heard feel a proprietary interest in the business. They have a stake. They're part of it. Employees who feel ignored can easily develop an "us versus them" mentality. Bitching becomes part of the corporate culture. It can even become a form of entertainment, almost a competitive sport.

"You think your problem is bad, just listen to this."

"If you think he got screwed, wait until you hear what they did to me."

And everybody's got a built-in excuse for anything that goes wrong, for any goal they don't achieve.

A few years back, a newsletter for healthcare providers offered caregivers suggestions for taking care of themselves. Among them: Learn to recognize the difference between complaining that actually relieves stress and complaining that only reinforces negative stress. Not a bad idea—for individuals and for companies. Enlightened businesses provide people with an outlet, then help them focus on the positive.

That's why at companies like Delta Airlines, any employee can take his or her concerns directly to any level of management. The janitor can sit down and discuss his problem with the president. The president will address it and let the janitor know what happens. Other companies have created employee ombudsmen or set up anonymous e-mail systems to gather input. Still others use employee focus groups.

WHY HELP THE COMPETITION SCALE THE WALLS?

I once saw an experienced manager empty an employee suggestion box, unread, straight into the trash. Noticing me watching, he laughed. "It's always the same old garbage," he said. "Why should I waste my time paying attention to garbage?"

I wish I could say I immediately zapped him with an inspired response. But the truth is I didn't think of a good reply until later that day when I was relaxing with a drink aboard the plane headed home. That's when I remembered that in the early 16th century, the garbage outside the city walls of Paris got so high the king was afraid a hostile army would scale the garbage and climb over the walls.

You've got to pay attention to your garbage, whether you're a company or you're an individual. You can't ignore the negatives of a situation, and you can't pretend they don't exist.

Companies and the individuals that make them up succeed by dealing with the real world. Not by dealing with a world they might like to believe in but can never really exist—no matter how Pollyannaish they try to be. There is some truth, of course, in even the most Pollyannaish of visions. But the difference between truth and some truth is the difference between an updated auto club map and a map as we might like it to be, leaving out the detours and sharp turns and washed out bridges and mountains and all those boring cornfields on I-80 between Denver and Pennsylvania.

MAKING PEACE WITH THE NEGATIVES

It's okay to put a dose of reality in your positive thinking. As an individual, it's okay to realize that you have problems, that you can fail, that your career has problems, that your product has problems, that your company has problems. It's not only okay, it's vital for your own sanity, for your peace of mind, for your integrity—integrity as I said, meaning wholeness, oneness, as opposed to two-faced. And ultimately, it's vital for your own success.

Nothing is more negative than trying to hide from your problems. Nothing is more positive than recognizing your problems and trying to deal with them.

As I said before, ethical salespeople need to find a way to make peace with the negative aspects of their products in order to sell those products to themselves or anyone else. The rest of us need to find a way to make peace with the negative aspects of our careers and our business lives in order to be able to sell those careers and lives to ourselves, and maintain our sense of integrity.

A person who has made peace with the negatives and who has that sense of integrity feels that what she does for a living is an expression of who she is and who she would like to be. Or at the very least, that it's not a contradiction of who she is and who she would like to be. That person brings greater commitment to the job and greater genuine, long-lasting enthusiasm than any Pollyanna possibly can.

Obviously no job, no company, no situation, no life can ever be perfect. The idea here is not to achieve employment bliss. As Malcolm Forbes said, "If you have a job without aggravations, you don't have a job." The idea is to work on eliminating the contradictions between who you are or who you'd like to be and what you're doing in your work.

ON BALANCE

"Expensive! You bet our widgets are expensive," a sales rep might declare to a prospect. "They're twice as expensive as anything the competition sells! And that's exactly what allows us to custom fit them to every application, and make them the best value on the market."

Some of us make peace with the negatives in our jobs the same way that sales rep made peace with his product's negatives: by realizing that the positives are part and parcel of the negatives. And that on balance, the product or the job is still a superior deal.

Yes, I don't have the career I would have liked and I certainly don't make as much money as I'd like to. But the work is pleasant and with my educational background I'm actually lucky to have this job.

Making peace *on balance* simply requires understanding and weighing the trade-offs. How much is it worth to you in salary to live in that wonderful small town? How much extra stress are you willing to endure for the chance for rapid promotion?

You're selling the situation to yourself and determining just what it takes to get you to take ownership of it—to commit to it. What does it take to make the sale—to yourself, to your family, and maybe to your friends as well?

"Things themselves don't hurt or hinder us," the Stoic philosopher Epictetus said. "Nor do people. It is our attitudes and reactions that give us trouble. . . . We cannot choose our external circumstances, but we can choose how we respond to them."

Unfortunately things do sometimes hinder us—Epictetus was never hit by a car or he might have felt differently—and so do people. People with guns and knives can be particularly irksome. And we've all dealt with people and things at work that would have given Epictetus a run for his money. Still, as he said, we choose how we respond to circumstances.

We know that. It's just that we seldom act like we do.

> **TIP:** It's much harder to change the world than it is to change how we respond to the world. Believe me. I've tried both.

So it's certainly possible to make peace with the negative aspects of a situation by convincing ourselves that, on balance, the job, the career, the life, is a superior deal for us. You make peace with the negatives, then put them behind you and focus on the positive.

And sometimes this works. Being realistic doesn't mean you can't and you shouldn't try to make the best of the reality around you. In fact, being realistic makes that easier. The more rooted you are in reality, the better prepared you'll be to deal with the inevitable twists and turns of reality. The more firmly you're grounded in reality, the more you can withstand the inevitable downturns that reality is going to throw your way. Because you've weighed the positives against the negatives and you know that, on balance, it's honestly better to be where you are than not to be.

You've already learned how to weigh and accept the bad. You're less likely to get caught in the Manoogian death spiral.

Still, whenever you're balancing anything, the balance is always subject to change. A new boss or a lost promotion, an alteration in pay scale or shift in corporate direction—one major change or a number of smaller ones—could make your career much less promising. You need to be able to reevaluate your decision at comfortable intervals to make sure the balance hasn't changed enough to tip the scales in another direction.

"On balance, I was sold on being a doctor until just recently. But now maybe I'd be better off selling Amway."

If you find yourself reevaluating the situation on a daily basis—or a weekly basis or anywhere near that frequently—you're not sold. You haven't actually made peace with the negatives, you just think you have. And those negatives are probably hurting your performance. They're definitely hurting your quality of life. Unfortunately this is all too often the case with on-balance decisions.

Far too often, perhaps even most of the time, on balance the negatives you're dealing with are too great to make a lasting peace with. The glass you're contemplating looks half empty too much of the time.

That's when you've got to find a way to fill the glass.

4

Filling the Glass

Sometimes, when a salesperson honestly acknowledges her product's negatives and weighs them against the pluses, she finds that on balance the product is less than a superior deal for the customer—sometimes far less.

She can't sell herself on her own product.

Sometimes once you or I have acknowledged the negatives in our jobs or our companies and weighed them against the pluses, we find that, on balance, whether the glass is half full or half empty, it sure as hell isn't full enough. What we believe we should be doing in our careers or our lives doesn't match up well with what we actually find ourselves doing. We can't sell ourselves on our situation.

We need to find a way to fill up the glass.

SUCCESS

There are as many ways to fill that glass as there are half full and half empty glasses. But here's the key point: the glass has to be filled, and you've got to find a way to do it. If you can't honestly justify to yourself what you are doing with your life, if you aren't working toward goals in which you honestly believe, you are never going to be—by your own standards—successful. Never. *Never!*

No matter what you may achieve. No matter how successful others may think you've become.

This may be one of those remembered truths Plato was talking about. We all know that it's true. Yet we frequently act like amnesia victims with absolutely no recollection of it.

Sam Walton was the founder of Wal-Mart and one of the richest men in the world. Many considered him the prototypical entrepreneur, a role model, even a hero.

"I blew it." That, apparently, is what Walton said as he lay dying. According to Kerry L. Johnson, author of *Mastering the Game*, billionaire Walton said that "he barely knew his youngest son, he even neglected his grandchildren and his wife stayed with him out of commitment."

I don't know if Sam Walton was a failure. If this story is true, then he was—by his own standards, regardless of what he achieved. At the very least, he failed to reconcile the values he expressed on his deathbed with the values he'd lived his life by.

If he'd made that reconciliation, Walton would have had a more successful life—a life more completely in tune with what he believed in. He may have even had a more successful business—again by his own standards—a business more in accord with his actual beliefs. I'm even enough of an optimist to think that a powerful force like Sam Walton functioning without the restraints of conflicting values might have created an even larger empire.

Filling the Glass is all about reconciliation: reconciling what we do with what we believe we should be doing—what we really believe.

You cannot be truly successful without doing it.

And, as I said, there are a million possible ways to do it. What is keeping your glass from being full and what can you do about it?

PUT YOUR VALUES TO WORK FOR YOU

Many religions believe in a final judgment. If you had to make a final judgment on your life, like the one Sam Walton made, what would that judgment be?

What are your real values? What's really important to you? It's not the purpose of this book to judge your values. That's up to you. The purpose of this book is to help you to get those values, whatever they might be, working for you. Few careers are value-neutral. If there's a conflict between what you truly value in life and what you find yourself valuing on the job, either your job or your life is going to suffer—probably both.

Again, this is about integrity. Being one person as opposed to being two-faced.

> **TIP:** Finding a way to do your job that's in tune with the way you really believe you should be living your life can make you far more effective on the job.

At the very least, it should make you happier.

Ron Campbell, the salesperson who thought his company's machines were overpriced, fills the glass for himself and adds water to his customer's glass by making sure the value-added services he provides are worth far more than the extra money his products cost. Norma Landry, the church secretary who was so concerned about her bishop's constant focus on fund-raising, fills the glass by making sure that every nickel raised does the most possible good.

You fill the glass according to your own values.

THE MAHATMA MARKETPLACE: BE THE CHANGE

"What I hate most about my job," a middle manager once confided, "is who it forces me to become and how it makes me act."

"So," I asked, "what would happen if you became who you'd like to be, and acted how you'd like to act?"

"Well . . . well, actually, I'm not sure."

"Would they fire you?"

"No, they wouldn't do that."

"Could you still do your job?" I asked.

"Actually, I could probably do it a lot better. But I'd be bucking the culture of the whole corporation."

So the question is, do you think that corporate culture needs bucking? And do you feel strongly enough about it to do it?"

> **TIP:** Neither the job nor the company makes us who we are. We make us who we are.

"Who you are is your decision, not the company's. If you have a problem with the standards or the values or the ethics of the company you're in, you don't have to accept them. You don't have to make a show of opposition; you can simply remember who you are and perform accordingly. That's called integrity. It's also called leadership—even if nobody is following. You may catch some flak, you may even be vilified. But often you'll find that ultimately you will be respected.

How much respect are you ever likely to get for turning yourself into somebody you're not?

And if you're successful, your values will spread. You may even be promoted. Sometimes you can simply *be* the change you want to see. Gandhi said that. Nobody's done a "Gandhi on business" book—*The Mahatma Marketplace?*—at least not yet. But this is a first-rate piece of business advice. Sometimes you can fill the glass just by doing your best to be the person you want to be within your job.

TIP: The job doesn't make the person, the person makes the job.

WHAT ARE YOU INDUSTRIOUS ABOUT?

However you decide to do it, filling the glass ultimately entails developing a vision for your career and a compatible vision for your life. Just as a company needs a vision, so do we as individuals: to keep us on track, to motivate us, and to keep us aware of who we are, why we are who we are, and why that person has value, to ourselves and to others.

As Thoreau said, "It is not enough to be industrious: so are the ants. What are you industrious about?"

Just as companies develop a mission statement designed to show how their vision functions in the marketplace, you should develop a mission statement for how you'd like your vision to function on the job and in your career.

This is not the same as simply setting goals. "Getting to be the CEO" is a goal. "Getting to be CEO by helping each of my people develop to their fullest potential" is a vision.

Past generations frequently filled the glass by enduring the drudgery of the job in order to achieve some long-term goal: a better life for their family or an eventual business of their own. Where others saw themselves as condemned to a life of backbreaking labor, these people had a vision strong enough to give their work value to themselves and to others. They weren't working on the railroad or in the cotton fields: they were working on a dream.

Many of those dreams came true. But often that left the children and grandchildren of those dreamers lacking a dream of their own—at least a dream they could find as meaningful.

TIP: Have a vision for your work. Develop a mission.

PROFUNDITY NOT REQUIRED

Your vision doesn't have to be profound. Say you come up with a great new type of boots. You know they're just what people need. They're warmer, more comfortable, and more flexible than anything on the market. You do some direct mail advertising. The orders start coming in. Then the boots start coming back—with the leather tops separating from the rubber soles. Ninety out of the first hundred pairs are returned. Refunding that much money will come close to driving you out of business. You've already spent most of the receipts tooling up for the anticipated demand. What do you do?

If you're L.L. Bean, you have a vision and the decision is virtually made. You make the refunds: no hassles, no questions asked. And you begin to establish a reputation that's worth more than the price of 100,000 pairs of boots.

Having a vision doesn't mean you have to run around claiming to be working for world peace or feeding the hungry. This is your life, not a Miss America contest. You're not looking for brownie points. You're not trying to impress anyone. This is for you. And again, we're not talking about morality or altruism here, we're talking about what you would like your work and your business life to be.

In other words, if you could somehow manage to conduct your career in tune with this vision, your final judgment on at least the business part of your own life would be pretty much what you would want it to be.

Have a vision. Do your best to live by it.

You will not succeed, at least not completely. You aren't perfect. Don't beat yourself up when you fail, but don't let failure in the past excuse failure in the future. Acknowledge the failure, learn from it, then forget it and do your best to do better from that point on. The harder you try, the closer you keep to your own personal vision, the better you'll feel about yourself and your career. Even the fact that you're making the effort may help you overcome the dissonance you have in your life.

The effort itself can start filling that glass for you.

WHAT WORKS BEST

Like most people, I'm in favor of morality. Like many of us, I consider it particularly important in other people—people like yourself. Many of whom, as we know, can't entirely be trusted. But, let me repeat, this is not, *not* about morality. We're trying to fill the glass here, not the chalice. This is about doing what works best—what works best for you as a person, and in most cases what will also work best for you as a worker and a leader.

The values we're talking about here are yours, not mine. Whatever those values may be. Conflicting values sap your energy and increase doubt. Reducing the disconnect between the person you want to be and the person you actually are when you're doing your job will make you more effective, more honest, more confident and decisive, and will vastly improve your credibility. In most cases, that will make you far more effective at work.

THE MOST WORTHWHILE GOAL

Once you have a vision, you might find that one of the best ways of filling the glass involves working or managing for the most worthwhile goal within that vision. It might be the most worthwhile goal for you personally, or for your family. Or you might fill the glass by working for the most worthwhile goal for some or all of the stakeholders of your company.

> **TACTIC:** Like Ron Campbell, your goal might be to give the best customer service possible. Even for those of us who aren't salespeople, customer service is often an excellent way to make up for shortcomings in a product, a department, or a company.

Find a way of improving customer service and you'll often find a way of improving your career. Obviously, customers are the ultimate focus of any business. And as Jan Carlzon of SAS, the Scandinavian airline, used to say, "If you don't serve the customer, you serve somebody who does."

TACTIC: Try treating your internal customers—even those who work for you—the way top salespeople treat their most important accounts. This means service. It means respect and courtesy and taking the time and the trouble to build rapport. It also means getting their input before making decisions—recommendations—and their buy-in afterward.

TIP: Dictators dictate. Leaders sell. Their subordinates, their peers, and sometimes even their superiors, follow because they wish to follow. In situations where you lack the authority to have people taken out and shot, try leadership.

TACTIC: Sometimes you can make the very experience of dealing with you something that will help fill the glass for those around you. That in itself can help fill the glass for you.

When Dustin took over as shipping's liaison with manufacturing, the two departments had more hostility for each other than for the competition. "With his unfailing good humor, understanding of the processes, and willingness to do whatever must be done, he brings people together and creates solutions," says one manufacturing foreman. "With Dustin, it's always *our* problems. Before, it was always *your* problem. *Your* problems never seem to get fixed as quickly as *our* problems do."

Angela was hired for what appeared to be a dead-end receptionist job. Then, as she says, she "asked questions, read manuals, made phone calls, and talked to everyone who knew anything," and made herself an expert on every piece of software used in the office. Now, like Ron Campbell, she's become an indispensable resource—not only for her fellow workers but for management as well.

"We literally could not run this department without Angela," her boss insists. She's become the highest paid clerical person on the staff—by far."

> **TACTIC:** Some people fill the glass by working toward making their companies better corporate citizens. One directory publishing executive carved out his own niche as the company environmental activist. His recycling program turned the potentially devastating issue of phone book disposal into an environmental triumph and, not incidentally, a public relations and competitive triumph as well.

A heavy equipment company had a "minor restructuring"—at least that's what the corporate officers considered it. The next day, the vice president of manufacturing was scheduled for a routine visit to the plant where the layoffs would be taking place. She was amazed to find a large and bitter demonstration.

"One sign read, 'A businessman is just a criminal who's incorporated,'" she says. "That got to me. It wasn't the way I saw myself. It wasn't the way I saw the people I worked with. Hell, I danced naked at Woodstock. And that was only a few decades, and won't say how many pounds, ago."

So she decided to develop an expertise in community issues. Her program to subsidize vocational training programs in local community colleges has turned an inadequate hiring pool into a steady stream of highly qualified workers. It's just one part of a much larger strategy to strengthen the bonds between the local communities and what they've often come to feel is *their* plant.

> **TACTIC:** Many people try to fill the glass by working for change within their company. Whether you're an executive or a worker or an owner, the old adage is usually true. Five percent of us make things happen, 10 percent watch things happen, 85 percent wonder what happened. We're all familiar with the medieval business guru who said, "Grant me the serenity to accept the things I cannot change, the courage to change the

things I can, and the wisdom to know the difference." Thirteenth-century MBAs referred to this as Saint Frankie A's Differentiating Paradigm, and it's a still an excellent model for setting priorities in a corporate environment.

If the company is willing to listen, you have the right, even the obligation, to pass your suggestions up the chain of command to those who can make the change. If they never hear what's wrong, they can't be expected to do anything about it. And passing on information is part of what they're paying you to do. In a survey of companies listed in *The 100 Best Companies to Work for in America,* the majority of the respondents said that the most common mistake dissatisfied employees make is not giving the company an opportunity to work things out before they quit.

For those of you who work for the one of the 100 *worst* companies to work for in America, the most common employee mistake is letting the boss know you are dissatisfied. After that, you might as well quit.

Someone once said that if you have time to whine and complain about something, you have time to do something about it. Trust me, as human beings we can whine and complain about any number of things we can't do anything about. And a few other things may take a bit longer to fix than they do to complain about. But I will grant that often, if you have time to whine and complain about something, you have time to *start* doing something about it. Often, however, doing something about it involves simply bringing the problem to the attention of someone who has the power to act. In other words, whining and complaining in a way that doesn't sound like whining and complaining.

Occasionally, like perhaps 99.9 percent of the time, sending the problem up the corporate ladder yields no discernable results. And you have to find another way to fill the glass.

TACTIC: Some employees do it by becoming like the "skunk works" types Tom Peters talks about: working undercover with a group of likeminded peers to turn their company into the kind of company it should be. Reporter Bob Woodward once claimed that, "all good work is done in defiance of management." An overstatement, but not without a kernel of truth.

TACTIC: Many CEOs devote themselves to doing the best possible job for the stockholders—the people who own the company. That's who they see themselves as working for, that's who they feel they owe their greatest allegiance to. If that's what they truly believe, there's nothing wrong with that. The stockholders usually include pension funds and armies of little old ladies and little old men. And even the richest investors have a right to make a profit. If they don't, they're going to take their capital elsewhere, which means no company and no benefits for any of the other stakeholders.

Of course there are stockholders, and then there are stockholders.

"You bet I work for the stockholders," one CEO told me recently. "But I work for the long-term stockholders—the people who have faith in the corporation and in me and who've cast their lot with us. I'm not nearly as interested in seeing that short-term investors—the speculators—make a profit. I've watched too many CEOs try to become Wall Street heroes. They slash R&D and advertising, and decimate the workforce. They devour the company's seed corn. They run up short-term stock prices—usually netting themselves a fortune—and destroy the company."

In 1995, American Airlines was vastly larger than ValuJet, and it had 50 times the profit. Yet the stock market was so infatuated with ValuJet's shortsighted cost-cutting that—by market capitalization—ValuJet was actually worth more than American Airlines. The fact that their accident incidence was 14 times the major carrier average was immaterial. This particular Wall Street darling crashed when one of its DC-9s went down in the Florida Everglades. The crash killed 109 people and—eventually—the company.

TIP: Having a job means devoting your life—or a great deal of your life—to something. You'll be far happier and probably far more successful if you make it something you consider worthwhile.

You can't necessarily transform your job. But you can ask yourself what you consider to be the most worthwhile goal for the job you have.

You can't fill the glass if deep down inside you don't really believe in what you are doing. But can't you believe in making people's lives better, whether it's the lives of the people who work for you, the lives of your customers, or the lives of your stockholders or any other group?

NUMBER ONE

"Do you know who I'm working for?" an ambitious executive once asked me over a couple of drinks in a hotel bar. "Do you know whose interests I keep uppermost in my mind when I manage? Mine. I look out for Number One. And I don't have a problem with that."

"Neither do I." I said. "Not in the slightest."

Are you working for your own benefit? Of course you are. We all are. There's not a thing wrong with that. Filling the glass is all about doing what's best for you. That's why you're trying to make peace with the negative in the first place—so you'll feel better about what you're doing with your life. But human beings being what we are, working strictly for our own material gain often isn't enough to completely satisfy us. If it's enough for you, fine. This is about doing what works best and is most satisfying for you. This is about self-interest—enlightened self-interest, but self-interest all the same.

This is not about sacrificing yourself for the sake of someone else. It's about helping them while helping yourself, according to whatever your values might be.

Helping others get what they want is not only satisfying, it can be extremely profitable. Isn't that, after all, what capitalism is all about?

> **TACTIC:** Some people manage to fill the glass simply by helping others with problems similar to their own.

Janice is part of a group trying to deal with the workplace dilemmas caused by their early-onset Alzheimer's disease. "There are no big solutions," she says, "But we've solved a lot of little ones. And the support I can give them and they give me has been more rewarding than anything else I've ever experienced in the workplace."

There are an infinite number of ways to fill the glass. We'll be looking at others throughout the book.

CHAPTER | **5**

Fill Their Glass First

If you're a manager, often—very often—you have to fill the glass for those you manage before you can fill your own. There are as many ways of doing that as there are people to be managed—at least people who believe their careers should be one thing but find the reality to be considerably less. And obviously the same techniques that can help you or me can also help them.

But as a manager, as a leader, you've also got other tools at your disposal, tools of motivation and reward.

What do you do when the job simply isn't meaningful or satisfying enough for your people? What do you do when they're asking themselves, *Why am I wasting my time here?* Money is seldom an adequate answer.

Warren Buffett claims that he really only has two duties. The first is allocating capital. "The second is to help 15 or 20 senior managers keep a group of people enthused about what they do when they have no financial need whatsoever to do it. At least three-quarters of the managers that we have are rich beyond any possible financial need, and therefore my job is to help my senior people keep them interested enough to want to jump out of bed at six o'clock in the morning and work with all of the enthusiasm they did when they were poor and starting out. If I do those two things, they do the innovation."

Those who work for you may not be quite that wealthy. But few of us are going to leap enthusiastically out of bed every day at 6:00 AM just for the money anyway. We may crawl out. We aren't going to leap. So how can you fill the glass for your people and fill it so high that you can generate that kind of excitement and enthusiasm?

Well—short of filling their morning coffee cup with liquid amphetamine—you probably can't. But you can certainly do a far better job than most companies are doing now.

WELCOME TO THE WEASEL-OCRACY

Salespeople are motivated by having a goal, a way to judge their progress toward that goal, and rewards for reaching it. To keep them motivated long term, the goal and the rewards have to be both meaningful to them and attainable. And the more control they have over the outcome, the better. You and I are no different, and neither are your people.

One the other hand . . .

A large financial services corporation "cannot, after extensive study, uncover any reasonable explanation" for why so many of their best people either turn down promotions or leave for management opportunities elsewhere—in some cases lower-paying management opportunities. They should try talking to some of their employees.

"The company brags about being a meritocracy," a financial planner named Jonathan, says, "And there's no question that some outstanding people have risen high in the ranks. But too often it's more a luckocracy. Too often, damn good people with years of first-rate service get demoted simply because the economy in their region goes into the tank. Being surrounded by demoted ex-managers doesn't give you a warm and fuzzy feeling for your own chances. Then too, we've got some low-grade morons who got promoted simply because they happened to be occupying a desk in an area where the economy turned around."

"I've got an MBA," a planner named Bill added, "which the company was nice enough to pay for and which I'll probably never use. At least not around here. I've already turned down three promotions." Jonathan hasn't quite finished his MBA or he'd realize that fundamentally this company is neither a meritocracy nor a luck-ocracy. Technically it's actually a weasel-ocracy. Too many of our so-called "leaders" have gotten where they are because of their outstanding *following* skills. They know just who to play up to and when: always kissing just the right posterior at just the right time. They protect their own butts by never taking a risk or seizing an opportunity—never doing any real leading."

Jonathan nodded. "Take the GM who currently runs this division. His last boss—our previous VP—had a mustache, wore three-piece suits, and wire-rim glasses; and he had his Day-Timer surgically attached to his right hand. So, coincidentally enough, did our GM."

"When they walked into a room it looked like Tweedle-dum and Tweedle-dumber," Bill added.

"You never saw such a shameless toady. Then the VP was demoted in favor of new blood. The very next time I saw the GM, the glasses were replaced by contacts, the mustache was gone, and the Day-Timer forgotten. Fortunately, the new female VP is big on pantsuits or this particular 'leader' would be sporting dresses and pantyhose."

"And they wonder why the upward path in this company leads right out the front door," Bill grumbled. "Somebody once said it takes intelligence and ingenuity and years of application to ruin a large corporation. Stupidity and spinelessness can also do a pretty fair job."

THE PRONOUN TEST

We hear so much about leadership. And we all know leadership starts with vision. Take, for example, Japanese industrialist Konosuke Matsushita, founder of Panasonic. In 1932, Matsushita told his 1,100 employees, "The mission of a manufacturer is to overcome poverty, to relieve society as a whole from misery and bring it wealth. Beginning today, this far-reaching dream, this sacred calling, will be our ideal and our mission, and its fulfillment the responsibility of each one of us."

You can certainly disagree with Matsushita's conception of a manufacturing company's mission. You argue whether or not Panasonic ever actually tried to live up to this ideal. But what you can't deny is that this is a clear, dramatic mission statement that employees could find worthy of rallying around, worthy of devoting their shared effort to. And you can't deny the company's success in becoming the world's largest manufacturer of electronics.

It's certainly a lot better than what was provided by the owner of one floundering furniture manufacturer.

"Vision?" his second in commanded wondered. "Lee doesn't have a clue where he wants the company to go. But he's inordinately proud of the fact that he's willing to work himself and all the rest of us to death to get there."

Then there's the cigarette company Janette Hawthorne worked for. "When it came to noble sentiments, their mission statement read like the U.N. charter. It could have been written by Thomas Jefferson or Mother Teresa. Coming from this particular company, it was a sick joke and that's the way everyone treated it."

> **TIP:** Vision without substance is not vision, it's illusion. Illusion has no long-term motivating power. It's worse than no vision at all because it creates distrust and cynicism.

And vision is a two-way street. It comes down from the top of the corporate ladder. But it should also rise up from the individuals who make up the company, each of whom should have a vision for what they'd like their life to be.

The more compatible those two visions are, the more powerful the total effect will be.

People love to feel they're part of something special. Helping them feel part of something bigger than themselves, part of a team, can go a long way toward filling their glasses—along with your glass as a manager and the company's glass as well. The more being part of that team gels with the vision they have for their own life, the easier this will be.

Former U.S. Secretary of Labor Robert B. Reich talks about what he calls the pronoun test. He asks employees about the company they work for. "If the answers I get back describe the company in terms like *they* and *them,* then I know it's one kind of company. If the answers are put in terms like *we* or *us,* I know it's a different kind of company."

TEAM SPORTS

Too frequently, however, businesses extol and even demand teamwork then set up situations, which destroy any possible team spirit.

> **TIP:** Don't expect team players if you haven't made it a team sport.

If you want team play, then set up competitions in which one employee wins and others lose, you aren't going to get team play. At least not among those employees.

If some employees have to work significantly harder than others who are supposed to be part of the same team, how are they going to feel? Especially if some of those they're outworking are supposed to be leading the team. How would you feel?

And, though my CEO friends don't want to hear it, there's also the issue of compensation. In 1990, the average CEO made about 45 times what his average worker made; today it's 450 times. Companies lose money and their CEOs get $70 million. Companies don't reach their targets and their boards of directors redefine the targets—making sure the top executives get their bloated bonuses. Business writer Charles R. Morris calls it "affirmative action for the managerially challenged."

If you're one of those CEOs, you may be absolutely certain you're worth 450 times what one of your average workers is worth. But I want to hear you explaining that to those particular "teammates."

"[The CEO] made over $10 million last year; I made $29,000," is the way one of those average workers put it. "That tells me how he values himself and how he values me. If we all bust our butts like he's asking, next year I may make as much as $29,900. And he'll make $20 million. How can we be on the same team when we're not even in the same league?"

"It is more apparent every day that our managers are making decisions that will influence their bonuses, stock options, et cetera, not decisions for the good of the company," insists an employee of a major chemical company.

AT&T's board of directors fired their president after just nine months saying he lacked "intellectual leadership." He got a severance package worth $26 million. To me, getting $26 million plus for nine months' work sounds like pretty solid evidence of intelligence. *Paying $26 million for nine months' work may not be the best possible example of "intellectual leadership" on the part of the board of directors.*

On the other hand, Silicon Valley companies are attracting and retaining top people by sharing stock options not just with top executives, but throughout the company—in some cases that includes the janitor. Lynn Parker, who runs Parker LePla, a 22-person PR agency in Seattle, Washington, distributes nearly 40 percent of profits to employees. Her stock option plan vests everyone after six months. Only five people have left the company in the last six years. "Unless your people experience some type of ownership," she says, "you're going to have turnover."

> **TIP:** If I don't win when the team wins, I'm not on the team. And it will never take more than one victory for me to figure that out.

PROLONGING THE JOURNEY

Managers who aren't loyal to their people can't expect loyalty in return. Companies that complain about employee loyalty have usually done nothing to earn loyalty, often routinely lying to employees, demanding sacrifices that are never rewarded, shunting them aside and casting them off in the name of good business. That particular weaselocracy that Bill and Jonathan complained about routinely takes top-performing managers and sticks them in problem markets. Fair enough. What isn't fair is that these managers are paid on an inflexible bonus and override system. This means their reward for doing a superior job and for helping the company out is a massive cut in pay and frequently a poor evaluation if they fail to turn the market around quickly enough.

And upper management cannot understand the lack of loyalty throughout the company. Or why they have the highest turnover rate in their industry.

During the Civil War, a reporter asked General Ulysses S. Grant how long it would take him to reach Richmond. "I will agree to be there in about four days," Grant answered. "That is, if General Lee becomes a party to the agreement. But if he objects, the trip will undoubtedly be prolonged."

When supposed teammates aren't really teammates, the journey toward the goal will undoubtedly be prolonged.

Sidney Harman is chairman of Harman International, maker of high-end sound systems like JBL and Infinity. "We attract people who over time become persuaded that this company is their company and they are going to give it their all," he told PBS's *Surviving the Bottom Line.* "When people determine to give it their all, the levels of productivity you see will blow your mind."

To help employees see the company as *their* company, Harman International does everything possible to avoid layoffs. When demand is down, the company keeps production workers busy in security or maintenance or landscaping rather than downsizing them. They're paid their normal wages. Employees benefit and Harman International retains its highly trained, loyal workforce.

To keep the channels of communication open between management and labor, every single executive spends time every month on the production line. Sidney Harman also discourages the use of temps. And there's no such thing as a permanent temp. If a temp stays past a certain point, he or she becomes a regular worker with full benefits.

Nowadays this may seem like radical, outside-the-box thinking. Or maybe it's inside a box so out of fashion that few other companies ever bother to look inside. Either way, it's turned Harman International into an industry leader, a company with $1.4 billion in annual sales. Ed Boyd, senior vice president of manufacturing, says, "I've worked for four corporations on three continents and this is by far the most motivated group of individuals I've ever been associated with."

That's a team.

STUDYING THEIR THINKING

One recent study found that "management recognition of the importance of personal and family life" was the most important factor in creating employee loyalty. It also found that employees who were allowed to spend a moderate amount of time on personal matters during work time—even if it was merely making a few personal phone calls—were more committed to their employers than those who weren't.

Yet in a recent survey of CEOs by the Conference Board, only one percent cited "helping employees achieve work-life balance" as their top concern. Well, it might not be number one, but it had better be up there. In still another study—this one done by the Families and Work Institute and funded by corporations like AT&T, Xerox, Allstate, American Express, and IBM—38 percent of workers said employees who put personal or family needs ahead of their jobs were not looked upon favorably by their employer.

TIP: Any manager who expects his people to put the company's needs ahead of their own needs and the needs of their loved ones is not bright enough to be a manager. How many managers put company needs ahead of their own?

TIP: Too many.

According to the Associated Press, the Families and Work Institute study "paints a portrait of a hard worker who feels burned out from balancing work and family life yet cares intensely about performing well on the job."

In the words of AT&T spokesman Burke Stinson, "The study validates what we'd believed for a long while." When employees get more freedom to take care of their family priorities, productivity does not suffer, just the opposite. "Employees who feel as if they're being treated fairly will treat their employers at least as fairly in return."

And factors like employment security, flexible scheduling, and supportive work relationships reduce burnout, increase loyalty, and generate greater effort.

Of course whenever studies like these are done, the question some always ask is, Why do employers have to fund studies to discover what their employees are thinking?

SIMPLE TRUTHS

Managers should never forget these three simple truths:

1. You can never expect your people to have a greater vision for the company than the one that your actions demonstrate that you have.
2. If your people believe the company is trying to take advantage of them, many will try to take advantage of the company. Some will succeed.
3. You can never expect your people to be more ethical than you are. Even if you've never done anything against them, if they see you cutting corners with customers, why shouldn't they cut corners with you?

MAXIE FLOWERS

TIP: Never expect more of your people than you expect from yourself.

Maxie Weisberg, AKA Maxie Flowers, has been a bookie in St. Paul, Minnesota, for 40 years. Maxie has an IQ in the 50s. The state would like to prosecute him for bookmaking, but he insists that what he is doing is no worse than the state lottery.

"What's the difference?" he asks.

Maxie honestly can't see the difference. And because of that, psychologists and the courts have determined that he's incapable of distinguishing between right and wrong. Which means the state can't prosecute him.

If the winters were a little warmer, I'd give serious thought to moving to Minnesota and becoming a bookie, because I can't see the difference either. To me, it looks as though the state wants to prosecute Maxie for horning in on their gambling business. (And they probably don't mind the $700,000 they've confiscated from their repeated raids on his ramshackle house.)

Obviously, I'm just being facetious. Any normal person can see the difference between illegal bookmaking and a state lottery. Maxie only deals with people who seek him out; he doesn't promote his business on TV and radio and tempt people who can't afford it into throwing their money away. And of course, with Maxie the odds of winning are millions of times greater than they are with the state.

Let me repeat: Never expect more from your people than you expect from yourself.

That doesn't mean you shouldn't expect a lot from your people. And help them to expect a lot from themselves. It simply means that you have to demand at least as much from yourself.

PURSUING HAPPINESS?

As I said, helping your people to fill the glass is part of what management is all about, and having that as a goal can go a long way toward filling the glass for you. Fight for your people. Listen to them. Explain what you expect them to do, how the work is worthwhile to the company and to them, then give them the resources, the aid, encouragement, and feedback so they can do a job you'll both be proud of. Help them to reach their goals and do it in accordance with their vision.

Few things in life are more rewarding than helping others grow and succeed. Especially if you helped give them the faith in themselves to try to succeed in the first place.

> **TIP:** Help your people feel better about themselves.

David Myers is a professor of psychology at Hope College and the author of *The Pursuit of Happiness*. Myers says, "Your happiness is like your cholesterol level. Both are genetically influenced, yet both are—to a certain extent—under your control." No surprise, self-esteem is the trait most strongly linked to happiness. You wouldn't expect a high degree of bliss among self-loathers and potential suicides. Happiness also is associated with health, intelligence, and a feeling of being in control of one's life.

You can't do much about the health of those who work for you. You can do precious little about their intelligence. But you can do something about giving them the feeling of being in control of their working lives. And you often can do a great deal about the way they think about themselves.

Which means you have the power to make other people happy—to one extent or another. That's another one of those truths that we all know but seldom seem to remember. When it comes right down to it, we all have that power; as a boss you simply have more.

> **INCREDIBLY OBVIOUS TIP:** Make the people around you happy, and you'll be surrounded by happy people.

> **INCREDIBLY OBVIOUS COROLLARY:** Most of us are happier when we're surrounded by happy people.

DISTINGUISHING THE CARROT FROM THE STICK

Every manager and every organization pays lip service to leading by empowerment and positive reinforcement. "They swear they believe in the carrot not the stick," one ex-manager told me of his former employer. "But a lot of people seem to be getting brutalized by that carrot." ("Brutalized" is actually my word; the phrase he used was considerably more graphic—and painful to imagine.)

He showed me several postcards from his former coworkers. One read, "The flogging will continue until morale improves." Another quoted Steven Wright, "For every action there is an equal and opposite criticism."

I was reminded of a Fortune 500 vice president who brought me to a corporate management conference a few years back to deliver a presentation on the benefits of empowerment. It was very well received; the vice president himself was so inspired that he immediately leaped up and told all his minions that they'd better be empowered from that moment on, "Or believe me heads are going to roll." He added, in all seriousness, "Just make sure you clear anything you want to do with me first."

"He just empowered them to do nothing but claim to be empowered," one of the other speakers whispered to me.

"Not quite," I said. "He *ordered* them to claim to be empowered."

Try treating those you supervise as partners, not peons. As Booker T. Washington observed, "Few things help an individual more than to place responsibility on him, and to let him know you trust him."

"Management is simple," one award-winning manager claims. "I create incentives, small rewards, recognitions. I believe in my people, and I show them how much I believe in them. I get them to want to live up to my high opinion, and then I give them the freedom to do just that."

We all need to be appreciated. There's a joke about a guy who's stranded on a tiny desert island. One day he's walking on the beach and he stumbles across a woman, washed up just above the surf line. She's in bad shape and as he reaches her, she stops breathing. Quickly he administers mouth-to-mouth resuscitation. After a few frightening seconds, she starts breathing again and opens her eyes.

"You saved my life," she insists gratefully.

She brushes the hair back from her face. That's when he realizes that he's stranded on a desert island with the biggest box office star and the most gorgeous and most famous beauty of the day. To avoid litigation, we'll call her Tasmalia Thistlemore.

Time passes. The island is warm with plenty of fruit. They build a comfortable hut. It's like Eden. Tasmalia falls deeply in love with him, and making love becomes their major form of entertainment. Then one day, she notices he looks depressed. She asks him what could possibly be wrong in such an idyllic existence.

"Is there anything I can do?" she wonders.

"Well, actually," he replies, "there is something."

"Anything, darling."

"Would you mind putting on my shirt?"

That puzzles her, but she says, "Of course not," and puts on the shirt.

"Now could you put on my pants?"

"Sure, if you think it will make you feel better."

"Good. Now put on my coat and draw a mustache on your face." She goes along with that too. Then he says, "Now, would you please start walking down the beach and head around the island?"

She starts out, and he sets off in the opposite direction. Fifteen minutes later they meet on the far side of the island.

He rushes up to her, grabs her by the shoulders, and says, "Man, you will never believe who I'm sleeping with!"

We all need appreciation and recognition. Appreciate your people. Help them discover their self-worth and their potential.

TIP: Mark Twain said that great people make you feel that you too can become great. Make others feel that they can become great and maybe you won't be a great person, but you will get great results.

When Emery Air Freight started encouraging supervisors to use positive feedback—telling workers when they were doing a good job rather than stressing the negative—customer service improved and sales increased. After three years, the company estimated the new system had made them $3 million.

100 UNSUPERVISED DECISIONS A DAY

Employees work best when they're being themselves, when they're fully committed, when they're contributing their own ideas. The average worker supposedly makes 100 unsupervised decisions a day. If they're looking over their shoulder on every one them, they're going to walk into a lot of walls.

Catalyst, a nonprofit group that seeks to advance women in business, commissioned a study of businesspeople to discover what was most important to them in a career. At the very top of the list were the emotional benefits like supportive management, freedom to do the job on their own, and control over their output.

> **TIP:** Financial compensation is important. But you can't buy loyalty, enthusiasm, commitment, or devotion. You have to earn it.

THE BIG CARROT

> **TACTIC:** A salesperson's pay is determined by his or her production. You may even decide that filling the glass for your people includes giving them a percentage of the profits—even a piece of the business.

A study at the University of Michigan found that companies with at least partial worker ownership average one and a half times the profits of traditional companies in their fields. Give away a piece and everybody makes more.

According to the American Compensation Association, 63 percent of U.S. companies now use incentives, bonuses, and other profit-sharing arrangements to tie at least part of their workers' pay to their performance. In 1990, only 15 percent did.

One out of every three businesses offers stock options to employees below the level of executive. In Silicon Valley, they talk about *growthcos,* companies that use options to compensate workers, and *stodgecos,* old-line companies that don't. We may be developing an entire class of "worker capitalists," employees who share the risks and share the profits.

Karl Marx would have been delighted. Or appalled, I'm not sure which.

"People aren't coming to work as factory workers but as business owners," Michael Stipicevic, plant manager for Unilever's Cartersville, Georgia, plant told the *Los Angeles Times*. "They're saying this is my machine, my plant." Unilever's "goal-sharing" pay plan has produced a torrent of cost savings ideas. Half of the first year savings are returned to the workers.

TIP: Speak softly and carry a big carrot.

PEARL HARBOR COMMENDATIONS

Reward behavior you wish to encourage, and only that behavior. Don't claim you want long-range planning, then base bonuses on the short-term fix. Don't expect innovative thinking if you give the best evaluations to employees who march lockstep to the company beat. Don't look for streamlining and promote those who create ever more complicated controls. Don't expect cost cutting when departments that exhaust this year's allocation get more money next year, and those who don't spend every cent face cutbacks.

TIP: Rewarding accomplishment is usually more effective than rewarding behavior. Whenever possible, set quantifiable goals, track progress toward those goals, then reward their accomplishment.

Reward each employee according to what motivates him or her personally: more responsibility, more recognition, pats on the back, perks and privileges, more freedom, more challenges, fancier offices, exposure to decision makers, titles, parking spaces, staffing, more flexible hours, the opportunity for more creativity. Even a lunch or dinner with you can be an extremely meaningful reward for some people. Just as it could be the worst possible punishment for others.

Additional training can be a particularly effective reward. It demonstrates the commitment the company has in the employee's future. Yet it's giving them something they give right back to the business.

Never reward indiscriminately. In Granada there were more medals awarded than there were soldiers in the campaign. You don't find a lot of people bragging about their Granada combat citations or framing them and hanging them over the mantle.

I know of one manager who sends out a steady torrent of "You're Fantastic" cards. Everyone gets them. For everything. All the cards are the same, and none ever mentions a specific reason for the acknowledgement.

"He probably fills them out in advance at home at night then writes in the name as needed," one of his clerical people decided.

Most of the cards quickly find their way into the trash. Some people do save them: for the "Pearl Harbor files" they keep to defend against possible disciplinary action or dismissal. And more and more of these people are keeping Pearl Harbor files. Though all they ever hear from the boss is how wonderful they are, he's developed such a reputation for insincerity that nobody trusts him.

Once while flying back from a successful European trip, George H. W. Bush took the time to personally write 40 notes of appreciation to various members of his presidential staff. When aides compared the various notes, they discovered that every single one of them was different. To me, the sheer volume of notes might call in question their sincerity and devalue the worth of any one of them. But I'll bet each of those 40 people appreciated his or her note, and most of them probably still have them.

TACTIC: Compliment people who deserve it. Always individualize the compliment with specifics. When the same compliment is given repeatedly to several different people, it rings false, even when it isn't.

TIP: Compliment the action, not the individual's character.

"Gee, you're so intelligent," is general, may be embarrassing and can sound insincere. But, "Damn, that was a smart idea you had in the meeting today," rings true, and it's less likely to make the recipient self-conscious.

THE HAWTHORNE EFFECT

TIP: Benefit from the Hawthorne effect.

This is a phenomenon first noted way back in 1924—several years before the era's leading "can-do" guru, Herbert Hoover, led the nation into the Depression. Elton Mayo was trying to study the effect of lighting on productivity at a Western Electric plant in Hawthorne, Illinois. He divided workers into two groups. For the test group, he increased the illumination in their work area. Productivity went up. For the control group, he left the lighting the same. Productivity went up.

That made no sense to Mayo, so he tried another study. He took a group of female workers, gave them regularly scheduled rest periods, company-paid lunches, and shorter work weeks. Productivity went up. Eighteen months later, all those perks were eliminated. And productivity? It went up once again.

Mayo concluded that productivity increased every time he paid attention to workers.

TIP: Pay attention to your people.

You might never get them to leap out of bed at 6:00 AM with delight at the prospect of heading off to work. But you can make them a lot happier and a lot more productive once they arrive. And you can keep them from ever asking, "Why am I wasting my time here?"

Of course there's always the school of management exemplified by the CEO who told *Fortune* magazine, "Leadership is demonstrated when the ability to inflict pain is confirmed." If that's what you believe and you think that fills the glass for you, good luck to you.

You're going to need it.

CHAPTER 6

Self-Esteem: A Tirade

If you value yourself more, if you have a higher opinion of yourself, you will probably be able to accomplish more. The positive thinkers are right about that. Only too many of them forget to include the *probably*. They tell us, you can if you think you can.

At a rubber chicken dinner, a fairly well-known positive-thinking guru of the Pollyanna school was seated next to a rising young corporate executive. Both were scheduled to speak after the meal. While they were eating, the guru explained to his less enlightened companion that—in spite of appearances to the contrary—every man and woman is entirely the master of his or her own fate.

This is something we'd all like to believe. And it seems that the more successful we are, the more we want to believe it. It makes the universe far less capricious and threatening. It makes our place within it far more secure. It also reinforces our individual merit: "We're successful because we're good and we work hard. Luck has nothing to do with it." Still this particular rising young corporate executive wasn't convinced.

"You don't think you've made it on your own?" the guru asked in surprise.

"Largely. My own efforts were probably the biggest factor. But I could have been who I am and done everything I did and still have fallen short or even failed. I have to admit there was a bit of luck—a few fortunate accidents along the way."

"Luck and accident are the failure's excuse," the guru insisted. Unfortunately, being of a somewhat dramatic turn of mind, he waved his arm to emphasize the point. A busboy was passing behind him carrying a tray of water glasses. The guru knocked one right into his own lap—just as the master of ceremonies stepped up to the microphone to introduce him. He gave his entire presentation standing behind the lectern, so few noticed he was wet, cold, and uncomfortable. Still, the speech wasn't up to his normal rousing standards.

Next it was the young executive's turn to speak. He moved out from behind the podium and stepped in front of the lead table.

"Accidents happen," he began. He picked up a glass of water and held it up. Tilting it until it was about ready to spill, he held it over the head of the company CEO seated behind the table. The CEO looked up. The audience tittered nervously. Then the executive walked down the length of the table, holding the glass over the heads of each of the confused dignitaries.

"And into every life some rain must fall," the executive continued. He turned to the audience. Then he slowly poured the water over his own head, drenching himself and his obviously expensive suit. The audience actually gasped, then the gasp yielded to scattered laughter. "But rain is just rain. They say you can drown in a teaspoon full of water. Too often too many of us drown in what may be a bit more than a teaspoon but hardly ever qualifies as an actual flood."

"So what do you do in a real flood?" the irritated guru called out.

"Swim—just as long and as hard as you can." The executive smiled. "A little water doesn't have to be a problem. But pretending to be dry can't keep you from being all wet."

Pollyanna positive thinkers say, you can if you think you can. I say, you've got a far better chance if you think you can. Certainly you can't if you're sure you can't.

But let's get real here. The streets are full of people who are unshakably convinced they can do all manner of delusional and megalomaniacal things. They can not. Crazy people step off rooftops absolutely certain they can fly. The term *loony bird* does not come from the fact that they succeed.

"Circumstances?" Napoleon sneered. "What are circumstances? I make circumstances." And he did. To a certain extent. For a while. Until circumstances and overconfidence unmade him.

TIP: If you're absolutely, 100 percent positive, without the slightest trace of a doubt that you can do something, get a second opinion.

MAGIC

"Don't be so literal," the positive thinkers tell me. But I tell them that one of the reasons why so many of us have so much trouble maintaining the type of positive attitude they would have us maintain is that they consistently overstate their case. That's part of the reason why so many try it, then crash and burn so quickly when they discover it doesn't work exactly the way they were told it would.

There's a world of difference between appropriate positive thinking based on reality and the type of simplistic, magical thinking that is so often espoused. Affirmations are fine and so is goal-setting. Mindless affirmations and empty goal-setting frequently remind me of the chanters who believe that if they repeat a particular combination of syllables devoutly enough and frequently enough, they'll get whatever they're chanting for. Want a new car? Chant. If you believe strongly enough and chant long enough, you'll get the car. No work required, no effort toward the goal: just chanting.

YOUR PLACE ON THE CONTINUUM

You can't if you're sure you can't. But many of us have trouble filling the glass—have trouble living the business life we feel we should be living—because of our lack of self-esteem. Of course, sometimes one of the reasons we don't hold ourselves in higher esteem is due to the very fact that we are not living that life.

This is the place where a self-help book is supposed to pat you on the back and tell you that you are a valuable human being, so you should hold yourself in higher esteem.

I'm not going to tell you that.

I don't even know you. You know yourself a lot better than I do. You are, when it comes right down to it, the world's foremost authority on you. And if you don't think much of yourself, who am I to contradict you? Maybe you know something I don't know.

Obviously, you are a valuable human being to yourself. You are the only you that you have. But your value to the rest of us—to the rest of humanity—depends on what you're doing for us.

What have you done for any of us lately? Maybe, not much. So as far as this "I'm okay, you're okay" stuff goes, maybe you're not so okay. It's not as if everybody is. The universe has produced Charles Manson, Jeffrey Dahmer, and Adolf Hitler. They weren't okay. And to be frank, I'm still not all that convinced about Attila the Hun. To me, those guys are on the bad end of a bad/good continuum that leads ultimately to those people who donate their kidneys to complete strangers and Mother Teresa. In between those extremes, it passes through Benito Mussolini; Al Capone; Richard Nixon; the salesperson who sells some poor little old lady an overpriced annuity she doesn't need; the driver who runs a red light because she doesn't have any patience, annoying and aggravating everyone else at the intersection and maybe even risking somebody else's life; and the bozo who talks in the movie theater because he's too self-centered to care that nobody around him wants to listen to him babble while they're paying $8 to watch a film. None of these people are all that okay—at least not when they are doing what they're doing.

Continuing across the continuum, we have the guy who gives an occasional buck to somebody in need, the woman who donates regularly to the United Way, the volunteer who gives several hours a month to help the homeless, etc., etc. We all have our places somewhere on the okay-dom continuum. And though most of us don't swing from Hitler to Mother Teresa, we do swing along it at different times of our lives, on different days, even in different hours.

Obviously, we don't all have the same values. So each of us is going to have our own perception of the bad/good continuum. But still, on balance—by our own standards—some of us aren't so okay at all, no matter how much we try to justify some of the things we do.

> **TIP:** If you want to improve your self-esteem, try earning it. Socrates said, "The nearest way to glory is to strive to be what you wish to be thought to be." It's also the nearest way to self-esteem.

Try to be a better person by your own standards. Maybe then you'll think better of yourself. Maybe then you'll believe those affirmations about what a worthwhile and valuable human being you are.

IMPROVE THE PRODUCT, LET THE IMAGE TAKE CARE OF ITSELF

I'm all for self-esteem. Too many people stop themselves before they ever start. They can't do it because they're certain they can't do it. And positive thinking is a wonderful thing. It's been said pessimists are only good for one thing: borrowing money from. Because they don't expect it back.

But Pollyanna positive thinking and the more Pollyanna aspects of the self-esteem movement are the logical outgrowths of 1950's-style selling and marketing: the mind-set that it's easier to improve the way people think about a product—improve its image—than to actually improve the product.

"Let's not worry about making you a better person, Mr. Manson. Let's just improve your self-esteem, and maybe that will make you better."

Yes, in most cases you probably can if only you believe you can. Human potential being what it is, you should never, *never* limit yourself by selling yourself short. And if you're a manager, you want to help your people avoid selling themselves short. You want to help them realize just how much they're capable of accomplishing.

But, for yourself, if the reason for your low self-esteem is that you're not living up to your own standards, then perhaps the best way to improve that self-esteem is to work on improving the product—the self you aren't esteeming. Do that, and you may find that the esteem—self and otherwise—takes care of itself.

TIP: Reality counts.

And a better product makes for an easier sale. Particularly when you're selling to yourself.

CHAPTER | **7**

Filling and Filling and Filling— More Tactics

There are as many ways of filling the glass as there are half full/half empty glasses. What's important is to discover what it would take to fill your glass, then set about doing it.

"For me, it wasn't a matter of not living the life I thought I should live," says Eleanor Adams, president of an international consulting firm. "I had no life. My days were filled with an infinite to-do list and a Day-Timer the size of the Manhattan phone directory."

How did Eleanor fill her glass? "I realized that perpetual motion without ever having a moment to think is not the idea behind my job. Achieving results is."

The last time we talked she said, "The better I get at what I do, the less I work."

Peter Drucker says that while being efficient means doing things right, being effective means doing the right things. But how many of us feel like the industrial designer who once told me, "We're far too busy around here to ever get anything done."

Organizational development expert Thomas Quick tells a story about a young man who was promoted to head the shipping department and had to work with an older and more experienced crew. After a few days, he cut a deal with them: if he didn't insist that they return to work immediately when their break ended, they would work harder.

The crew's productivity increased by 20 percent. Then the new supervisor's boss happened to catch them sitting around a few minutes after the official end of their break. Summoning the young man into his office, he angrily insisted that rules were rules and enforcing those rules was what supervision was all about. He didn't want to hear any reasons for granting exceptions.

So the rules were enforced. And production dropped back to where it had been. The men lost, the supervisor lost, and the corporation lost.

> **TACTIC:** Focus on results, not activity. Whenever possible, get your boss to do the same.

DO YOU WANT IT TUESDAY OR . . .

Lisa Garibaldi overcame her overwork problem simply by building some air into her schedule.

"I'm known around here for always cooperating on whatever needs to be done and for never ducking assignments," she says. "I'm proud of that, and I want it to continue. But nowadays I always try to negotiate enough extra time into any assignment to make sure I can produce the high-quality work my boss has come to expect. I try avoiding drop-dead deadlines that are likely to make me the one dropping dead."

The company gets better work and a less frazzled employee; and Lisa has a job she looks forward to going to. "I doubt if anyone who ever worked themselves to death felt a great sense of accomplishment at the achievement," she says.

> **TACTIC:** Get your manager to provide you with clearly defined goals. Negotiate to make the goals and the timeframe fair.

When screenwriter George S. Kaufman was told by the head of the studio that a script absolutely had to be completed by Tuesday, Kaufman replied, "Do you want it Tuesday or do you want it good?"

> **TIP:** Hard work is productive. Overwork usually isn't. That's why we call it *overwork*.

"Employee burnout is a greater problem for the business than it is for the employee," one human resources director insists. "The employee just starts looking for another job, and when they get a better one, they leave. We have to find and train a replacement. That can take a great deal of time and money. So why are so many intelligent businesses burning their people out?"

> **TIP:** As a manager, you can only burn out your most motivated people. The others are unlikely to let you work them that hard.

STRETCHING

> **TACTIC:** Jacque Daniel is a networking expert and a public speaking coach in Brea, California. For Jacque, filling the glass can be as simple as setting herself new goals. "One goal—if it's the right goal for you—can rekindle your desire and change your whole life," she insists.

Sometimes you can fill the glass by stretching yourself. You may find that doing your job to the best of your abilities makes the job more enjoyable. You may not. Still, it's worth a try. Worst case scenario: you might end up working a little harder and doing a better job for a few days.

There are those who claim that there are no bad jobs. And that if you apply yourself to the best of your abilities, any job will lead to something better. I'd love to believe that. But I've seen too many people busting their butts for companies that couldn't care less, for companies that, when they get more from employees, insist on even more. And more. Still, with any organization worth working for—and probably the organization you work for now—the following tip does apply.

> **TIP:** If you do a superior job, even at the most menial task, you will usually be given a chance to do a superior job at a higher level.

Business expert Dan Kennedy talks about a young entrepreneur who started out mowing lawns. He worked for himself so he didn't have a supervisor he could impress nor an organization he could move up in.

His marketing plan was to simply do the best possible job the first time he mowed a customer's lawn, then contract to do the same thing regularly. Beyond that, he scheduled appointments and kept them. His equipment was clean and so were his uniformed employees—once he got employees. He put out a newsletter.

His business now grosses over $1 million a year.

He hasn't done anything new or anything particularly complicated. He mows lawns. He does landscaping. He just does it very well.

> **TIP:** Nowadays we're all looking for the next great breakthrough idea. But often the biggest breakthroughs come in doing something exceedingly well rather than in doing something exceedingly different.

Mozart—arguably the greatest creative talent of all time—said, "I have never made the slightest effort to compose anything original." He merely tried to create the best possible music.

Many of us lack confidence because of what we perceive as a shortfall in education. Frequently, like much of what saps our confidence, this has more to do with perception than reality. More than 40 of *Forbes'* "200 Best Small Companies" are run by people who never made it past high school. Some of America's worst-run companies are run by people whose résumés are packed with impressive educational credentials and what appear to be intimidating levels of experience.

This doesn't mean that you shouldn't take advantage of every possible opportunity for learning and growth. You may just develop a few impressive talents of your own. And the alternative to continued growth and learning is stagnation.

"When your job no longer demands more than you have, do something else," Harlan Cleveland writes in *Future Executive.* I love that quote, because he's saying that your job *should* demand more than you have; that you should never be intimidated when that's the case; that you should have to stretch yourself.

TACTIC: Hone your skills and cultivate new ones. Prepare yourself for your next position inside or outside your present organization, inside or outside your present field.

Beyond the experience and training that businesses offer internally, many encourage employees to continue their formal education. And more and more colleges have programs geared for working adults: with accelerated programs, evening and weekend classes, off-campus sites, even distance learning over the Internet. When Sara Tailor decided to pursue a master's degree in information management to help in her new job, the average age of the students in her management class was 40. Almost 20 percent of them already held advanced degrees. Many were getting tuition reimbursement from their employers. Others were receiving financial aid from the school.

If meager earnings are part of the reason for your half empty glass, consider this: According to the University Continuing Education Association, college graduates with bachelor's degrees earn an average of $36,980. Those with master's degrees earn $47,609 and those with professional degrees like JD, DDS, or MBA earn $85,322.

YOU CAN ALWAYS ASK

TACTIC: In today's more flexible working environment, you might discover you can get your boss to help you obtain whatever it is you feel you need to fill your glass: more training, more responsibility, more freedom. Maybe life would become wonderful if only you could telecommute. Or maybe you'd like to redesign your job. Ask. You might be surprised.

Keith works for a software company. He used to deal with all types of businesses, but nowadays he's in such demand by the company's insurance agency clientele that he has no time for anything else.

"That's because over the years I've convinced the brass to shell out money for me to take every insurance course and earn every insurance license you can imagine," Keith explains. "They fought it at first. But I told them that picking up all that knowledge and earning all those designations would set me apart—would differentiate me and the company—from all the competition we faced in the insurance market. And I was right."

The agencies know that no one understands their business better than Keith does. And his company is delighted to have paid for training that at the time no one else thought Keith needed.

Ask. But don't just ask—sell the idea. What's in it for the company? And if possible, what's in it for the person approving the request? How will it make you a more valuable employee now or in the future? If they balk, you might offer to earn what you want: working with your boss to set firm goals for you to reach that will trigger the reward.

CHEAPER THAN THERAPY

TACTIC: The simplest solution is often the best. Sometimes filling the glass is as easy as . . . well, filling a glass.

When Dawn moved to a new town and took a new job at what seemed like a large impersonal company, she soon found herself feeling left out and alienated from her fellow workers. This deep psychological problem was remedied by filling a glass—a glass candy dish—and putting the candy on her desk with a "Help yourself" sign. After a couple of days, the sign was no longer necessary. Soon Dawn knew everyone who ever visited her department, including a few—like the chairman of the board—who dropped by just for the sweets. She felt as much a part of the organization as those who had been there for 15 or 20 years.

SEX. NOW.

Obviously, these tactics—and the others I've discussed and will be discussing—constitute only a few of the many potential ways of filling the glass. But sometimes the glass can't be filled. Sometimes in your career, as in sales, on balance "the product" is inferior. It may work for others but it doesn't work for you. There simply isn't enough value for you there. And no matter how you might try, no matter what you do, you can't make the product a value. When you honestly acknowledge the negatives, you just can't sell it to yourself.

When that happens, you have to find another product—one you *can* sell with integrity. You need to change your job, your company, your career, or all three.

A fairly successful individual named Warren Buffett once remarked that he worried about people who claimed they were going to work at a job they disliked for a number of years before doing what they really wanted to do. "That's like saving sex for your old age," Buffet said. "Not a very good idea."

> **TACTIC:** Sometimes you can remedy an unsatisfactory job situation with a lateral move within your company. You can honestly tell the powers that be that you're requesting it to broaden your experience. You never have to mention that you're also trying to get out from under a drooling troglodyte of a boss.

> **TACTIC:** Sometimes you can create your own position within the company.

Alan Mickelson was an *sttst*. "*Sttst*—that's the sound a snake makes when you chop off its head in mid-hiss," he jokes. "Actually, it's senior telephone technical support technician. And I'd been a senior telephone technical support technician for so long that I knew what the customers were going to say before they said it. I was getting to the point where I was about ready to chop off my own head. Or somebody else's."

Alan desperately needed a new challenge. But there were only three telephone technical support managers in his region. And none of them were likely to be going anywhere in the next few years. He had virtually no chance of promotion.

"I asked myself what needs the company had that I could satisfy," he says. "The answer was right in front of me."

With so few managers and so much turnover among the techs, new techs were never adequately trained. Alan proposed a system of regional trainers: experienced senior techs who would do nothing else but work with techs who needed help. It took 11 months, but the proposal was accepted.

Alan created his own job, and jobs for 12 other trainers like him. Nowadays, he loves what he does; he also makes more money. The company has significantly better trained techs, customer satisfaction is up, and turnover is down.

"That one simple idea may have had more impact on our technical support systems than anything any of the rest of us have done in the last couple of years," the vice president of operations insists.

TACTIC: Consider a job swap.

Norman Smith had been a high school guidance counselor for 29 years. He'd heard about people swapping positions—sometimes even between companies. He thought it would be great experience if he could switch places for a year with a university admissions officer. After getting his boss's approval, he sent out 80 letters proposing the idea to universities around the country. He got 78 rejections, but two acceptances. He ended up switching places with an admissions officer from nearby American International College. Not only was it a change for both of them, but each reported learning tricks that helped when they returned to their old position—and each earned a new respect for what the other did.

QUITTING TIME

But maybe you realize that you can never get where you want to go while a part of your present company. Perhaps the only life you can honestly sell yourself on is that of an Arctic explorer, and your present job can't accommodate the time you'll need to give it a try.

Or maybe you realize that you can never get where you want to go and still maintain your integrity if you stay at your present company. You've got to either change the values in the company or get yourself out.

As a friend of mine puts it, "I rent the corporation the use of my talents, my education, and my concentration. I rent them my productivity. They're paying a fair price, and I want to give them even more than their money's worth. But they aren't buying my soul, my self-respect, or the respect I see in the eyes of the people I work with when they look at me. That's not in the bargain."

You need to know when to quit.

Most of us don't want to leave the job we have until we've found another one. You are far more hirable while you're somebody else's employee. You're also much more likely to be able to negotiate a better deal. Nobody wants someone nobody wants, whether in love or employment. Nobody wants somebody else's discards either. Which also means you probably don't want to get yourself fired. No matter how satisfying it might be to tell one or more "hypocritical morons" off, you may someday want a reference from those very morons—in the hope that they'll be hypocritical enough to make it a good one.

FEEDING A DREAM WITHOUT STARVING THE DREAMER

TACTIC: If you're leaving your job to pursue an unfulfilled dream, the first question is of course, *Could you start fulfilling that dream while still an employee?* Could you begin in your spare time? Or could you talk the company into a leave of absence?

TIP: A regular paycheck can help feed a dream.

That said, I once quit a lucrative full-time job with what amounted to part-time hours, because it was so easy I was afraid I'd hang onto it forever and use it as an excuse to keep from doing what I wanted to do. I could have filled the glass the safe way. But I was afraid I never would.

When Michael Dainard resigned as director of marketing for CBS television stations, he created a ten-year plan for succeeding in his new career as a writer. The plan led him to write *Breaking Free from Corporate Bondage*. In it, he recommends researching your new potential career path thoroughly and understanding the possible downside and how long it might take you to succeed. He also recommends formulating a detailed plan of your own—working out the finances and a timetable—covering what, where, when, how, and how much.

A certain amount of fear is healthy. It will inspire caution and help keep your planning realistic. Dainard warns that family and friends may resist the change—particularly if your present situation is comfortable. If that discourages you, you may not be psychologically ready to make the move anyway.

HOW JEANETTE MADE $450,000

I would love to be able to tell you to "follow your bliss." I'd love to be able to tell you that if you don't love what you are doing, go do something you love. That's the easy answer and it's a good one. Unfortunately like a lot of good answers it's not always possible.

We've all heard the stories. Larry quits his position as a nuclear engineer to pursue his true love darning wall tapestries. In six months, he turns it into a million-dollar operation.

Jeanette hates her dead-end jobs and the fact that she keeps getting fired. Then one day some self-appointed authority (much like myself) asks her what she likes to do for fun.

"I just love to design my own clothing," Jeanette replies. "I could sketch new styles for hours."

Now—after following whatever advice the authority gave her— Jeanette earns $450,000 a year as a top couturière.

That's how the stories go. But the stark reality is that most of the time the Jeanettes of the world don't make it. Much of the time their clothing wouldn't be fit to soak up oil spills. Not always. But often. That's why there aren't a lot of $450,000 a year couturières milling around.

I like to play golf and make love to beautiful women. Nobody is willing to pay me to do either. (That may be a reflection on my abilities, though I'd like to believe otherwise.)

We'd all like our fantasies to come true. We'd all like to be rich, successful, and creative. And maybe you should keep trying. It's not up to me to say you shouldn't. But there really isn't room for everyone's dreams to come true. Too many of us have the same dreams; too many of us want the same elite positions. There's a lot more room for salespeople in this country than for stand-up comedians, more room for ad copywriters than for novelists.

Positive thinking that's rooted in reality acknowledges that, then tries to make the very best and the very most out of the incredible possibilities that are open to each of us. For some of us, that may lead to the pursuit and even the fulfillment of those original dreams. For others, it may lead to new dreams. Dreams, which may turn out to be even better, even more worthy, and more satisfying when accomplished.

Whatever you decide to do, don't play the victim. It's great fun to wallow in the mud of victimhood. But nobody is going to want some muddy SOB tracking dirt into their business.

Take control of your choices. If you can't sell the job you've got to yourself, is there always a better alternative? Maybe not invariably, but so close to invariably that I've never encountered a case where there wasn't one. This is America. Nobody is forcing you to do anything.

DIFFERING IDEAS

"One of the reasons why I have no regular job and why I haven't had a regular job for years, is quite simply that my ideas differ from those of the gentlemen who hand out jobs." That's what Vincent van Gogh said. Maybe you're the same.

Maybe filling the glass for you means starting your own business, building something of your own. As I implied when I was talking about Jeanette the couturière, you might not want to count on having the artistic ability to become the next Yves St. Laurent or Calvin Klein. You might not want to count on having the artistic ability of Calvin Coolidge. But that doesn't mean you have to force your ideas to conform to those of the gentlemen—and ladies—who hand out the jobs. You can still create your own job.

$85 MILLION WORTH OF CAT LITTER

Maybe you can come up with the perfect product for a great niche start-up business. Ed Lowe invented the cat litter industry almost single-handedly, starting out peddling five pound bags with handwritten labels, driving from pet shop to pet shop. It's not high fashion or wall tapestry; it's just an $85 million a year business.

Gail Frankel realized that every other mother had the same problems she did lugging around baby, purse, and packages. She came up with a gizmo for attaching packages to strollers. Her Kel-Gar Inc. now sells $3 million worth of gizmos a year. So many stay-at-home mothers are starting their own businesses nowadays that they've already got their own buzzword: *mamapreneurs*. The new technology gives them the freedom to do just about anything at home. Those of us who aren't moms have the same freedom.

But high technology is hardly a requirement. One day a friend of mine got tired of looking for a job. He picked up a squeegee and a bucket and headed off down the street looking for buildings with dirty windows. Today he runs one of the most successful janitorial businesses in southern Indiana.

Here's a "stop me if you've heard this one" type of story, which also happens to be true. Right after I finished college in the 1970s, my partner Paul Sheehan and I started a coupon business on less than a shoestring. One of our first clients was, if possible, even smaller than we were: a young kinky-haired kid with a single copier and a shop so tiny that he had to push the machine out on the sidewalk every day to do business. His nickname gave the business its name—Kinko's. That was the first of more than 1,000 locations.

Twenty years ago, 45 cab drivers in Madison, Wisconsin, were "tired of being ripped off" by the cab companies they worked for. They pooled every penny they could scrape together, got a bank loan, and started a co-op, Union Cab of Madison. It's now a 100-vehicle, $5 million a year business. And while some of the member/owners might be able to make more money elsewhere, at Union they have a voice in the business. They don't have to make compromises in their lifestyles, self-respect, or work environment that they don't choose to make. Their boss, the general manager, works for them.

A co-op of home health care aides, Cooperative Home Care Associates, is comprised largely of women who used to be on welfare. Few competitors can match their training program, and they pay themselves 20 percent more than the industry average.

People have built businesses out of walking dogs or waiting for repairmen or hawking newspapers, flowers, or even fresh-brewed coffee to motorists stuck in traffic. In Japan, a former boxer charged $9 a minute to let passers-by work off their stress by treating him as a human punching bag.

Maybe that doesn't sound like much of a job to you. Maybe it sounds better than the job you've got right now.

For true entrepreneurial courage it's hard to beat single mom Theresa Gladden. Unemployed, she had $50 to last her 45 days. Instead of trying to stretch the money, she invested it in socks. Not stocks, socks. Then she decorated a cart, pushed her fears aside and sold the socks on the street in the middle of Harlem. It got her through the crunch and today she's part of the co-op of home health care aides I mentioned earlier. Whenever I hear myself or anyone else with a full stomach, a fat paycheck, and money in the bank pontificating about risk-taking, I think of Theresa.

Starting a business is not for everyone. It's seldom easy. It's never a sure thing. But as a great marketing man once said, "Every crowd has a silver lining." The opportunities are always there.

> **TACTIC:** Look for a problem, a frustration, an annoyance, a want, a hope, or a dream: a need you can fulfill. If enough people have that need, you're in business.

> **TIP:** Your biggest weakness could turn out to be your most marketable quality.

Maybe you're a detail freak or maybe you're strictly big picture; a compulsive organizer or compulsively disorganized; antisocial or overly social; lethargic or so full of energy you can't sit still. Why not find a career that turns your potential negatives into positives rather than one that makes them liabilities?

JUST SIT DOWN AND CONSULT

> **TACTIC:** Perhaps like myself and so many other otherwise unemployable entrepreneurs, you can go into consulting. A consultant, Eric Severeid said, is simply "an ordinary guy more than 50 miles from home." Still, you might be amazed at how many people or companies are willing to pay for the hard-earned knowledge you've acquired over the years. What are your strongest skills? Who out there might benefit from them?

If nothing else perhaps you've got a special talent for sitting down that you could pass on to others. The Seattle Police Department recently required 26 employees to attend a training class on how to sit in a chair. This coming after chairs rolled out from under two workers and a third hurt her back when her adjustable seat abruptly slipped. If time permitted, the instructor was also going to cover other office terrors, like open cabinet drawers.

You could do that.

CHAPTER | **8**

Become Your
Own Guru

You are about to embark on an hour that can transform your life.

Of course, you've heard that before. That's what motivational speakers and various gurus always tell you. What I'll tell you is that any hour can be an hour that transforms your life. It's simply up to you to choose that hour to make the transformation.

Let me suggest that it might as well be this one. If you're going to make changes, you've got to make them sometime. Why not start now? If for no other reason than you've already paid for the book, opened it, and bent back the spine. Why not protect your investment and find a way to make the thing really work for you?

Really work. *Really* is the operative term here. *Really* meaning *in reality.* Reality is—for lack of a better word—real. We can't ignore it and expect to function successfully within it. There are too many real-world walls to bump into, real-world doors we need to be able to open.

ACKNOWLEDGING REALITY

The way we think about that reality is determined first by how accurately we perceive it and second by our attitude toward that perception.

How accurately we perceive it *and* our attitude toward that perception. For years, every guru out there has been telling us that we create and control our own attitudes. We all know that's basically true. Those attitudes in turn have a great deal to do with the quality of our lives and whether we ever achieve whatever it is each of us decides is success.

Unfortunately, the attitude gurus, particularly the Pollyannas, frequently ignore the importance of perceiving reality as accurately as possible and concentrate solely on trying to get us to adjust our attitudes toward that perception. *Every day in every way I'm getting better and better and better.* Unlikely. And, beyond a fragile, short-term morale boost, not particularly helpful.

It's far more constructive to keep your positive thinking based on reality: *Today I did an excellent job helping Fred with that problem but confronting Patrice like that was a mistake. Still, I can see that all my work is beginning to pay off and I know if I keep working on it I'll continue to improve.*

Never let your positive thinking obstruct the reality in a haze of wishful thinking. Acknowledge the reality: perceive it as accurately as possible, so it can be dealt with effectively. Always realizing that—as the gurus keep telling us—we are responsible for our own attitudes toward that perception. We are responsible for our own attitudes and our own happiness. As we all know, there are a million ways of reacting to any situation, and as Shakespeare said, "There is nothing either good or bad but thinking makes it so."

Your boss may be 100 percent wrong. But you are 100 percent responsible for how you react and how she affects you and your behavior now and in the future.

We all know that, don't we?

The gurus, the self-help authorities, and business experts have also told us that we have the power to change whatever we need to change in our lives. We all know that's also true—at least it is within reason, within some obvious limitations the gurus usually prefer to ignore. But how long has it been since you first came to believe or to understand that truth? And in that time, how many of the changes that you wanted or needed to make have you actually made?

If you're like most of us, probably not nearly as many as you'd like.

TODAY IS NOT THE FIRST DAY
OF THE REST OF YOUR LIFE

> **TIP:** Think of Sam Walton. And ask yourself how much closer to death, how much closer to the end of the ride you are than you were the first time you were told—the first time you realized—that, more than anything else, you are the controlling factor in your own life?

What are you waiting for? What are we all waiting for? We've heard it a thousand times, from every guru out there. We spend so much money on self-improvement in this country you'd think by now most of us would be damn close to perfection. We make guru after guru wealthy—for telling us things that for the most part we all recognize as true. Then we don't do much of anything about it. It's a good thing gurus don't give refunds. If they had to return the money of every person who failed to follow their advice, we'd have a major problem in this country with starving gurus, and I don't think any of us want that.

It's time. What are you waiting for?

> **TIP:** Today is *not* the first day of the rest of your life. Yesterday was.

The future is getting closer by the minute. If it gets any closer it will be the past. Of course we all have reasons for not making the changes we know we should make. There are always reasons. But to quote that great American philosopher, Ann Landers, "Stop feeling sorry for yourself and get moving." To quote Calvin Coolidge, "We cannot do everything at once, but we can do something at once."

Do something at once.

You don't have to do everything. Just get started. *Sic parvis magna:* Great things have small beginnings.

A multinational publishing company once paid $800 a head for their entire 900-person sales force to attend a two-day seminar designed to teach them how to overcome their reluctance to make cold calls. At the conclusion, one participant turned to another and said, "I've found a better cure for call reluctance, and it's free: JGOYFDAMTC."

"What?" her friend asked.

"JGOYFDAMTC. Just get off your fat duff and make the call."

Sometimes you've just got to get off your duff and do it. There's always a reason for not doing it right now; there's always a reason for waiting for some mythical right moment, for some propitious wind. The Romans, who knew a more than a little about getting things done, used to say, "If there is no wind, row."

TIP: Row.

Or drift. The choice is yours.

YOUR CHOICE

Change is difficult. Every day for years Konrad Lorenz, the anthropologist, would take one route to work, then take a second route going home. When he tried reversing the routes—taking the "out" route in and the "in" route out—the change generated so much anxiety, he never did it again. Makes you feel positively well-adjusted and amazingly flexible by comparison, doesn't it?

"When you're through changing," Will Rogers said, "you're through."

I can keep throwing quotes at you, but here's another simple truth. Neither me, nor Will Rogers, nor Ann Landers, nor Calvin Coolidge, nor anybody else can motivate you to make the changes you want to make. The gurus, the business experts, the psychologists, the motivational speakers, the dead Romans—the self-appointed authorities like myself—can only point out the trail. It's up to you to decide that it's a trail you want to take. It's up to you to make yourself get up and walk it.

There's only one person who can be CEO of the corporation of you. There's only one person who's responsible for that corporate culture and for the productivity of that corporation. And that's you, not Stephen Covey, Zig Ziglar, or Tony Robbins. You're the only one who can decide what your goals are, and you're the only one who can provide the motivation to get you there.

Lincoln could have remained a struggling Illinois lawyer. He would have lived longer. Jonas Salk could have been a pharmacist, Einstein a clerk. FDR could have been an invalid.

Think about whomever it is that you most admire. Those people could have been less—much less. While they were living they had that choice.

You and I are living, and we still have it.

> **TIP:** Try becoming your own favorite guru, your own favorite motivational speaker.

Start thinking of being your own guru as part of your job description, part of what you have to do. Part of what you're being paid to do. Part of what you want to do. Self-help means just that, helping yourself. Be your own guru. You already know most of the answers. Start applying them.

As a general and later as secretary of state, George Marshall helped pull the world through one of the grimmest eras we've ever known: World War II and its immediate aftermath. "Gentlemen," Marshall once said to his staff, "enlisted men may be entitled to morale problems, but officers are not. I expect all officers in this department to take care of their own morale. No one is taking care of my morale."

Be your own guru.

MOTIVATION FOR WHAT?

Before you can motivate yourself, of course, you've got to decide what your goals really are. "If you don't know where you're going, you might end up somewhere else." That quote comes from the immortal—if somewhat deceased—Casey Stengel, perhaps second only to Attila in management acumen.

When I was a sales manager, I once had a rep who told me that his goal was to be the number-one salesperson in the division.

"No, it isn't," I answered. "Your goal is to be number five."

"What? How do you know what I want?"

"Just a dumb guess. It's the same dumb guess I make when I'm following a guy up a staircase and he stops at the second floor rather than continuing to climb. I figure that his goal was the second floor. When I see a sprinter run full speed down the track for a hundred yards then stop—and he's a big strong guy and he's not pulling up lame—I figure his goal was to run 100 yards."

"Obviously."

"Obviously," I agreed. "Now, I've never seen you pull up lame, but I do see that as long as you're one of the top five reps in the division you never even bother to run. But if you fall to sixth or seventh, then you're making extra calls and working harder in those calls, and you don't play golf on Friday afternoon. . . ."

"I don't pla . . ." he started, trailing off when he saw that he was about to toss away any remaining credibility.

"Once you get back up to number five," I continued, "it's back to business as usual. You're comfortable with your standing, you're comfortable with your income. So no matter what you might *think* your goal is, your real goal is to be number five."

> **TIP:** If you want to know what your real goals are, look at what you do. Where are those activities likely to get you? If that's not your real goal, it might as well be.

> **TIP:** If you'd like to be an immortal like Casey Stengel, the best time for racking up the necessary accomplishments is *prior* to death.

There's nothing wrong with not racing to win. It's a choice you make and it's a valid one. Your goals are your own. Just don't kid yourself about what you're doing. Or where you're going to be when that particular race is over.

You've got to understand what you really want. Whatever it is, if you really do want it, you've got to be willing to do all the things that it takes to make it happen. And you've got to provide the motivation yourself, the constant motivation, to make sure those things get done. Whatever your goals, Zig Ziglar can't be with you every moment of the day, when all the thousands of little decisions that lead toward or away from those goals have to be made.

BREAKING FREE OF THE PACK

Filling the glass is about reconciling the disconnects between what you're actually doing and what you believe you should be doing. Filling the glass doesn't mean that you won't have to make sacrifices to get what you want. It simply means that you make certain you actually want whatever it is you're making those sacrifices to achieve.

The key of course is pursuing the success that *you* wish to achieve— whatever that may be. You can't be afraid of having different goals, of filling your glass in ways that are different from the ways those around you fill theirs.

We've all heard that if you're not the lead dog, the view never changes. And that's true—unless you break free of the pack and find a trail of your own. Then you'll be free of the harness and you won't have some bozo from some other species cracking the whip over your head. And even if you're heading for the same destination, you may well get there first because you don't have to pull a sled full of somebody else's baggage.

TIP: There may be more to life than being the lead dog.

Again, the key is to pursue the goals you really want to pursue. Not the goals you think you should have. Not the goals your boss or your parents or your brothers and sisters or your friends or even your wife think you should have. Not the goals you have because you feel you need to keep up with the Joneses, or because somebody else might decide that you're not a success.

HEADING HOME—WITH OR WITHOUT MRS. GAUGUIN

You can accept somebody else's goals for your own but you can never borrow their desire to do the work necessary to reach those goals. Writer Willa Cather said it, and it applies to whatever we do, "There is only one thing—desire. And before it, when it is big, all is little." You can succeed—at least as the world measures success—without following your desire. You can follow your desire and not succeed: not as you measure success nor as anyone else does. You can follow a desire and lose your own sense of integrity.

I'm not saying you should quit your job, abandon your family and move off to the South Seas to paint. That might have worked for Gauguin but it probably won't work for you. It certainly didn't work for Mrs. Gauguin and the kids.

But working for goals that aren't really your own is like running uphill. You can get to where you're going but it's not going to be easy. It doesn't matter if everyone has to look up to you once you get there, if that's not where you want to be.

On the other hand, if you can harness your desire—a desire to do the work or a desire to reach the goal, or better yet, both—you've got an engine and the fuel to drive it. Not an unstoppable engine. Nothing is unstoppable. No destination is ever guaranteed. But as close to unstoppable as you are ever likely to get. Compared to running uphill toward a cold and unwelcoming peak, you're heading home. It's not necessarily an easy trip or smooth journey, but it is mostly downhill.

Again, I'm not saying "follow your bliss." It might be that easy for some, but not for me and maybe not for you. Maybe there's no way that anything that gives you bliss will earn you a penny. Or you may not be able to meet your financial obligations on what your bliss might bring. Maybe you don't have a bliss.

What I *am* talking about is, once again, what works best. It's very simple:

1. What do you want from your working life?
2. Is there a way to get there? Or as close to there as possible?
3. Are you willing to do what it takes to get there? Some of it is going to be work. Maybe a lot of it. Some of it is going to be less than pleasant—though none of it should compromise your self-esteem or your self-image.

ANCIENT GURUS, HEARSAY, AND A BAD DAY AT THE OFFICE

In *The Way of Man,* theologian Martin Buber tells the story of a great teacher. One day one of his pupils asked of him, "Show me one general way to the service of God."

The teacher answered, "It is impossible to tell men what way they should take. For one way to serve God is through learning, another through prayer, another through fasting, and still another through eating. Everyone should carefully observe what way his heart draws him to, and then choose this way with all his strength."

William Bridges recounted that story in *Creating You & Co.* (So I'm telling you about Bridges telling his readers about Martin Buber telling his readers about something a famous guru told one of his disciples. Is this the accumulated wisdom of humankind passed down through the ages or is it distorted hearsay and rumor?) Bridges says that each of us has a "lifework," a "productive activity which is particularly fitting for us . . . [that] satisfies our unique desires, capitalizes on our singular abilities, and makes use of our individual assets . . . it reaches down to how and what we are, to the structure and grain of our nature . . . it is the very stuff that makes us *us*."

Maybe. Though this strikes me as the occupational equivalent of the idea that each one of us has a particular soulmate somewhere on the planet. I think you can waste a lot of your life and pass up some pretty great relationships if you're waiting for the one perfect mythical love to appear on the horizon.

Still as the Chinese proverb says, "If Heaven made him, Earth can find some use for him." There's no question that we are each far better suited for one path than another—just as we are far more suited to one person than another. There's no question we want to find a path that fits in with who we really are, with what we really want, just as we want to find a relationship that does the same.

But you ain't Cinderella; nobody's chasing after you with glass footwear. No matter how suitable a career you manage to build for yourself, you've got to work on making it work—on making it fit who you are. Just as you have to work on making a relationship fit. No matter how suitable for you it might be.

If you're not willing to do what's necessary, you probably don't really want it. I've written a couple of novels. I enjoy writing them; I've even gotten a few decent reviews. I'd like to be an award-winning novelist, but I'm not willing to do what's necessary to give it a shot, to get as close to that goal as possible. I neither desire to do the work nor to succeed as a novelist enough to make the necessary effort.

Of course, desire doesn't necessarily make the road easy. It may be extremely difficult. That's where the power of desire comes in. Because nothing you or I have to deal with in our careers is likely to be any more difficult than what Donald Wyman had to do back in 1993 when he was having a bad day at the office.

WHY I NEVER DATED BRIGITTE BARDOT

Donald was a woodsman. A tree fell on him, breaking his left leg and pinning the leg beneath it. He called for help for an hour, then realized that no one was close enough to hear him. If he stayed where he was, he'd die. It was just a matter of time.

So Donald pulled out his pocket knife. He cut off his own leg, just below the knee. He cut through the skin, the muscle, then—with that pocket knife—sawed through the broken bone.

He crawled 90 feet uphill to a bulldozer. He dragged himself up and in and drove to his truck. He hauled himself from the bulldozer to the truck, then worked the standard transmission with his right leg and his hand while holding onto the shoestring he'd tied as a tourniquet with the other hand. He reached help just as he was slipping into shock.

That's what desire can do. Now tell me how difficult it is to do the things you have to do to reach your goals.

Is desire enough? I could fill the rest of this chapter with guru quotes that seem to indicate it is, stretching back to at least 1819, when William Hazlitt said, "A strong passion for any object will ensure success, for the desire of the end will point out the means." Epigrams like that sound wonderful but if it were really true when I was 12 I would have been dating Brigitte Bardot. No one on this planet has ever wanted anything more.

That's what I liked about the original *Rocky* movie—as opposed to Rockys II through XXXIV. It wasn't the standard "desire overcomes all odds" story line. Rocky does everything he can possibly do to prepare for the fight with Apollo Creed. But the night before, he faces the reality. As an unranked club fighter with little experience and less training, he has no reasonable chance of beating one of the greatest heavyweight fighters that ever lived. No matter how much he wants it, no matter how positive his thinking, it's not going to happen. In spite of that, he's still determined to take maximum advantage of his talents and his opportunity. He's going to give winning his best shot—why not? But his real goal becomes to go the distance with the champion—something no one else has ever done. He fits his goal to the reality and succeeds on his own terms.

To me that's far more inspiring than the typical "zillion-to-one shot beats the champ" story—because it has a much greater ring of truth.

Few Pollyannas would have scripted the movie for Rocky to lose the fight. But I'll bet that even fewer would have put their money on him if the fight had been real.

POLLYANNA HERESY

Here's a bit of reality-based positive thinking that's Pollyanna heresy. We've all been told that if we want something we should never, ever give up. *Never, ever* is a long time. I don't believe *never, ever* is for most of us. Remember all those people in true-life never-ever-give-up stories that we hear about are the ones who ultimately reached their goal. The screenwriter whose 29th script was plucked out of the trash to become the box-office bonanza. The catcher who spent 13 years in the minor leagues before becoming rookie of the year at age 32. The entrepreneur who finally stumbled on the next pet rock after enduring years of starvation and bankruptcy.

Statistically, for every against-all-odds, never-ever-give-up success, there are hundreds, maybe thousands of others who succumbed to the odds and failed—for one reason or another. That's why the odds being bucked were as great as they were.

Most of those who didn't make it weren't as tenacious or as hard-working as the one who succeeded. But many of them were. Most of them weren't as talented. Many were. The one who succeeds will tell you that they believed in themselves and that they always knew they would make it. So did most of the ones that failed.

At some point, maybe some of those who didn't make it—and maybe even some of those who did—would have been happier if they had cut their losses and found something else to do that made them happy. A musical-comedy playwright once told me that no one should try to make it in his field unless they absolutely *had* to write musical comedies: unless their desire was such that they really had no other choice.

Try. Try hard and try smart. If I had to list the single characteristic I considered the most important in sales or any other type of success, I would say *persistence*. If at first you don't succeed, learn everything you can from the first effort and try again. And again and again. But sometimes what you eventually learn might be that you should try something else. Or some other variation. Another heretic, Simon de Beauvoir said, "In the face of an obstacle which is impossible to overcome, stubbornness is stupid." We all know that. Most of us even act on it. We just try to pretend it isn't true.

The *never, ever* quit situation may be only for those who, psychologically or otherwise, absolutely have to do what they're never, ever going to give up. And for those for whom the effort itself is a greater reward than anything else they might be doing, or who can pursue their *never, ever* while still having a rich, rewarding life at the same time.

Max Filer became a lawyer in 1991 at age 61. He passed the bar on his 48th try, 25 years after he'd first taken it in 1966. During that time, he worked as a machinist, raised seven children—two of whom became lawyers—and served four terms on the Compton, California, city council.

INTERPRETING DREAMS

You may have a dream. Maybe it's a dream you should never, ever give up. Or maybe it's only a dream and nothing more—though even then it might be telling you something about what you really want in the day-to-day world around you. I used to have a dream about becoming a professional baseball player. I never did much about it, and I was never particularly good at baseball. But what did I really want? What appealed to me about being a ballplayer?

Well, I always liked the idea of traveling around the country, visiting different cities. And, to be frank, I liked the idea of getting a certain amount—not too much—of attention, and having people look up to me. Which is why being a speaker and a consultant—a professional pontificator—appeals to me more than being a full-time sales executive or a full-time writer, though it took me years to figure that out. To be honest, baseball tends to bore me; speaking never does. It's like the old joke: Follow your dreams—just not the one where you're walking down Main Street naked.

> **TIP:** If you want to fill the glass, you've got to know what you really want. Not what you think you want or you think you should want.

You may be great at something and love it, but not great enough to make a living. Or you may be great at something that society doesn't particularly value, or doesn't value enough in the way you want to do it for you to make the kind of living you want. I have a friend who's an excellent visual artist, but he was never able to earn much money doing it. He's also the world's greatest car and truck packer. He can squeeze more boxes and furniture into a car or a truck than anyone I've ever seen. If vehicle packing were a major professional sport, he would be the Michael Jordan of it, making $50 or $60 million a year. Unfortunately for my friend, our society happens to value throwing a ball through a metal ring more than it values cramming a car full of old possessions. So he's taken his spacial relationship talent into radiography, where he can figure just how to maneuver equipment and patients to get exactly the right images of exactly the right internal body parts.

All that said, drive the engine of your desire as much as you can, as far as you can.

PUTTING YOURSELF INTO THE PATH OF THE GODS

Big goals are great motivators. They energize us, they make us come alive. They stretch us, and stretch our conception of reality. Basing your positive thinking on reality does not mean putting limitations on yourself that don't exist. Stretch your reality.

"We grow great by dreams. All big men are dreamers . . . some of us let these great dreams die, but others nourish and protect them, nurse them through bad days till they bring them to the sunshine and light which come always to those who sincerely hope that their dreams will come true."

Woodrow Wilson said that. He probably said it before his failure to get the United States into the League of Nations, his stroke, and the ultimate repudiation of his policies by the American people. Dreams don't always come true, but if you don't pursue them they *never* come true. And Wilson did go from college professor to American president and world hero. If that's a failure, it's one that's better than a lot of successes.

Someone once said if you want to walk with the gods, first of all you've got to put yourself in their path.

TIP: No matter how big your career goal might be, never expect your job to single-handedly fix a life that isn't otherwise working or to single-handedly prove to the world that you're not the person you're secretly terrified you might be.

That's too much to ask of a mere career. If you try to use it to do that, you're likely to hurt the career, yourself, and those around you. On the other hand, your career can be the perfect vehicle for proving to yourself that you aren't the person you're worried about being—and for demonstrating to yourself the type of potential you do have and the type of amazing growth you can achieve.

Big goals are wonderful, but only if they really are your goals. And only if trying to meet them isn't going to devastate the other aspects of your life. Companies often impose unrealistic goals upon us. Whenever possible, correct them. Nowadays many of us are coming to realize that frequently these goals aren't worth the misery we have to put ourselves through to reach them. Often they're counterproductive, driving people to a point where they can't push themselves any further.

TIP: A man's reach should exceed his grasp. But if you tear your arm out of the socket reaching, you can't grasp anything.

TIP: Not living up to someone else's goals and expectations doesn't make anyone a failure.

TIP: Sometimes success should be measured not by the goals we reach but by the life we've lived. Living well is not only the best revenge, it's not a bad goal in itself.

When you truly set your own goals, you may find that you're no longer in any type of competition—that the people you thought you were competing against don't even have the same goals you have. They aren't seeking the exact same mix of the various elements that make up a life: family, work, friends, challenge, spirituality, relaxation, etc.

TIP: Never compare yourself to anyone who's not even running the same race.

THE SHORTHAND OF SELLING

Here's a simple truth: *There may not be any simple truths.* Yet selling is often a matter of supplying shorthand ways of thinking about complicated problems, allowing the prospect to evaluate complex situations and come to a decision. That's why analogies, stories, metaphors, and quotes work so well. As General Electric CEO Jack Welsh said, "Simple messages travel faster, simple designs reach the market faster, and elimination of clutter allows faster decision making."

Wyatt Technologies, a client of mine, manufactures light-scattering equipment for measuring absolute molecular weight in polymers. It may require a Ph.D. to fully explain why their methodology is superior to their competition's; many of their prospects and at least one of their consultants—me—couldn't understand it, even from a Ph.D. But everyone could grasp the shorthand metaphor we came up with: "It's like using a speedometer to measure the speed of your car rather than an altimeter. The altimeter will do the job—roughly. If you're willing to do some complicated figuring. The speedometer gives you the exact speed immediately."

Consider finding shorthand ways to sell your goals to yourself—to remind yourself of what you are doing and why you are doing it. So you can keep yourself motivated. Which means keeping yourself sold.

San Diego Charger defensive tackle Norman Hand wears a pair of Miami Dolphin shorts under his Charger shorts. Hand was cut by the Dolphins. "Every time I'm tired . . . I raise up my Miami Dolphins shorts and they remind me."

I once watched a top-level executive completely demotivate an assistant with a few harsh, astonishingly ill-chosen words. I noticed he was wearing a pair of shoes that probably cost more than the assistant made in a month.

"In your business," I asked him after the assistant left, "your shoes are more important than your attitude, right?"

"No, of course not."

"So what exactly do those expensive shoes do for your business?"

"They *help* my attitude."

"Good. Switch them on, will you?" Fortunately he laughed, and his mood lightened immediately. From that point on, he used to talk about switching on his shoes when he needed to adjust his attitude. He started thinking of himself as "the man in the electric shoes."

Salespeople used to say they sold on a smile and a shoeshine. Nowadays too many executives—too many of all of us—are all shoeshine and no smile. We wouldn't think of wearing shoes that pinch and bind but we'll wear an attitude that chafes ourselves and everyone around us. You can change your attitude even quicker than you can change your shoes. That can change your entire day and the day of those that have to deal with you. A visualization like this—as silly as it might seem—can be an effective shorthand way of recovering the attitude you want.

MORE REALITY

> **TIP:** A salesperson should never lie to a customer. Particularly when the customer is himself.

That's why filling the glass is central to being your own guru. It's far easier to motivate yourself when you really do believe in what you are doing, and that belief is supported by reality—not just Pollyanna positive thinking. You can only fool yourself and those around you for so long. When reality rears its ugly head and you discover you've been lying to yourself, all the gurus in the world won't be able to help you, even if by all outward appearances you're succeeding.

In fact the more you appear to be succeeding, the worse you may feel, because the more you're likely to feel like a fraud, the more you're likely to feel you're misleading those around you. That can lead to lack of effort or to quitting, cynicism, or self-delusion, none of which are particularly great long-term motivators.

You've got to be your own guru. Make it part of your job description. Any hour can transform your life. Any hour that you choose. Why not make it this one?

OTHER GURUS

Of course being your own guru doesn't mean that you don't pick up every scrap of knowledge and any technique that works from whomever or wherever you can. That makes you an even better guru to yourself. Pick up everything you can, but pick up nothing unquestioned.

Question authority, question gurus. Tom Peters is as insightful and influential an observer of American business as anyone out there. But two-thirds of the companies extolled in his huge best-seller *In Search of Excellence* underperformed the S&P 500 in the decade following the book's publication.

Business gurus sometimes lose sight of the realities of the workplace—for those of us who ever understood those realities in the first place. I remember one speaker telling a group of assembly workers that being fired no longer has the stigma that it once did.

"Many individuals end up improving their situation after being dismissed," he insisted, "just like Lee Iacocca did when he was fired from Ford and went to Chrysler."

One member of the audience caught a small distinction that seemed to have escaped the speaker. "May I respectfully submit," she said, "that if I get my butt fired, my chances of being hired to run one of our major competitors may not be all that great. And that I may well be looking at a pay package that's a little lower than the millions Mr. Iacocca got from Chrysler. I haven't done any conclusive studies on this you understand, that's just my gut feeling."

"Well, Iacocca's just one example," the guru explained.

"And probably a rather typical one," another worker muttered. "If a bit dated."

After being summarily fired by his own handpicked board of directors, business guru Al Dunlop was reportedly getting $100,000 per appearance for giving audiences leadership advice, perhaps because Attila the Hun wasn't available.

John A. Byrne is the author of *Chainsaw,* a book on "Chainsaw Al Dunlop." Byrne writes, "He anointed himself America's best CEO. But Al Dunlop drove Sunbeam into the ground." His methods were credited with jacking Sunbeam stock up to quick short-term value of $50 per share then dropping it to a long-term value below $6.

Among Dunlop's advice to his audiences, "If you want a friend, buy a dog." I would suggest to "Chainsaw Al" that if you need to buy a friend—and one from another species at that—that you might want to examine your methods a bit more closely.

My all-time favorite business guru is at least nominally a spiritual guru: a guy who supposedly came back from a near-death experience to sell a never-ending series of tapes and self-help books. A key tenet of his teaching is that you can't borrow his books and tapes and still get whatever it is that his disciples are getting. I guess all the spiritual value somehow seeps out of them in the transfer. If you don't buy your own, they don't work. I don't quite understand it myself but I do love the concept. (I understand the recording industry is looking into it even as we speak.) This guy may be good as a spiritual guru, but as a business guru he's without peer.

TIP: Marketing has its own truths, which are often hidden from the heart.

And let me just add that if you borrowed this book or stole it or even bought it secondhand, don't let me or my attorneys catch you trying to live by one of its precepts.

Stephen Covey is certainly one of our most successful business gurus. *The Seven Habits of Highly Effective People* has sold nearly 13 million copies. At one point he was advising 82 of the top 100 companies on how to run their businesses. Then he teamed up with Hyrum W. Smith, the guru who created the Franklin Day Planner and best-selling author of *The 10 Natural Laws of Successful Time and Life Management.* Talk about guru wonderland: here's a guy who in the 1980s talked every yuppie in America into lugging around 40-pound appointment books that they had to take a course to use.

"We intend to apply our expertise to our own merger," Covey declared when Franklin Covey was created, "thereby creating a model merger for corporate industry."

According to *Business Week,* "It turned out to be a model all right, not the kind Covey had in mind. A bloated bureaucracy, poor planning, and internal bickering helped turn Franklin Covey Co. into a poster child for highly ineffective organizations." The current plan is for the two management gurus to concentrate on writing and speaking and let others manage the company.

"In other words," one less than charitable observer told me, "now that they've proven they can't run their own company, they'll stick to telling the rest of us how to run ours."

At age 66 after collecting tens of millions of dollars selling management advice, Covey says, "It's much different when you go through it than when you look at it from some academic ivory tower."

Is that the sound of gloating you hear from a writer who'll never approach the kind of superstar status Covey has achieved—a writer who would have to admit that he agrees with much of what Stephen Covey has to say?

Absolutely. As a good example of our relative stature, a while back, Covey and I happened to be in the same town on the same day. I gave a workshop for one of the area's fastest growing companies. It was extremely well attended, incredibly well received, and I was—I have to admit—very well compensated for it. On the other hand, Covey's workshop was the lead story on the evening news. No one is ever likely to give me the chance to run a company the size of Franklin Covey into the ground. I'll have to do it secondhand—with my advice.

TIP: Question the best. Question accepted wisdom. Question the flavor of the month.

TIP: Question me. Question everything in this book.

Question conventional wisdom. Earl Nightingale said, "Whatever the majority of people is doing, under any given circumstances, if you do the exact opposite, you will probably never make another mistake as long as you live."

Question Earl. And all the others I've quoted in this chapter.

CHAPTER | **9**

Thinking Outside
the Cliché

Being your own guru sometimes involves innovative thinking and finding innovative ways to fill the glass. Today conventional wisdom tells us we have to think outside the box. But truly innovative outside-the-box thinking comes from questioning conventional wisdom, questioning the basic premises we all tend to agree on.

There's an island in Micronesia where the people have 17 different systems of counting, depending on what's being counted. One system is for stick-shaped objects, one for round things, one for fish, etc. It's almost impossible to get them to think in terms of numbers as numbers. You ask them what three and two is; they'll ask you three and two what?

They are locked into their world view, just as we are.

At the first session of a political science seminar at an Ivy League university, the thinking ran the gamut: from slightly left-of-center Republican to slightly right-of-center Democrat. The professor opened the second session with a statement.

"Maybe in a truly just society," he said, "we would say to one baby, 'Your forbears grew rich from polluting the air and raping the earth and exploiting child labor. Well, I'm sorry but because of that, you'll have to go live in Harlem in a ghetto with all the other children of wealthy undesirables.' Then to another infant we might say, 'Your forbears worked six days a week in the fields from sun up to sundown, with never a vacation or hope of bettering themselves or putting anything away to better their families. They could be beaten and bought and sold like a piece of machinery. Though they didn't have to be as well cared for because they were cheaper and easier to replace—by owners who could never imagine working that hard themselves. Well, because they had to do that, you get to go live in this beautiful estate in the country, with servants and maids and governesses and every imaginable advantage. You'll get to go to the finest schools so you can have the best possible career. Not that you really need a career because we're also going to give you more money than you could ever spend no matter how much you might care to spend or how long you live. The money is going to be worth even more because those children of the wealthy in the ghettos with no education are, for the most part, only going to be able to get grunt jobs. And whatever they do for society—like picking crops and hauling garbage, or working in fast food outlets—we're only going to value those hours of their life at a fraction of what we value the hours from your life. So everything you wish to buy is going to cost a whole lot less than it would have if we paid them a living wage. They don't really deserve a living wage because their forbears were rich thieves. Yours on the other hand were hard workers—not that they had a choice—who never harmed a soul out of greed to make a dollar.'"

The professor paused for a moment, then added, "Maybe this is exactly what we should do, in line with the Puritan ethic and the ideals upon which this country was founded: that honest hard work should be rewarded."

"So you'd like us to punish the children for the sins of their fathers," a prelaw student demanded accusingly.

"Whereas" the professor replied, "right now we're rewarding the children for the sins of their fathers. Obviously it's ridiculous to settle the sins of the fathers on the children. But maybe we shouldn't be so quick to settle the advantages of the fathers on the children either."

Do you agree? Probably not. But the thought was original. It helped the students see a few old assumptions in a new way. It got them to spend a few moments testing their own beliefs, at the very least reselling those beliefs to themselves as preferable to the alternatives being advocated.

A CERTAIN ASPECT OF FOOLISHNESS

Someone once said that discovery consists of seeing what everybody has seen and thinking what nobody has thought. In business, we're often afraid to suggest novel ideas for fear of being laughed at. But as Alfred Lord Whitehead noted, "Almost all new ideas have a certain aspect of foolishness when they are first proposed."

Sometimes they don't merely appear foolish. Sometimes they are foolish. Gail Borden had an idea for curing yellow fever by refrigerating the victims until their whole bodies were covered with frost—and keeping them that way for an entire week. His next idea was for a "terraqueous machine," a combination horse-drawn wagon and sailboat. It worked poorly on land and capsized immediately when it hit the water. Then he came up with dehydrated meat biscuits, which *Scientific American* actually hailed as "one of the most valuable inventions that has been brought forward." Others found them "absolutely disgusting." The Army decided that they not only tasted awful and failed to satisfy hunger, but they produced headaches, nausea, and "great muscular depression."

Borden's next foolish idea was for condensed milk—and a $3 billion a year business was born.

"At first a new theory is attacked as absurd," psychologist and philosopher William James said. "Then it is admitted to be true but obvious and insignificant; finally it is seen to be so important that its adversaries claim they themselves discovered it."

IBM founder Thomas J. Watson once suggested we should be less concerned about being laughed at than about "the stigma of conformity." I don't know how it is at IBM, but in most organizations there is no stigma attached to conformity. No matter how mind-numbing it might be. If there's a stigma it's attached to nonconformity, no matter how much management might rhapsodize about thinking outside the box.

"Somehow every organization must make room for inner-directed, obstreperous, creative people, sworn enemies of routine and the status quo, always ready to upset the apple cart by thinking up new and better ways of doing things." That's how Admiral Hiram Rickover put it.

ESCAPING THE BOX—EVEN WHEN THERE ARE BARS ON THE WINDOWS

TACTIC: One of my favorite ways to generate innovative thinking is to list several possible solutions to a problem, then consider the exact opposite of each. Do any of the opposites make sense? How good a case could you make for any of them if you had to sell them to someone? Do any of them sound better than the first group? What about combining an approach with its opposite?

You may not come up with an immediate solution, but you will gain a new perspective on the problem—and that may provide a starting point.

Another of my favorites comes from Jack Foster's book, *How to Get Ideas.* Foster tells of an older office building that housed far more workers than it was ever designed to handle. The problem was that the building had only two elevators. During peak hours it seemed to take forever to get one.

Foster notes that there were several possible solutions the manager of the building could have chosen. She could have had new elevators installed on the outside of the building. She could have had escalators built into one of the stairwells. She might have given perks or prizes for workers who arrived early or departed late. She could have established programs encouraging workers to use the stairs, especially those with offices on the lower floors. She could have asked the various tenant companies to stagger their hours.

How did she solve the problem?

With mirrors. She installed ceiling-to-floor, wall-to-wall mirrors in all the elevator areas. And it worked. Because, just as she figured, people didn't mind waiting as much if they could spend their time looking at themselves—and perhaps surreptitiously sneaking a peak at the others waiting with them.

Confronted with too few elevators, the manager solved a different problem. Or more accurately, she examined the reality and uncovered and then solved the real problem: the irritation people felt at having to wait.

Any assumptions can be challenged. Every assumption should be.

TACTIC: When you're looking to fill the glass, it's always worthwhile to try digging deeper, asking yourself, "What's the real problem here?" Is it not enough elevators or is it something else altogether?

TIP: When you disagree with a company policy, ask yourself what they're really trying to accomplish. What other options can you offer? Maybe you can put up a few mirrors rather than build them an elevator.

It's like the joke about the three men's clothing shops that opened in the same building all adjacent to each other. It quickly became apparent that there was no way all three could survive.

The man who ran the store at one end of the building had a degree in merchandising. He created a beautiful window display and fronted it with posters proclaiming, "Year-End Clearance." The businessman at the other end had an MBA in marketing. He took out newspaper, TV, and radio ads, did direct marketing, and tied it all together with two huge window signs that screamed, "Final Close-Out Sale."

The woman in the middle had no degrees. She'd worked her way up from clerk. She knew very little about marketing and advertising. But she did come up with a banner to hang across her storefront. It read simply, "Main Entrance."

In February 1999, an inmate in a city jail was granted a private phone call. Instead of calling his lawyer or his girlfriend, this guy called the jail itself. Pretending to be a police official, he instructed them to take a certain prisoner (himself) from jail over to a certain address (his girlfriend's house) and to leave him there. They did. According to the chief of police, the transfer request was so bizarre that everyone thought it had to be on the up and up.

Talk about outside-the-box thinking. There's a self-help book in this guy—if anyone can track him down.

THINKING OUTSIDE THE FAD

TIP: Sometimes the first thing we need to question in order to think outside the box is the very idea of thinking outside the box.

Sometimes the clichés, the buzzwords, and the management fads seem to take a life of their own. How many companies seemed to go through downsizing and/or reengineering for the sake of downsizing or reengineering, with no specific, well thought out goals and no clear picture of the long-term effects? They were bound and determined to save money, no matter how much it cost.

Substituting clichés for thought can cripple business as badly as it cripples government. A few years back, when *focus* was the word of the moment, I sat through a lengthy meeting in which a regional VP instructed his people to focus on 27 different variables. Twenty-seven! The man had no idea what the word *focus* even meant. And neither he nor his subordinates had any idea what he really wanted from them.

We've all learned that we have to embrace change, and we've learned it with such devotion that change has sometimes become an end in itself rather than a means to an end.

"We've been told so often that we're living in an era of constant change that by gosh we are going to change—constantly," is the way one frustrated manufacturing executive put it. "So we change the good and the excellent as well as the mediocre and the bad. I don't know how it is with other companies, but around here we're sacrificing too much of what we do best. Ask why, and the only justification you're given— and as managers the only explanation we give—comes in the form of the latest management cliché. Whatever that might be this week."

"It's management by parody," one of his peers added. "Because what they're doing is usually a parody of the original idea that generated the cliché in the first place. That's why Dilbert has become so popular. Not because it's so outlandish, because it's so true."

"I'll give you an old cliché," the first executive said. "We're reinventing wheels everywhere you look. Only with the new paradigms the wheels can't be round. Round wheels, that was the old, inside-the-box thinking. So the new wheels don't roll as well as the old ones did."

Sometimes getting outside the box means looking back into some of those old boxes we may have abandoned. Thinking outside the box means opening up potential solutions. If you ignore what's currently in the box, simply because it's inside the box, you may succeed in being novel at the expense of the tried and true.

Round wheels roll exceedingly well. No one who's his or her own guru should be afraid to admit that.

CHAPTER | **10**

Add Water

"Do you want to buy some magazines?"

If you stood on a corner and asked passersby that question, how many people do you think you'd have to ask before someone said, yes or even, maybe?

When I was 16, I sold magazine subscriptions door to door. In the neighborhoods we worked, on Saturdays and early evenings, people would occasionally come to the door whom we didn't want to waste our time pitching. They'd be drunk or crazy or underage or so obviously impoverished they'd never pass the credit check. To get rid of one of them as quickly as possible, we only had to ask one question, "Would you like to buy some magazines?"

The answer was always immediate, and it was always, "No." No one ever even asked what magazines we were selling.

It's like the old saw about a guy standing on a corner propositioning every passing woman, figuring that sooner or later one would say yes. Maybe. But by the time it happened he might be too old to be able to do anything about it.

David Oglivy, founder of the Oglivy & Mather ad agency, said, "In the modern world of business, it is useless to be a creative original thinker unless you can also sell what you create. Management cannot be expected to recognize a good idea unless it is presented to them by a good salesman."

"In my 35 years or so of observing people in organizations," organizational expert Thomas L. Quick notes, "I've concluded beyond question that the people who get things done and who are most effective in getting the results they want are those with superb selling skills."

You and your ideas and your vision are your products. How well have you been selling them to those you need to reach? Have you been keeping your own strongest selling points hidden, hoping that they're self-evident, or figuring that the upper echelon of the company should be able to puzzle them out on their own? Are you even sure what the most effective selling points might be to them?

If you want one of your people to reach new heights, how well have you sold that vision to her, in a way that she'll understand not only intellectually but emotionally and motivationally? Are you even sure what the most effective selling points might be to her?

Besides being CEO of the company of you, you've also got to be the national sales manager and the number-one salesperson. If you aren't selling yourself and your ideas, who is?

Who?

Too frequently when we want something in business, we simply ask our bosses, our subordinates, our coworkers, or even our customers, "Would you like to buy some magazines?" Without doing any selling. You need to ask; if you don't ask you don't get. But if all you do is ask, you've got about as much chance of getting satisfaction as that horny guy on the street corner.

WIIFM

TIP: People are more likely to comply with a request if given a reason—even if the reason makes no sense.

Can I cut in front of you to use the copy machine?

Would you let me, if I asked you that question?

In one study, a researcher asked people just that: if she could cut in line at a copying machine. When she asked, "Excuse me, I have five pages, may I use the Xerox machine?" only 60 percent of those asked allowed her to cut in front of them. But when she used the exact same words but added, "because I have to make some copies," almost everyone allowed her to. She'd given them a reason, a "because." It worked even when the "because" made no sense.

> **TIP:** Reasons for agreement and commitment—selling points—work even better when they do make sense.

Obviously, the more water a salesperson can add to the customer's glass—the better he can make the deal, the greater the benefit to the customer, the more the salesperson can marshal his honesty and his honest enthusiasm—the more sense that deal will tend to make to that customer. The same holds true for those of us who aren't salespeople, when we're trying to influence those around us.

You might not be able to fill someone else's glass. But you can at least add water—as much water as possible.

> **TIP:** Understand the problems of your superiors, your peers, and your subordinates. Figure out what their goals are. Discover where those goals intersect with yours.

> **TIP:** Selling your ideas sometimes means spending more time perfecting saleable ideas.

Always maximize the WIIFM. Every salesperson knows what the WIIFM is. Which is why it's amazing how often some of them seem to forget how to use it. The WIIFM is the *what's in it for me—me* of course being the person you're trying to influence. What's in it for them in advancing your cause? What are they likely to buy into? Why would they buy into it? If they don't recognize that they have a need for whatever you're trying to advance, how can you create that need?

What's in it for them?

An architect in a third-world country designed a high-rise apartment building for an area that was prone to earthquakes. During the construction, he discovered that his company had ordered substandard steel for the project. So what did he do about it? He considered bursting into the company president's office, pointing fingers, and pounding the table. He considered threats. He considered appealing to ethics. He even considered begging and pleading.

Instead he waited until he met with the president for his normal weekly progress report. After they covered a few routine matters, the architect calmly said, "You know they've ordered a different steel than the one we specified. It's really not that bad. It's almost as strong, and it's considerably less expensive. Normally I might be okay with it. But as close as we are to a major fault zone here, it leaves us open to a huge problem."

He pulled a newspaper clipping out of his briefcase and passed it across the desk. It was a story about several Turkish contractors who were forced to flee their country—a couple were even stoned in the streets—after the 1999 earthquake.

"It's the same grade of steel these poor bastards used," the architect explained. "Perfectly acceptable under most circumstances. But we're in this for the long haul and sooner or later we're going to have an earthquake. They'll be politicians looking to shift the blame for their own lack of preparedness and we'll be making ourselves the perfect scapegoats. We'll be completely ruined."

Not a thing about the law breaking, no accusations about who changed the order on the steel, nothing about the 250 residents of the building who could be killed. Instead, "We'll be completely ruined." The strongest selling point was that, long-term, this was not a strategy that would work for the president or the company.

Obviously, this is an extreme example. Most of the time we're not dealing with illegalities, we're not dealing with life and death. But no matter how big or small the issue, you're far more likely to get what you want by persuading people that it's in their best interests than by ordering them or asking them or pleading with them or hoping they'll stumble upon the idea of giving it to you on their own.

This is a lesson even salespeople are slow to learn. Studies have consistently found they spend too much time talking about themselves and their products instead of discussing the customer and the customer's needs.

WHO'S DOING WHAT FOR WHOM?

"How can you do this to me?" I once overheard a salesperson whining to a customer who'd gone over to the competition.

The customer wasn't doing anything to her. The salesperson simply had failed to prove that her product made good business sense to the customer. Too frequently in business, our attitude toward the people around us is, "How can you do this to me?" rather than showing them how what we're advocating makes good business sense to them.

Davis Parsons knew that his manager abhorred doing the budgeting. The work was tedious, and though it didn't take her that many hours, it tied her to headquarters. She knew her time would be better spent out in the field. When Davis was turned down for his raise, he offered to take on a few extra duties to justify the additional money, including the budgeting. His boss found him the money and freed up enough of his time so Davis could take on the extra work.

A POTENT STRATEGY

The legitimate purpose of ethical selling should be to get what you want by helping others get what they want. Helping others get what they want is not philanthropy, it's a potent strategy for success. After creating a true deal, we sell by showing people the benefits, by demonstrating the *what's in it for me* to each of the *me's* we want to sell. It's astonishing what you can achieve, in sales, in a career, in any aspect of life, by helping people get what they want.

A convenience store is a convenience store, right? Maybe. But the average QuikTrip store pumps 3 million gallons of gas while its rivals average less than 750,000. They average $2 million in merchandise sales while 7-11 averages less than $1 million. How? They pay store managers almost twice as much as the competition. They offer all workers monthly profit-sharing bonuses. They provide stock options along with benefits like homeowners insurance and childcare reimbursement accounts. They cut profits to offer their customers better pricing and generate massive repeat business: though price-sensitive shoppers are notorious for their lack of loyalty. Their stores are clean and up to date.

And if you're worried about cheap gas, theirs is low-priced but it's guaranteed. If your car develops fuel-related problems from tanking up at QuikTrip, they'll reimburse you for the repairs. Without a receipt. Your word is your proof of purchase. If a mechanic attests that the repairs were fuel related, QuikTrip pays. A marketing person might call that a gimmick. A salesperson would call it proving value. Your bank may treat you like a convicted felon if you accidentally bounce a $15 check, but a convenience store takes your word for hundreds of dollars worth of repairs. QuikTrip is not just working on filling tanks; they're working on filling the glass—they're adding water to the glasses of their employees and their customers.

> **TIP:** Concentrate on *what's in it for them* and the *what's in it for you* will take care of itself.

Show the person you're dealing with how what you're proposing will make his or her life or job or numbers better, more convenient, more cost-efficient. Show what it will do for the impression others— particularly their superiors—have of them. Demonstrate your concern for their well-being. Provide them with reassurance, perhaps explaining how similar plans have worked for others.

In other words, prove value.

"I was being sexually hassled and harassed—sexually *harassled*— by a hygienically challenged coworker," a female aerospace worker reports. "My boss bathed a little more often, but beyond that he wasn't much more enlightened than the harasser. So instead of going to him with a complaint for him to cram into his "forget" file, I tried to show him how this kind of thing was interfering with team-building, wasting company time, and screwing up the goals he needed to reach for that promotion he'd been struggling for."

Did the woman have a right to complain? Absolutely. But selling the boss on the idea that stopping the harassment was in his own best interest worked far better than any complaint would have.

She was not complaining; she was creating a need. In this particular case, it was a need the boss didn't realize he had: the need to keep the harassler from screwing up his team and his goals.

SELL SOLUTIONS

Can salespeople sometimes force, coerce, threaten, or browbeat customers into a sale? Absolutely. They can and they do. And sometimes we can do the same with bosses, subordinates, and coworkers. But how happy is that customer, boss, subordinate, or coworker going to be about it? How wholeheartedly are they going to support the decision we forced them into? What's going to happen the next time we want something from them?

So you sell: yourself, your ideas, your proposals. Much like you might sell a product. Of course you can't really sell a product. The best salesperson in the country can't sell a product. Nobody can. What you can sell are solutions. You uncover needs and prove value and sell solutions to those who have those needs.

When clients hire me as a consultant or a speaker, I always keep in mind that they aren't really buying me. They're buying the belief that I'm going to make them money. That I'm going improve productivity and the bottom line. That I'm going to make them look good. And that people—particularly their superiors—are going to think that they made the best possible use of the funds they were allocated.

Let's say you'd like a raise. You might be able to sell the boss on the idea simply by meeting preset goals and specifying exactly what you've done for him and the company since your last pay increase. Normally bosses don't have to be told that it's in their best interest to keep producers producing and to keep their best people happy. But sometimes they do.

Everybody in the accounting department knew Angela was indispensable, her boss included. Angela deserved a raise. But getting her one would have taken a major effort on his part. He'd have had to take it to his manager then fight on up the line. So Angela never asked him for a pay increase. Instead she told him how much she loved working in accounting. And how she'd love to be able to make her career there. The problem she had—which without her ever mentioning it immediately became *his* problem—was that the head of credit had been talking up a position in his department. A much better paying position.

Starting almost immediately and continuing over the next few months, Angela's boss found her several raises along with a promotion in grade. A year later she was making 33 percent more money for the exact same job. Her boss told her, "I wanted to make sure you were making so much you could never afford to leave."

She didn't sell herself. She didn't sell fairness. She didn't sell her need for a raise. She sold a solution to her boss's problem.

You don't want a bigger office because you're a power-mad empire builder. You want it because it would improve your productivity—and the department's—by giving you the meeting space you need. Or because you're bringing in clients who'll feel slighted if forced to deal with someone the company values so little they don't even provide them with a decent office. Or at least a door.

You're not selling your reallocation proposal. You're selling security and peace of mind. You're selling the opportunity for your boss and her boss to look good and make their numbers and make points with their superiors—and ultimately receive higher evaluations, bigger raises, and faster promotions. And the same goes when you're selling to a subordinate or a peer.

WHEN YOU CAN'T FIND PERFECT PEOPLE

At one of my workshops an attendee who introduced himself to the group as Mr. Lansdorf stood up and asked me, "What can I do about working for a corporation full of stiffs?" In spite of the fact that the company paid quite well, Mr. Lansdorf's people never performed the way he hoped they would when he hired them. His coworkers weren't much better. As for his boss, "He couldn't care less about my problems. He'd like to be able to forget about my whole department."

"So what exactly do you want?" I asked.

"What I'd like is for people to do the job they're supposed to do—the way they're supposed to do it."

"Which means?" I asked.

"To do something beyond the minimum—to go the extra mile for the company. Everybody expects something for nothing."

"Don't you?"

"Hey, I earn my money," Mr. Lansdorf insisted. "I go way beyond the minimum."

"And it gets you?"

"Nothing, that's the point. It gets me nothing."

"So how long are you going to keep doing that?"

"Not much longer, believe me."

"But you want others to go beyond the minimum without putting something it in for them? Aren't you the one who's expecting for something for nothing?"

"I want people to do what they *should* do."

"So what we're talking about is morality and ethics? What people *should* do?"

"Exactly." he said.

"So as a manager, your ability to manage is based on people doing what they should do? Otherwise you can't get the results you want?"

"No, of course not. Nobody does what they should. At least nobody in my company."

"So wouldn't you be better off trying to find a way to manage—to get the results you need—with the people you've got rather than the perfect people who do what they should and apparently don't exist? Or at least don't exist in your company?"

"Obviously."

Obviously. *Bingo!* I thought. I felt like Socrates, teaching with my questions. Of course later someone reminded me of the famous report given by a third-grader: "Socrates was a Greek philosopher who went around giving people advice. They poisoned him."

So much for the Socratic method.

Obviously, Lansdorf said. If it was so obvious, why had he been asking his people to go the extra mile when there was really no advantage in it for them? Even if they went along in order to stay on his good side, how enthusiastic would they be?

YOU CAN'T SELL AN EMPTY GLASS

Why do we all so frequently act like Mr. Lansdorf? Trish asks her boss to go out of his way for her and help get her promoted. There's nothing in it for him. If anything, losing Trish will make his job more difficult. He's a nice guy. He may help her. But wouldn't he go along far more willingly if he was doing it to gain another ally in management, to earn points with the company for having developed another manager, or to free up Trish's spot so he can reward—and keep from losing—that great new talent he's been grooming on the rung below hers?

It's *obvious:* You can't sell anybody anything if you don't offer them some benefit. You can't motivate anyone by offering them an empty glass, by asking, in effect, "Do you want to buy some magazines?" It's obvious. And we all forget it. Constantly. We hope ethics or morality or religion or character will make up for the lack of incentive.

Does your idea of character tell you that when there's little or nothing in it for you that you should devote yourself unstintingly to providing for someone else's welfare? If so, please call, I've got a job for you.

> **TIP:** If I believe that playing by your rules, systems, procedures, traditions, or morality guarantees that I'm going to lose, do not expect me to play by them.

Bosses who tell you they can't hire good workers are usually telling you they're poor bosses. They're telling you they aren't adding enough water to the glass, they aren't providing sufficient incentive for people to meet their standards.

This is business. Both sides are hoping to benefit from the transaction. Otherwise it's not business, it's charity.

> **TIP:** In business, you never want to rely on charity.

Add as much water to the glass as you realistically can—for your superiors, your coworkers, your subordinates—the way Ron Campbell did for his customers. Do what you have to do to make sure that what you offer is truly a deal. You'll be amazed at the results.

Mr. Lansdorf considered himself a hardheaded realist. He certainly was no positive thinker. But he was a bigger Pollyanna than any of them. At least the positive thinker Pollyannas provide the temporary incentive of a bit of feel-good smoke and mirrors. Lansdorf expected to get results without offering anything.

Do slaves work hard? Not when they don't have to. Wage slaves work as hard as they have to and no harder. Who wants people working for him or her who are nothing but wage slaves? Who wants to work for or work with someone who's nothing but a wage slave?

The more of a stake your people—bosses, coworkers, subordinates—have in a project (or a company), the harder they will work. The less of a stake, the less they will work.

MAKE IT EASIER TO SAY YES

I know this is business and everyone is being paid. Perhaps they're even being paid to do exactly what you're trying to get them to do. Will they be paid even if they don't do it? Will life go on without causing them a major problem? If so, then it doesn't really matter if they are being paid, does it? He who's got the gold may make the rules. The problem is this particular "he" will have to spend a lot of that gold forcing people to follow those rules. Forcing them to do what they are supposed to do, and getting the kinds of results you get when you force people to perform.

Lansdorf was upset because his people didn't perform as they were supposed to. That's what managing is all about. If people performed as they were supposed to, beyond training there wouldn't be much need for managers.

Buyers are supposed to buy. At least that's what salespeople believe. But buyers never buy if you simply ask if they want to buy some magazines.

Are you setting up situations where it's easier for people to say No than Yes? Or to just go through the motions—which is sometimes worse than just flat-out refusing to do it?

What's in it for them?

Add as much water to their glass as you can. That's the first rule of sales. As I tell salespeople, even if it really somehow was the buyer's fault for not buying, you're the one without the sale. Make them want the magazines.

Then don't be afraid to ask for the order.

ASK FOR THE ORDER

We're often reluctant to ask for what we want, particularly when we have to ask superiors. Nobody likes to be turned down. Often we'd rather not ask than ask and be told No. Perhaps the reasoning is, *I may not have gotten what I want but at least I wasn't rejected. At least my boss, coworker, subordinate, rival, whatever, doesn't know that I want it.*

Better they should know. You may have heard something about squeaky wheels. "Around here," they used to say at one high-turnover company, "the squeaky wheel gets greased." Squeak too much or in too irritating or inconvenient a manner and that could happen. But a good employee who makes her desires clear and makes a strong case for those desires puts her boss under a burden, even if the boss has to deny that particular request at that time. A good boss will try to make it up to her and look for opportunities to do just that.

Don't be afraid to ask, whether you're dealing with bosses or coworkers or subordinates. Hinting around will get you nowhere. Not unless the WIIFM is more overwhelming than it's ever likely to be. Hints are too easy to dodge; they make it too easy to avoid making a commitment.

> **TIP:** Horatio Alger is dead. No one is going to take it upon themselves to discover your wonderfulness or the wonderfulness of your ideas. It's been said that if you're doing a good job and nobody needs to pay attention to you, nobody will. Consider it said again.

Ask. And that means ask verbally. Novice salespeople are easily put off by prospects who tell them to leave their literature or their card "and I'll call you." Reports and proposals are often the leave-behind literature of the business world. And sometimes they get as much attention.

Vannevar Bush, the cofounder of Raytheon, was a longtime advisor to Franklin Roosevelt. He made it a point to present his proposals in person and always did his best to get an immediate decision. "I always tried to come out of the [Oval] Office still in possession of any paper or report I took in," he writes in his book, *Pieces of the Action.*

In his memoir, *I'll Always Have Paris,* Art Buchwald tells a supposedly true story. An American movie company contacted its manager in France. They told him a VIP TV station owner was coming to Paris by himself. The manager was to do everything possible to make the trip enjoyable.

The station owner arrived, and he had only had one request: "a female companion for dinner." The manager made a few calls. Eventually he came up with a beautiful, high-class call girl. She wasn't cheap but he agreed to pay her on a daily basis. And yes, he'd pay the full, all-night rate. She wasn't to ask the station owner for money.

That evening, the manager introduced the VIP to his "dinner companion." The morning after, she came by his office to collect her cash.

And the morning after that. This went on for five straight days. Eventually, the manager decided to call the station owner at his Paris hotel, hoping to find out how the hefty "PR expenditure" was working and how much longer it might continue.

They chatted pleasantly for a few minutes, then the manager tactfully asked, "So how are things going with the young lady?"

"Just great," the station owner enthused. "I think tonight I'm going to get lucky."

TIP: If you never ask, you never get.

Add water to their glass. The more you add, the higher you fill it, the easier it will be to ask. You might even get lucky.

CHAPTER | **11**

Bring Out the Prospect in Yourself

In psychology, there are almost as many different systems of classifying human beings as there are psychologists. Sales trainers—at least those who don't divide people into two types—love to divide everyone into four types. The four types never seem to match up from one training program to the next. But no matter what those types might be— thinkers, relaters, feelers, drivers, gropers, droolers, whatever—the trainers always insist that each of the types has to be approached in a specific way if the sale is to be made.

I could never keep it all straight. And I've never known a halfway decent sales rep who ever paid much attention to any of it in a sales call. Still, having the ability to relate to others on their own terms is the most powerful—if perhaps the most subtle—sales skill there is. It's even more effective for nonsalespeople, who usually don't have to overcome the type of massive initial resistance salespeople encounter.

EMPATHIZING ENGINEERS

Samuel Metters, CEO of the engineering firm Metters Industries, told *Technology* magazine that in spite of the technical proficiency of its people, at one time the company had trouble generating repeat business. "I remember presenting a proposal to a government agency and watching my employees ram our ideas down the representative's throat. If the government had to choose between Metters Industries and a company with equal technical resources, the decision makers would choose the other company because we didn't understand how to treat people."

So Metters changed his conception of the ideal employee. "Now I look for [job] candidates who have . . . a warm side to their personality. I just hired a man whose ratio of social skills to technical skills is about 70 to 30. We're finally beginning to win those follow-up contracts."

Training and Development magazine recently reported on a study done at another major engineering firm. "[T]he most valued and productive engineers working in teams weren't those with the highest IQs or achievement test scores but those who excelled in rapport, empathy, cooperation, persuasion, and the ability to build consensus."

BRINGING OUT THE PROSPECT IN NORTHERN IRELAND

When I'm training salespeople, I like to talk about building rapport by "bringing out the prospect in yourself." Which really means bringing out that part of yourself that's most like the person you're dealing with. So they'll see you as someone like themselves, someone they can understand, someone who might be worthy of trust. We're all more likely to trust and—in a sales situation—to buy from people who are like ourselves.

George Mitchell was trying to bring together the Protestants and Catholics in Northern Ireland, to salvage the collapsing Good Friday Agreement. But David Trimble and his Ulster Unionists would sit on one side of the table. Gerry Adams and the Sinn Fein people would sit on the other. For hours at a time they'd blast each other, each blaming the other for the failure of the peace process.

So what did Mitchell do? He moved the talks out of the pressure cooker of Belfast to the comfortable, relaxed atmosphere of the U.S. Ambassador's residence in London. The conference table was replaced by upholstered chairs and overstuffed couches. The two sides took walks in the garden together and shared meals.

"I insisted there was no assigned seating at dinner," Mitchell said, according to the *Los Angeles Times,* "no nationalists on one side, unionists on the other. It was mixed up, random, and there were no negotiations. We talked about sports, family, fishing, things like that. And gradually the proper atmosphere was created."

They talked. They got to know each other. Then they discussed the issues; they negotiated face to face before committing their ideas to paper, where each would have a firm position to defend. When they didn't understand each other, Mitchell led them back into negotiations as often as it took. Frequently, he asked questions he thought needed to be asked.

"And then," an insider reported, "they helped each other to draft the documents they each wanted to see from the other side. Whoever would have imagined that?"

In other words, each put themselves in the other's position.

RELATABILITY

"No one ever buys from someone he can't relate to," a great natural salesman once told me. "To get what I want I've got to be 'relatable.'"

If you wish to persuade someone—to sell them on yourself, your vision, or your proposal—you've got to be "relatable." And to be the most "relatable," you've got to bring out that part of yourself that's most like that person. Each of us might have different predominant character traits, but all of us have virtually all of those traits within us, simply to differing degrees.

So this is not about faking or pretending. It's not about manipulation. It's not about acting. Or perhaps it's like the best acting, where a Brando or a DeNiro finds the character within himself. It's about understanding the person you're dealing with. And empathizing with him. And even liking him.

TIP: Try to like the person you're dealing with.

TIP: Try harder.

THE FIRST CASUALTY

You can try to like those you have to deal with. Or you can be like those mediocre salespeople who secretly despise their customers; who boast about "nailing" them or "slamming" them; who secretly resent their customers for the power those customers have over the rep's destiny.

"It's us against the other—the competitor, the corporate watchdog, the customer," is the way it was put in *The Force,* David Dorsey's revealing exploration of an old-style sales force at work.

And: "In certain moods, Pacetta [the sales manager] was known to call his best reps Assassins, and Nelson was so good, Pacetta called him a Paid Assassin, presumably ranking him higher than a mere amateur killer."

Who among us wouldn't be anxious to buy from a sales force with that type of mentality? Dorsey's book was written in 1994. Despite massive lip service to the contrary, this type of thinking is still far more prevalent than most people in sales care to admit.

And too many of us who aren't in sales develop a similar attitude toward coworkers, subordinates, and bosses. Frequently, they seem to hold our fate in their hands just like a customer seems to hold the fate of a sales rep. It's easy to start resenting them.

Try to like them. Try to respect them. If you think business is war, remember the first casualty of war is truth. And the first truth that dies is the truth that the enemy is a person much like ourselves, with good and bad qualities, with hopes and dreams. A person who probably believes in what she is doing exactly as much as we believe in what we're doing.

TIP: The other guy or gal is not the devil.

TIP: Be wary of people who try to demonize those they perceive as their opponents.

This kind of reverse-Pollyanna thinking might work fine if you want to fight wars all your life. It's a lot easier to kill a demon than it is to kill another human being who's basically just like you and me. Though even in a war, I'd argue that if you're running that war you're better off with an accurate, nonpropagandist view of the enemy.

But neither your coworkers, your subordinates, nor your boss should be the enemy. Not if you can possibly avoid it. Your customers—the customers of the company you work for—should never be the enemy. Too many of your competitors are anxious to have them as allies.

> **TIP:** We talk about internal customers, but try actually treating your fellow workers at least as well as a great salesperson treats his customers—instead of the way the paid assassins and demonizers treat theirs.

> **TIP:** Try smiling at them.

Creativity lecturer Mike Vance says Dale Carnegie's advice was basically, "Smile even if you don't feel like it," but what it should have been was, "Find a reason to smile so you *can* feel like it."

TWO MORE GURUS HEARD FROM

You don't have to trust those you work with—just like you don't have to trust customers. You might keep a very wary eye on them. On the other hand, they should be able to trust you.

> **TIP:** Jesus CEO (from the business book of the same name) and St. Frankie A. might have told us that sometimes you can better empathize with someone who's giving you problems by "hating the sin and not the sinner."

Your subordinate missed the meeting. He wasn't doing it to spite you. He had a reason. He probably even thought it was a good one. You may not see it that way—and you may have to impress that upon him—but the issue wasn't personal and you shouldn't make it so.

One management expert cites the famous scene in *The Wizard of Oz* in which Toto pulls back the curtain and reveals that the Wizard is a technologically augmented phony. Outraged after all she's been through and obviously taking the deception personally, Dorothy calls him a bad man.

"I'm not a bad man," the humbug replies. "I'm just a bad wizard."

We are all the heroes of our own stories. An astute philosopher named Ken Koserowski used to tell me, "Everybody is a jerk in somebody's eyes. But nobody's a jerk in their own." Most of your peers or subordinates or superiors are not really bad people. Some of them are just bad wizards. Sometimes very bad wizards. It's seldom personal and if you can avoid taking it that way, you'll be way ahead of the game.

A WISE LAMA

A good salesperson always tries to partner, to get on the same side of the table as the people she's dealing with. When she meets with opposition, she can't afford to take it personally, waste her energy, and destroy the possibility of developing a relationship. The Dalai Lama, for spiritual reasons, entreats us to practice an "inner disarmament of anger and jealousy." That makes great business sense as well.

Even if it is personal, how are you making the situation better by letting it get to you?

"No question my boss was a problem," an attendee e-mailed me a few months after a presentation. "But it's surprising how much it helps to remember what you said about me being paid to do the job the way she wants it done, to help her, not to make her life more difficult."

And from that moment on, this man and his boss lived happily ever after. Well . . . not quite. Truth in advertising forces me to admit that this guy found himself another position less than a year later. But at least he left on good terms. The way he'd talked about his boss during the workshop, I was happy that he'd left without bloodshed. In the guru business, some triumphs are smaller than others.

> **TIP:** The way we treat people has a lot to do with the way they treat us. Your boss is no different. Neither are your peers or your subordinates. Getting along with all of them is part of your job and part of how management will judge you.

Salespeople are paid to get along with their customers. You are paid to get along with those you work for, those you work with, and those who work for you. As well as the company's customers.

Even when they don't lead to bloodshed, dislike and resentment destroy empathy. Lack of empathy makes persuasion more difficult, whether you're trying to persuade your coworker, your boss, your subordinates, your customers, or yourself.

> **TIP:** Indignation, particularly righteous indignation, is more addictive than heroin. It's becoming the drug of choice for far too many of us. Thus the success of all those daytime talk shows on TV. Nothing kills empathy faster. I can personally attest to the difficulty, but try going cold turkey.

> **TIP:** Empathize with yourself. You're not the devil either.

STAY OUT OF THE PANTYHOSE

Sometimes when you "bring out the prospect in yourself," you'll discover that your manner will become similar to the other person's. Unconsciously, your posture may even mirror his or hers. Your body language, your gestures, expressions, your speech patterns, even your breathing may become similar.

"When I first tried this type of mirroring," one executive assistant reports, "I thought [the boss] would see right through it. I was sure he'd think I was sucking up to him. But he never even noticed. And the better I got at mirroring, the more he liked what I had to say and the more of my ideas he adopted. It's amazing."

That's all well and good. But be careful with this. Bringing out the prospect in yourself is a powerful strategy. Mimicking gestures and pretending to be someone you are not is not going to make either you, your boss, or anyone else you're dealing with happy in the long term. You don't want to be like the GM from that weasel-ocracy whom everyone expected to start wearing pantyhose once he began working for a woman.

And bringing out the prospect in yourself doesn't necessarily mean behaving like the other person. That's especially true if, at that particular moment, the individual is aggressive or antagonistic. There *is* a certain type of whiny screamer that can best be handled by screaming right back at him, but I wouldn't advise trying that without professional assistance (from either a sales or a psychiatric professional).

What this strategy does entail is understanding what would be motivating you—or that part of yourself that's most like this individual—if you were behaving like he is. Which means empathizing. And observing carefully. And listening—letting him have his say as you would like to have your say—and making it clear by everything you say and everything you do that you are listening.

So he will see you as someone like himself.

This is something we all do to one extent or another. As writer Sarah Orne Jewett said, "Tact is after all a kind of mind reading." And most of us have at least some small experience with tact. This is just exercising that "mind reading" at a higher level.

COMMUNICATE

Bringing out the prospect in yourself means communicating with the person in a way that person is comfortable with. You can certainly adapt to someone's style of communicating—you can accommodate that style—and still be 100 percent you. If she's businesslike and formal, she'll be uncomfortable if you're too relaxed too quickly. If she's more casual, she'll be uncomfortable if you're too rigid and businesslike. You don't want to approach a get-to-the-facts, cut-through-the-BS type the same way you approach a socializer—or someone who just happens to be in a socializing mood at the moment.

If you're dealing with a slow talker, you're going to lose him if you talk too fast. If he speaks rapidly you're going to frustrate him if you talk too slowly.

Here's a flash: Men and women are not the same. It's becoming a new cliché, but salespeople know that—as a general rule—there is some truth in the idea that it's better to stress information and solutions to problems when communicating with men and emphasize relationships when dealing with women.

Still, if women are really from Venus and men from Mars, then the two planets and their inhabitants are far more alike than they are different.

Nowadays we all understand how badly you can screw yourself up—and how easily you can offend—by relying on ethnic or cultural stereotypes when trying to get your message across. Still, it can help to have an understanding of different cultures, whether across national boundaries or within them. Different cultures are, well, different. The average volume of a breast implant in the United States is 33 percent larger than the average volume in Europe. Bankers and bikers tend to have different cultures, though the great thing about America—no, it has nothing to do with breast size—and the great thing about human beings in general is how much overlap there really is. Still, you need to be able to relate differently to a 28-year-old, long-haired biker than a middle-aged investment banker struggling with the gears of his first Ferrari.

> **TACTIC:** Speak to people in their own language, noting the terms they use and the concepts they're comfortable with. This is called communicating.

Be careful of misusing jargon; if you don't understand it, don't use it. You'll just be verifying your ignorance and confirming how different you are from the person you're talking to. It never hurts to toss in a bit of jargon to show expertise, but the operative term here is *a bit*. And make sure it's understood if it needs to be.

Jargon, euphemisms, psychobabble, unnaturally elevated business-speak, all raise barriers in people more frequently than they lower them. Even people who might mistake them for signs of intelligence are often turned off by the pomposity.

I was having a drink with a product manager at a corporate cocktail party when her boss came by and asked her, "What did you think of my presentation this morning?"

"As usual, Hank. You made me think of Lincoln."

"You always say that," he smiled.

"Just something about you."

"Lincoln?" I asked after Hank left. I'd heard the presentation. The Gettysburg address took seven minutes to deliver. Hank may have taken longer than that to thank the woman who introduced him, something many in that room will never forgive her for.

"Lincoln," the product manager insisted. "Every time Hank opens that erudite mouth of his, I think of Lincoln and what Lincoln said about another politician: that the guy could compress more words into smaller ideas than any man he'd ever met."

I had a friend with a low-wage, part-time job who was always broke. Until the 80s came along and he realized that he wasn't broke at all, he simply had a "cash-flow problem." It sounded so much better than telling people—or telling himself—that he only made $165 a week.

Bean counting becomes so much more "impactful," so much more impressive and precise when you say *metric* instead of number or measurement or system of measurement. A protocol that possesses "functionality" will run rings around one that merely has a function—not to mention one that simply *does* something. And that half-billion dollar high-tech start-up that's never made a penny in five years? No problem: they simply need to "monetize" their operation.

In its annual report, an airline company listed the millions of dollars it had received in an insurance payment as "involuntary conversion of a 747."

The plane crashed.

Aside from their inherent silliness, pretentiousness, and lack of clarity, far too often these kinds of phrases turn out to be euphemisms designed to camouflage a nasty reality. And we've all come to realize that. Or does anyone really believe that workers who lose their jobs through "right-sizing" feel a whole lot better about it than those who are downsized out the door? Or laid off?

> **TACTIC:** Be aware of the best time and place to approach those you're trying to influence. If your coworker doesn't like to talk shop outside of the office, don't corner him at his wife's birthday party with your latest proposal for manufacturing. If your boss is not a morning person, why are you talking to him at 8:15 AM before he's had his coffee? Or when he's late for a vital meeting or feeling overwhelmed on Monday morning or the day after returning from vacation?

Of course, people being people, they have a wonderful way of refusing to fit into the nice little boxes and categories we like to create for them. Sometimes the person who's normally a socializer will be all business. Sometimes the slow talker will be going a mile a minute. The woman who can't be bothered Monday morning will have nothing but time. That's why bringing out the prospect in yourself is an art, not a science. It's got to be done individual by individual, situation by situation, rather than according to some system of classifying personality types.

> **TIP:** You've got to be open to others. To who they are. To how they behave and communicate. To their opinions, their wants, and their needs.

Still, in spite of the vast industry devoted to human classification, no matter how you classify human beings, we are all more alike than we are different. It's precisely that fact which makes it possible for you to "bring out the prospect in yourself." As I said before, each of us might have different predominant character traits, but all of us have virtually all of those traits within us—simply to differing degrees.

UNRELATABLES

Are there people you can't relate too? Of course, there have always been and always will be. Are there any who aren't worth trying to relate to? Not if you want to sell them your vision or your proposal or yourself.

There may be a few people you work with that you want as little to do with as possible, just as there are prospects a salesperson might not want as customers. That's fine, provided you never do have to deal with them. And never, as they say, is a long time.

> **TIP:** Even those who aren't decision makers themselves can have a huge impact on decisions others make, especially when decisions are made in a group environment.

Winston Churchill said, "Never hold discussions with the monkey when the organ grinder is in the room." And it's true that you've got know who the decision maker is and you've got to convince that decision maker. But if you treat anybody like a monkey—if you ignore anyone in that room or snub anyone involved in the process—that person will do his or her best to make a monkey out of you.

> **TIP:** It's easier for decision makers to make decisions when those around them agree. Remember that when you decide someone isn't worth the effort of trying to relate to.

If you do make that effort, you might be surprised by what you discover. I know a woman who was judged by a fellow manager to be "the most incomprehensible and self-centered businessperson I've ever known. Successful in business, but completely unsuccessful at the business of being a person." Most of her colleagues shared that opinion. And I have to admit that when I first met her I felt much the same. Later I found out that among the things we hadn't comprehended in her "incomprehensibility" were clandestine acts of generosity with friends, acquaintances, and even strangers that put anything the rest of us had done to shame.

It was fun to make her the devil. But it not only got in the way of business, it wasn't accurate. I'd love to say that recognizing her generosity and granting humanity to her made it easy to deal with her. It didn't. But it did make it easier—considerably easier.

A man most of us would never have taken the trouble to get to know once said, "What am I in the eyes of most people? A good-for-nothing, an eccentric and disagreeable man, somebody who has no position in society and never will have. Very well, even if that were true, I should want to show by my work what there is in the heart of such an eccentric man, of such a nobody." That, again, was Vincent van Gogh. What would you give to have the chance to share a few glasses of wine with him now? (So what if you wouldn't be comfortable asking him to lend you an ear?)

It's hard to imagine anyone more difficult to relate to than van Gogh. Yet he may be the most popular painter of all time. He could hardly be that popular if, at some level at least, he wasn't astonishingly easy to relate to.

STARE CONFIDENTLY AT THE BRIDGE OF HIS NOSE?

Bringing out the prospect in yourself allows you to build rapport, creating a comfortable atmosphere and getting the person you're dealing with to relax.

TACTIC: Chances are he'll feel more comfortable in his office than in yours.

TACTIC: If he's a superior or a coworker and if you can get him seated instead of standing, you've gained more time for your presentation.

TACTIC: Nothing is more important for rapport building than good eye contact. If for some reason you have trouble meeting another person's eyes, look confidently at the bridge of his nose. He'll perceive it as eye contact and you'll be able to stare down a statue, if it comes to that. Just don't make it come to that. The idea behind eye contact is not to make the other person uncomfortable.

WHAT'S OVER THE MANTLE?

TACTIC: When you are in someone's office or work area, observe.

Door-to-door salespeople always used to comment on what was hanging over the mantle in their prospect's homes, because that's where people used to place whatever they were most proud of. And people's offices are usually crammed full of clues to their personalities, their attitudes, and their interests. It's a great place to find common ground, a great springboard for rapport-building conversation.

Note photos, trophies, plaques, and other memorabilia. What magazines do they read? The wall decorations people select say something about them. So do the cartoons and slogans they post. Chances are the guy interviewing you for that great new position didn't mount that huge framed poster on the wall behind him because he objected to what it had to say.

One day while I was consulting for a client in Louisiana, I was field training a rep named Chaz. Chaz had been getting a rather cold reception—at least cold for southwest Louisiana. In New York City, it would have been considered effusive. Suspiciously effusive. Still, though Chaz was a personable guy and the company thought he had tremendous potential, he'd been having difficulty building immediate rapport, and he was getting discouraged.

I'd no sooner talked with him about looking around the prospect's office than we walked into a body shop that had two full walls covered with baseball bats, baseball memorabilia, and baseball trophies. Chaz threw me a quick smile.

"Sold," I whispered. "It's only a question of how much."

The owner came over and Chaz introduced us. Now in this part of southwestern Louisiana, you normally have to spend 15 minutes trying to figure out who's kin to who before you can even consider talking business. But Chaz barely commented on the fact that he and the owner had the same last name. (As far as I could see half of the state was named Thibodeaux, anyway.) Instead he started right in talking baseball. The owner's eyes lit up like a night game at the old Astrodome. I knew that in a few minutes Chaz would make a solid presentation and that he'd be offering the owner an excellent product at a good price. But that's not why I knew he had the sale. I knew he had the sale because I knew that Chaz was wearing his LSU college baseball national championship ring, and that he'd quickly be working that into the conversation, along with the names of several well-known major-leaguer friends of his.

THE CRAM-AND-RAM MODE

Observe the environment. Observe the person. You can't master bringing out the prospect in yourself without paying careful attention to the other person. That means paying less attention to yourself and your internal dialogue and adjusting to accommodate the information that you're receiving. As every sales trainer in the world can attest, even simple listening seems difficult enough for most of us. Bringing out the prospect in yourself requires listening and observing at an even more profound level.

There's a story about me that's been reported in a couple of national publications. I've never confirmed it and I'm not going to now, but I am going to repeat it because it illustrates perfectly the point I want to make. (Now I'm passing on hearsay and rumor about myself, refusing to be an authority on my own life.)

I was working with a client—a well-known and powerful senator—on his personal selling skills. As *Selling Power* magazine reported the story:

> On Maher's second day in Washington, he set up a roleplay for the senator who quickly turned it into a filibuster. "Senator," Maher allegedly broke in, "shut up!"
>
> Stunned, the senator did just that—for a moment anyway. But every time he tried to speak, Maher interrupted, talking over him, refusing to let him squeeze in a syllable. When Maher started shaking a finger in the man's face and lecturing, the senator reached the point of apoplexy. That's when Maher flipped on the VCR and played a tape of the senator doing the exact same thing the day before—to another legislator, a less powerful man—but one whose vote the senator needed.

I work with some of the most intelligent people in the country. And I respect all my clients. But if I had done something like this, it would have been because sometimes you simply have to demonstrate to someone how his behavior makes the prospect, the person he's hoping to persuade, feel.

Most salespeople realize that the days are long gone when they can ram a product down the customer's throat and choke off his or her objections. The rest of us need to realize it as well. Particularly those of us in management. Because though we never try to do it with superiors and seldom try it with peers, too many of us are still in a cram-and-ram mode when it comes to our subordinates. Which doesn't tend to generate wholehearted, enthusiastic support.

A few years back, *Psychology Today* reported a study of top executives, comparing those who had gotten derailed in their careers with those who kept moving on up to senior management. The most common problem among the derailed? Insensitivity to others: an intimidating, bullying, abrasive style. Which means a lack of empathy, an inability to bring out the prospect in themselves.

You may think of yourself as the stereotypical tough boss with a heart of gold, "crusty but benign," like Lou Grant from the old *Mary Tyler Moore Show* and so many other TV and movie bosses. Those who work for you may not be getting the same picture.

Even many of us who'd never cram and ram are frequently guilty of not listening. Not observing. Once again, this is an especially serious problem in management. There's always a tendency for managers to talk too much and listen too little, to ramble on and waste our people's time.

People with less power have to act interested in what we say. So we start believing we're fascinating, and we talk too damn much. We know we should spend more time listening, but we seldom do.

If power corrupts, the first thing it corrupts is the little voice in our heads that tells us when to shut up.

TIP: Shut up.

FACT FINDING

Conventional wisdom in sales says, "He who talks the most loses." Like much of conventional wisdom, it's simply not true. First of all, if the customer loses when the salesperson wins, they're both going to end up losing eventually. Beyond that, it's a ridiculous overstatement. I've seen few—if any—sales in my life where the salesperson talked less than the customer.

The truth behind the overstatement is that the more the salesperson gets the prospect to talk—the more information the salesperson manages to gather, the more complete her fact finding—the more likely she is to make the sale.

You need to do more listening than any salesperson. Because you need your rapport—and your understanding—to be far more profound than the temporary, superficial rapport a salesperson needs to close a sale. Your rapport not only has to help you persuade when the time comes for persuasion, it has to help you and the person you're dealing with through the intricacies and the stresses of a long-term working relationship.

So you don't do your fact finding on an immediate, one-shot basis when you're trying to make a sale. You do yours gradually, over time. You have far more opportunity for observation than any salesperson ever has. Use it.

Listen. Discover what the people around you need. Ask questions. News reporters make a living out of getting people to provide information. According to reporters, the most seductive words in the English language are, "I'd like to hear your story."

Ask people about their story. Find out about them as people: their interests, hobbies, families, goals. Not only will it build rapport but it will also make them more interesting to you—and make them easier to work with. It will definitely make you a lot more interesting to them.

If you don't have a genuine interest and can't develop one, don't ask.

> **TIP:** Phony interest is worse than no interest at all, and eventually it will give itself away. The sharper the person you're dealing with is, the sooner he or she will realize you're a phony.

That's why most perceptive managers abhor butt-kissers; why so many glad-handing upper level executives are so despised by those they glad-hand. Nobody likes to be manipulated; nobody likes to be patronized.

If you don't honestly find that the people around you are more interesting than the office furniture or the potted plants, you probably don't know much about the people around you.

Take an interest, listen, observe. Then, when you're selling yourself, your vision, or your proposals, do even more listening and observing—and ask even more questions. That involves the person you're dealing with in the process, and helps turn you into a partner rather than an opponent. You're showing him that you're taking the trouble to find out exactly what he needs, that you want to satisfy those needs rather just forcing your ideas on him.

Beyond rapport building, the more you know about people, the more effectively you can reach them. What are their short-term and long-term goals: for themselves, for their subordinates, for the company? What are their plans for reaching those goals? What do they see as the biggest obstacles? What are their current problems? What would the ideal solution to any of these problems look like? What's the downside if these problems aren't solved?

How can you help?

Discover their hot buttons: involve them emotionally as well as intellectually. More of our supposedly rational decisions are made at the gut level than any of us like to admit.

"I also like to ask people about their values," a union negotiator once told me. "Not because that tells me much about what they value. You can only get that by watching them in action. But what they say about their values often tells you what kind of language you need to couch your proposal in to make it acceptable."

He must have known the VP from the "people-oriented" corporation who never fired anyone but provided a great many employees with "the opportunity to succeed elsewhere." Ironically this same VP was the first person I know of to be "promoted" right out of a company—when his superiors arranged to give him the opportunity to succeed as a minor functionary in an industry group.

Under the right circumstances, you may even want to take notes while you're asking your questions. It'll help you to remember, and it shows how important you consider the other person's input to be. It also works well when at least part of the reason for your questions is to allow an irate boss, peer, subordinate, or customer to vent.

If you think a question might appear intrusive, you can ask permission before you ask it. You can even explain why you're asking and the benefit to them of giving you the answer. That allows the other person to feel they're maintaining control.

"Do you mind if I ask you a personal question, Fred? I only want to know because it will help me decide if this transfer really is in everyone's best interests."

"Not a problem."

"Good. And feel free to tell me it's none of my business—but just how much money did you make last year?"

TACTIC: When in doubt, ask a question. That's a good general rule in a selling situation—or any other time for that matter.

Someone once said, "You can tell whether a man is clever by his answers. You can tell whether a man is wise by his questions."

Let your probing be conversational, not an interrogation. Listen to the answers and acknowledge them. Don't interrupt while listening. Practice letting the other person talk. Often we're much more interested in getting to our own comments. And we usually don't do a particularly good job of disguising that fact.

> **TACTIC:** If you want more information from someone, just gaze at her silently after she finishes her answer. She'll throw in more details to fill up the silence. It's an old trick trial lawyers use, and it works.

CAN'T YOU TELL SEXUAL DESIRE FROM ITCHY FEET?

The problem with gathering information, of course, is that the information you gather isn't always true. "Buyers are liars," is the charming adage of the old-style, combat-prone salesperson. And the more the other person sees his interests as differing from yours, the more he sees you as an opponent rather than a partner, the less likely he is to feel he owes you the truth.

> **TIP:** He doesn't necessarily owe you the truth.

Empathizing with someone, bringing out that aspect of yourself that's most like him, does not mean taking everything he says at face value. Maybe instead of pure, unadulterated objective truth, you're getting the company line, a negotiating position, or whatever answer he figures is most likely to appease you or motivate you or generate whatever response it is he's trying to generate in you.

Obviously you can't get what you want by helping people get what they want unless you can discover what they really want. And that may take additional probing. And listening. And observing. And understanding.

I always take those hard-and-fast explanations of body language with a little salt. I've sold to many people who were sitting back in their chairs with their arms crossed in front of them, supposedly in a defensive, closed-off position. Perhaps they were just cold or pensive or there were no arms on their chair. And in spite of what the experts may say, I've scientifically proven to my own satisfaction—or lack of satisfaction—that when a woman crosses her legs and lets her shoe dangle from her toes, it doesn't necessarily means that she wants me. The only itch she has may be in her feet.

Still, obviously, we do express ourselves in body language and facial expressions. Clenched fists, gritted teeth, and bulging eyeballs do tend to indicate anger. A loaded .357 Magnum pointed at your head probably is a sign of aggression. According to one body-language guru, "Boredom is communicated by placing the head in an open palm and dropping the chin in a nodding manner while allowing the eyelids to drop." If that person actually begins to snore, you may be losing his attention.

So while there is no foolproof body-language lie detector or anything close, there are certain signs that tend to indicate equivocation. Does the person hesitate before answering or hesitate while answering? Does his posture stiffen? Does his tone of voice rise at the end of sentences? Does he start fidgeting more or touching himself more frequently before or during responding?

I once had an employee who'd shrug his shoulders while answering whenever the answer was less than 100 percent forthright. Another would shake her head from side to side, as if to show her own doubt about what she was saying—a sure sign I needed to ask a few more questions.

The better you're able to bring out the prospect in yourself, the better your rapport, the better you are at convincing the person you're dealing with that you're trying to add water to his or her glass and not just fill up your own, the more likely you are to get the truth. You have a lot more time to develop a relationship than any salesperson ever gets. Use it. Make rapport-building another part of your job, just like it is for a salesperson. It could well be the most pleasurable part.

> **TIP:** If I can be 5 percent as interested in someone else as I am in myself, I'm going show that individual far more interest than 99.9 percent of the people they encounter. And I can build rapport.

TIP: There's no one on this planet who isn't at least 5 percent as interesting as I am. (There are damn few who'd find me 5 percent as interesting as they find themselves.)

MY FAVORITE TACTIC: Asking for help is one of the best ways to build rapport with someone you're having trouble with— or anyone else for that matter. It indicates respect, makes the other person feel needed, and implies that you consider her, her judgment, and/or her experience valuable. And not incidentally, it gets you help. Later, be sure to give credit where credit is due.

THE IDEAL CANDIDATE

I once asked a senior executive about the type of person he was seeking for a middle management opening. Midway through his response, he suddenly realized whom he was describing.

"I guess I'm looking for me," he said with a laugh. "Only younger."

If you're seeking a promotion, you're a good part of the way there if those who will be doing the promoting already perceive you as the type of person they're seeking. Which usually means a type of person like themselves. That's why there's always such a temptation to pretend to be someone you're not. But there's a 180-degree difference between imitating the prospect and bringing out the prospect in yourself.

TIP: Never act like the type of person you don't want to be.

TIP: Never act like the type of person you *do* want to be.

TIP: *Be* the type of person you want to be.

Be the person you want to be.

Just be damn certain that person *is* the person you want to be. If that person isn't you, isn't an extension of you, isn't really the person you'd like to become, then you need to find a way to succeed as the person you are and the person you want to be. That's called integrity. It's called filling the glass.

You can never be successful by becoming someone you don't want to be. That's the very definition of failure.

That should be obvious. You succeed by being and becoming the person you want to be. And finding a way to reach your goals as that person. It's far easier to sell yourself when you believe in yourself. Sell yourself out, and you may find nobody—yourself included—believes in you. And you'll never have the authority you need for true leadership. We've already got too many supposed leaders in business and in the world in general that no one believes in.

CHAPTER 12

Become an
Expert Witness

The CTO of the information technology company was more than a little irritated. "In our high-tech business," she said, "when people buy our products, they're really buying into our conception of the future. Some of us have an innovative vision for where our company can fit into that future. Unfortunately, right now the company simply reacts to the marketplace and the competition. The CEO's favorite saying is, 'It might be the early bird that gets the worm, but look what happens to the early worm. And it's the second mouse that gets the cheese.' Unfortunately, we're never even the second mouse, or the third. By the time we get there, the cheese is long gone. But every time any of us try to push through our point of view, the CEO turns the discussion into an argument. Which of course, we eventually have to let him win."

"We're losing out to birds, worms, mice, and cheese," another senior executive added. "Underneath it all, I think [the CEO] sees the logic behind what we're saying, but he's not comfortable acting on it. Which always leaves us on the verge of civil war."

ARGUMENTS YOU CAN'T WIN

These two executives were confronted with a basic sales problem. If a salesperson pushes, his prospect usually pushes back, and the salesperson loses. If the prospect pushes and the salesperson pushes back, the salesperson loses.

Every sales rep knows you can never win an argument with a prospect.

I've done a bit of expert witnessing. When you appear in court as an expert witness, you have a point of view and you express it. Then you get cross-examined. During the cross-examination, you quickly see what the opposing attorney is trying to get you to say, and the tendency as an expert is to contest every one of the points he's trying to make. After all, you're the expert, you've staked out your position, and he's attacking it. By extension, he's attacking you.

But the first thing the attorneys on your side will tell you is that if you do that, if you contest every one of his points, you lose all credibility as an impartial expert. Now it's hardly a secret that you're being paid big bucks by the side for which you're testifying, and that the reason you're getting that money is that—at least for the most part—you agree with their position. The jury understands that. And if they don't, the opposing attorney will be sure to point it out. You need to make your best possible case; you can be certain the other side will be making their best case. But the more you appear to be an instrument of objective truth, granting the other side their legitimate points, the more the points you make for your own side will be believed.

As a salesperson—and at times each of us is a salesperson—you always should present yourself as an expert witness. First, you make your best possible case. If you are an advocate, you don't have to pretend not to be. When I was selling, I'd go so far as to say, "Hey, I don't want you to forget I work on commission. The more you spend the more I make. Now I'm going explain why you need to be spending more and making me more money."

"Hey, I know it's in my self-interest to support the restructuring," you might imply or even say. "But that doesn't mean this isn't the best possible option for the corporation. And here's why."

> **TIP:** The more firmly that best possible case is rooted in reality, the more convincing it is likely to be, the easier it will be to remember, and the better it will stand up to cross-examination.

You make your case, then you grant the opposition—the doubting Thomas within the mind of each potential buyer—his legitimate points. His *legitimate* points. Once again, even as an advocate, the more you appear to be acting as an instrument of objective truth, the more effective your points—the points you need to make to make your case—will be.

> **TIP:** In a nonselling situation—when you're not acting as an advocate—and as a matter of common courtesy, effective people skills, and simply helping the other person get what he or she wants, this expert witnessing technique works equally well.

THE ABRAHAM LINCOLN SYNDROME

Marshall Feinstein is a department head for a large direct mail operation. His problem wasn't with his boss but with another department head. "You talk about telling—selling—the whole story, making sure we get in all our selling points. I'd like to see anyone try to do that with our director of marketing. This guy is obviously too busy and too important to listen to anybody else—and he has to make sure everybody knows that. I don't push him; he starts pushing the minute I open my mouth. I never get the chance to make my points. All I can do is push back or get run over."

"Does pushing back work?" I asked.

"Not really."

"It's the Abraham Lincoln syndrome," I said.

"The what?"

The Abraham Lincoln syndrome gets its name from an incident that occurred off the coast of Newfoundland in October of 1995. Here's an actual transcript of a communication between the aircraft carrier USS Abraham Lincoln and Canadian authorities:

> *Americans:* Please divert your course 15 degrees to the north to avoid a collision.
>
> *Canadians:* Recommend you divert *your* course 15 degrees to the south to avoid collision.
>
> *Americans:* This is the captain of a U.S. Navy ship. I say again, divert *your* course.
>
> *Canadians:* No, I say again, you divert *your* course.
>
> *Americans:* This is the aircraft carrier USS Lincoln, the second largest aircraft carrier in the United States Atlantic Fleet. We are accompanied by three destroyers, three cruisers, and numerous support vessels. I demand that you change your course 15 degrees

north, or countermeasures will be undertaken to ensure the safety of this ship.

Canadians: This is a lighthouse . . . your call.

When the person you're dealing with refuses to let you go where you want to go, divert your course. Start talking about whatever he insists on talking about. Be the expert witness and grant him his legitimate points. Then come back around and make your point a different way. In the course of the conversation you can usually work in the information you need to deliver, making all the points you need to make. You do need to tell—sell—the whole story. You need to make sure none of your most important selling points are left out. But smashing into lighthouses is not a successful navigational strategy—no matter how pushy those lighthouses might be.

"My supervisor is the ultimate bully," an accountant complained. "Management to him is intimidation. It's either fight back or let him treat you like something he needs to scrape off his shoe. Any psychologist who wants to understand why workers go postal should spend a few days working for this guy."

Expert witnessing is a particularly effective strategy for dealing with bullying bosses. Don't argue, expert-witness. Grant his legitimate points, then make yours. You'll not only maintain your self-respect, ultimately you'll probably earn his respect as well.

BUILDING EXPERTISE

The greater your credibility, the more effective you'll be as an expert witness. If someone doesn't respect you, he isn't going to respect your testimony. Which means you had better respect yourself as well. That doesn't mean arrogance, it means self-assurance. If you've got pertinent experience, expertise, or both, and the people with whom you're dealing aren't familiar with it, you might recap it in a nonbragging, nonthreatening way. Even if they are familiar with your expertise, a diplomatic reminder never hurts.

> **TACTIC:** Always strive to build and increase your credibility. The more credibility you have, the more impact every one of your ideas and proposals will have—automatically. Look for ways to build up your expertise both in general and on important specific topics.

> **TIP:** Read every industry publication you can get your hands on. You'll be amazed at how much better informed you'll be than your peers. You might even cut out and forward clippings to selected individuals with a tactful, "Just in case you missed this" note.

In one large corporation, the credit manager at one branch is so strong in his field that no one in the entire company will challenge anything he has to say about credit procedures. He's also generous with that expertise so he's become an indispensable resource. More than a resource, he's become a standard. If Larry says it's so, it is so—throughout the company.

Larry's a nice guy. But he's a nice guy who usually gets what he wants when credit issues are involved, simply because no one can contest him.

> **TACTIC:** If you're recognized as an authority, sometimes you can even control the criteria on which a decision is going to be based.

Anne O'Halloran advocated a system for new product development that would get the products to market faster than the system the vice president of operations wanted, though it also cost significantly more. Unfortunately for operations, Ann's expertise in development and implementation helped convince the powers-that-be that in this area speed was far more important than cost.

You already have experience and you already have expertise: about yourself, your vision, and probably about whatever it is you might be proposing. There are any number of ways of increasing the weight of your expert testimony. Like Larry, you can become an in-house resource. You can gain influence within a professional organization. You can write articles. You can talk with newspaper, magazine, newsletter, and journal editors and set yourself up as a source for stories related to your area of expertise. This works particularly well after you've had an article or two published to heighten your credibility. You can address local, regional, or even national groups on issues important to your business.

You may need to be careful about this type of self-promotion. If you're working for yourself, it can be an effective, low-cost way to get your name out. In the corporate world, some companies will love it. They'll write you up in their house organ and make you a local star. Others will be wary of a voice coming from inside the company they can't control. They'll start talking about loose cannons, and want to tie you down.

YELLOW PAGES STAR—THAT'S WHAT I ARE

When I was a manager in the Yellow Pages business, one of my boss's bosses always used to say of me, "He's the guy who wrote the book on the subject" because I had in fact written a book on the Yellow Pages. The additional prestige that gave me in that industry continues to this day. And I do mean this day. Just this morning, on the day I'm writing this, I happened to encounter a high-level Yellow Pages executive. His name wasn't familiar to me, but he remembered that we'd met briefly ten years before, and that he'd had his picture taken with me. He said he wished he'd gotten me to autograph his copy of my book. Understand, this is not *Gone with the Wind.* This is *Getting the Most from Your Yellow Pages Advertising,* a book that even my current literary agent probably doesn't know I wrote. Very little movie potential here and not a whole lot of star quality.

My boss's boss had probably never read the book. In fact I was told that he was intimidated by the fact that I'd written it. But it gave me much more authority than I ever would have had otherwise, and made any testimony I offered far more effective.

SUCH A MODEST BRAGGART

You need people to be aware of your expertise but that doesn't mean flaunting it. Your peers and superiors will resent that and look for ways to shoot you down. The best-case scenario is to become such an authority that others spread the word on you. Then you yourself can be as modest as possible. Failing that, find ways to make sure it's introduced that don't appear to be bragging. Humor can help.

When I was still in the Yellow Pages industry and I needed to throw my expert status around with someone who didn't know me, I'd say something like, "For what it's worth, this is who I am." Then I'd pull out a copy of my book and offer a very brief synopsis of my background. I'd give them a quick glance at the cover then flip to the back and the picture, proving that it was me.

"What's bizarre is that the publisher actually airbrushed more hair onto my picture," I'd say, handing them the book. "I guess they figured I was too bald to sell books."

Not high humor. But the person would always smile or laugh. The onus was off; I wasn't an obnoxious braggart, claiming to know more than they did. I was self-deprecating, but I got my point across. And as they looked over the book, they could see that I hadn't even bothered to point out the quote from *Time* on the front cover calling me, "easily the most respected authority on the subject" or the fact that I'd been the number-one salesperson in the world for one of the world's largest directory publishers.

I *was* a braggart. I made sure my credentials were as widely known inside and outside the industry as possible. Obviously I'm still mentioning them, even though by now I would hope they've been far surpassed by the credentials I've gained as a public speaker and a motivator and sales and management consultant. (See, I worked those in as well, and if you want to know just how awesome those credentials are, I'll be happy to arrange for somebody to let you know.) But I was also widely regarded as being exceptionally modest.

"With his track record and his credentials, it's amazing how modest he is," they used to say, right before reiterating for the umpteenth time, and often exaggerating, one or more of my accomplishments. Never realizing that it was that track record and those credentials that allowed me to be that modest. Never considering that if I really were modest, the entire industry wouldn't be so familiar with my achievements.

In my last assessment, my boss listed "self-promotion" as the one area in which I needed development. She said this while sitting beside a signed copy of my book, displayed where no visitor to her office could possibly miss it.

In some ways I'm as much a self-promoter as P.T. Barnum or Hulk Hogan, just not as blatant (or, one could argue, as successful). Showman Mike Todd said, "The meek shall inherit the earth . . . but not in our lifetime." Mike Todd's lifetime has concluded, but if the meek have taken over since he left, I must have missed it.

There's nothing wrong with a bit of hype to get you noticed and generate excitement—as long as you can deliver on what you promise. And as long as you never start believing it yourself. If you ever think your reputation or whatever acclaim you manage to generate makes you superior to those you work with, you might remember that you're never likely to make as large and as lasting an impression upon the rest of the human race as the great American guru, Ralph Waldo Emerson. And Emerson called fame "proof that people are gullible."

Neither you nor I are ever likely to receive a fraction of the public acclaim received by Hitler, Stalin, Nero, Caligula, Robespierre, or for that matter, the redoubtable Attila the Hun.

Still, as I asked earlier, if you aren't selling yourself, who is? If you aren't sold on yourself, who is?

In touting the virtues of arrogance, many gurus will tell you that you'd better be able to look the world squarely in the eye and proclaim that you're as good as it gets and that anyone on the planet should consider themselves lucky to have the chance to do business with you. If you can't do that, in the words of one, "They're going to chew you up like a cow working a cud."

I prefer to keep my self-promotion more subtle. Still, I never forget what could be called the first rule of expert witnessing or selling or even business: "If you choose to put a small value on yourself, you can be sure the world won't raise the price."

MAKE SENSE

That idea of subtlety brings up another point to remember when you're selling your ideas, your proposals, or yourself. If someone tells you that you've done a great selling job, you haven't. What he's saying is that he feels that he's being sold something he would never have bought into on his own. He may go along with you, but he won't be happy about it. He'll be more likely to change his mind after you leave the room, and he'll be far more reluctant to go along with you the next time.

What I'd much rather hear is simply, *You make a lot of sense.* People who say that don't feel sold; they feel their needs are being met. Of course, they may never have realized they had those needs until you spoke up. And they'll commit to the person that makes sense far more enthusiastically than they'll ever commit to anyone they consider a great salesperson.

TIP: Obviously, the more you appear to make sense, the more you enhance the weight of your expert testimony. But the more you can enhance the weight of your expert testimony, the more sense you'll appear to make.

BRANDING

TACTIC: Since you are your own product, consider a bit of branding. Branding is another type of selling shorthand, a way products position themselves, differentiating themselves from the competition. Developing expertise is just one way of branding.

What is it that gives you an edge over peers? Is there a way you can use that to create a name for yourself? Are you the most knowledgeable, the hardest working, the smartest, the most articulate, the best dressed, the most upbeat, the best motivator, the most reliable, or simply the most well rounded?

Position yourself, but cover all the other necessary bases too. Yes, you're a great motivator—that's what everyone thinks of when they think of you—but you can also do the nuts and bolts work it takes to get the job done.

What do you want people to think of when they think of you?

Sometimes it can be little more than a hook to make you more memorable, a way of distinguishing yourself from the faceless hordes surrounding you. In *Winning Office Politics,* Andrew DuBrin talks about a government bureaucrat, an ambitious economist named Terry who couldn't seem to stand out as a member of that ultimate faceless horde. Then he stumbled across a book on remembering names and faces.

"Remembering the names of many people I came in contact with in my job became an intriguing game," Terry said. "Gradually a number of people commented on [it] . . . My skill helped me phase into assignments that interfaced with people outside my department. My outside contacts led to a position with a much higher level GS rating than carried by the position of an entry-level economist. My career with the government had been launched because I finally found a way to stand out from the crowd."

Depending on how you position yourself, branding may directly increase the authority of your expert testimony or it may simply make you more memorable—which, when you do produce, will increase your authority.

> **TIP:** If you fail to produce, being more memorable simply means people won't forget your poor performance.

BORROWING EXPERTISE

Sometimes you can borrow additional weight for your expert testimony. The training department of a major utility recently spent six months developing a new on-the-job training course for customer service reps throughout the company. A lone customer service manager named Javier happened to see an advance copy.

"It was a six-month program, packed full of bells and whistles and gee-whiz graphics," he says. "It included Web-based instruction, a computer CD, 26 modules, several workbooks, and upon completion the employee got a framed diploma and an embossed leather briefcase. The letter included with the advance copy made it clear the VP of training had been involved in every aspect of development and considered it to be his major corporate achievement. All in all, it was the worst thing I'd ever seen in my life."

Even the most cursory glance made it clear that the training department's idealized version of what a customer service rep did had little to do with the actual job. But that wasn't the worst part. The reason the old program had been so ineffectual was that neither the customer service trainees nor their managers ever had nearly enough time to complete the required written reports. The new program freed up the managers by shifting all the reports to the reps.

"They wouldn't have had time to do their job, which was the only place they ever got any training of any practical value," Javier explains.

From Javier's point of view, the best-case scenario would be that the new program would be as widely ignored as the old one had been. Worst-case scenario, it would waste hours and hours of everyone's time; and it seemed that the program called for enough training department monitoring to make sure that this is exactly what would happen.

"Something had to be done," Javier says. "But I was only a customer service manager—barely clinging to the bottom rung of management." As hierarchical as the company was, he couldn't even directly approach the vice president of training, much less offer a critique of the man's pet project. Nobody was asking for Javier's input and no one would pay any attention if he offered it spontaneously through channels.

Javier was the expert. The problem—for Javier and for the corporation—was that no one was likely to listen to his expertise.

Fortunately for the customer service department, the company was a devotee of management fads. They moved from one fad to the next, usually catching it on the far downside, when the rest of the business world was moving on to something else. At this particular time they were instituting quality improvement teams. A memo had just been circulated, pushing to have as many teams as possible set up. No one would be eligible for a raise without participating in at least one.

Javier suggested a quality improvement team, headed by himself, designed to offer feedback from customer service managers on the new training program. It was approved by whatever minor functionary had gotten stuck with the duty of approving the teams—in all likelihood with no serious review. Javier selected the most experienced and most respected managers from across the country. The team held two conference calls. Then he tactfully reported to the vice president of training—not Javier's own concerns, but the concerns of the leading customer service managers throughout the company. *Tactfully.*

The training program was scrapped. And Javier's team was consulted every step of the way as the new program was developed.

TACTIC: You can put added weight behind your expert testimony by forming alliances, and gain the strength of numbers or of influential allies. Use your power diplomatically, especially when approaching higher-ups who might not appreciate anything that smacks of blackmail.

HOT AIR

TACTIC: Enhance your authority by always keeping any claims you make credible. Watch the hot air. Tie that hot-air balloon down to earth, and tie it down securely with hard, concrete facts. Use numbers if you've got them, the most specific ones available.

Specifics say that you did your homework and you know what you're talking about. Rough approximations might have come off the top of your head.

TIP: Using approximations in a negotiation is the same as announcing that there's room to dicker.

TECHNICAL EXPERTISE

If the subject is technical, being an authoritative expert witness doesn't mean you have to be a technical expert. And even if you are, you should avoid splashing around in your technical expertise, confusing the issue and those you're trying to convince.

Let's say you're proposing sweeping changes in the information available on the corporate intranet. You don't need to be an expert in the technology. You need to be an expert in what the technology will do for the company, and specifically for those you're trying to convince.

One of my clients manufactures and sells highly technical medical equipment. Their salespeople were inundating the physicians who were their prospects with scientific detail the doctors didn't understand, information they neither wanted nor needed. What they wanted to know, what they needed to know, was exactly the same as what any everyone else wants and needs to know when someone is trying to gain their commitment: *What's in it for me? What's in it for us?* What are the benefits to myself and my patients? You don't need to be able to build a space shuttle to get someone excited about flying in one.

AND WHEN YOU DON'T KNOW

TACTIC: When you have nothing to say, say nothing.
Particularly when you're new in an organization or when you're
uncomfortable in a job or in a situation, there's a tendency to
want to speak up—to speak up for the sake of speaking up—
especially in meetings. We feel if we keep our mouths shut,
people will think we know little or nothing about the subject
under discussion. If we actually do know little or nothing about
it, the desire becomes especially strong. Get me around a bunch
of guys at a construction site, and I can't shut my mouth.

In sales, we call this panic blathering.

The less you know, the more you want to interject something—anything—and usually what you interject serves to prove just how little
you actually do know. In an astonishingly short period of time, you can
damage your credibility in a way that can take months and even years
to repair.

Panic blathering.

I know it's difficult, but when the impulse to panic blather seizes
you, take a deep breath and think before you speak. Weigh your words
carefully and contribute only when you have something worthy of con-
tribution. A penetrating question—or even an admission of what you
don't know—is a greater sign of intelligence and even expertise than a
transparent pretense of knowledge.

TIP: Regardless of who you are or how new or experienced you
might be, when your expertise is questioned and you don't know
the answer, "I don't know" is usually the correct response.

My father was an attorney and a man who had an answer for everything. Ask him to elucidate the difference between Einstein's concept
of special relativity and just ordinary run-of-the-mill, day-to-day relativity and he'd give you a 20-minute oration without having any more
of a clue about any of it than you or me. But he was an excellent attorney, trained at Harvard Law, loved by his clients, and if you asked him
a question concerning the law, the response could well be, "I don't
know."

"I don't know," is powerful expert testimony. It makes everything you do know that much more believable. If you know where to find the answer and you can promise to do so, even better. "Let me find out and I'll get back to you on this by Friday, if that's soon enough." Then do it.

When Gary Ames was president of U.S. West Communications, whenever he got a tough question while addressing a group, he'd say something like, "Excellent question. While I generalize for the next 30 seconds, Jake Hanes, who's sitting out there in the back of the room, will be coming up with the correct answer. When I stop talking, Jake will give you all the specifics, because I don't have the slightest idea."

When Gary Ames told you what he did know, you believed him.

LEADERSHIP SECRETS OF ATTILA THE HUN

TACTIC: As an expert witness you need to have confidence in what you're proposing—in what you do know. And you need to exude that confidence. It's far easier to make someone else a believer when you're a believer yourself.

If you go to a doctor for a health problem, you want her to listen, evaluate, and investigate. When she makes her recommendation, you want to hear as much confidence as possible.

"Andrew, you've got the plague. Here's a prescription that will fix you right up," is a lot more reassuring than, "Andrew, I think you either have gout or it could be scurvy or possibly lupus. Then again, it might just be the flu or a bad cold. I'll write you a prescription. Maybe the drugs will make it go away, maybe they won't, and you might want to call me if you think they make it worse."

When you finish presenting your expert testimony, if you've done it well enough you should fully expect to carry the day. And that should be obvious to everyone present. You show it in your speech, your body language, and everything about you.

If you really do expect your testimony to prevail, those you're testifying to can't help but feel there's a reason for that confidence, that you honestly believe your position makes perfect and obvious sense. It becomes more difficult for them to give you an absolute, final No. Even if they don't say Yes, they may well be open to more persuasion or to a process of negotiation.

If you don't show confidence, you're announcing that you don't feel your expert testimony is even close to airtight. You're announcing that you expect to be turned down. If you don't appear to believe in what you're saying, why should anyone else believe you?

A subordinate I'd inherited once asked me, "Do you think it would be okay if I got some sort of raise, eventually at least?" Hardly a question asked by someone convinced of the overwhelming force of the argument he's just put forth. And this poor soul was supposed to be a salesperson. Maybe he was going for a pity raise.

A few months later, my best salesperson approached me for a pay increase. She concluded by saying, "So that's my case for the 20 percent raise. I know it's not time for my yearly review and I know 20 percent is a lot more than normal, but obviously these aren't normal circumstances. I just want to make sure I can count on your backing."

She didn't get the raise simply because she expected to get it. But she did get the raise. I got her more than she expected, bringing her into line with the top reps in the company. Which is what she deserved.

General Omar Bradley was commander of all U.S. forces for the invasion of Normandy. In his book, *A General's Life,* he tells of warning his commanders during preparations that they were never to show the slightest doubt about the eventual outcome of the mission.

"Even a trace of skepticism in the high command could be exaggerated to ruinous proportions at division, regiment, and battalion," he cautioned. "Yet to muster that confidence in success, the plan must genuinely support it."

If you've added enough water to the glass, your plan, your proposal, your vision should support that kind of confidence. If you have obvious faith in what you're saying, people are more likely to have faith in you. If you don't believe it yourself, you're going to have trouble getting anyone to follow you into the lunchroom, much less the beaches of Normandy. Unless you're a far better actor than most of us.

Confidence sells. And the closer confidence gets to absolute conviction, the more powerful it becomes. That's why crazy people can sometimes be so convincing. Hitler never had a moment's doubt or hesitation. He believed so absolutely an entire country was swept along in his insanity.

In the late 1980s, I was asked to consult on a start-up operation by a potential client who soon turned out to be a megalomaniac. The man was on drugs and under psychiatric care and absolutely convinced that he was going to revolutionize consumer purchasing. It was astonishing how many intelligent people he pulled into his fantasy, including a former high-ranking military officer and the chairman of the board of a leading Fortune 100 company. Investors were throwing money at him, and a telecommunications giant gave him several million dollars worth of equipment on credit. None of them were bothered by the fact that the man's conception of the business he was putting together changed hourly. And that, because of that, no one, least of all the poor man himself, had any idea of what the final product he was putting together might be.

Such is the power of confidence. The above model of course later became standard operating procedure for Internet start-ups.

Confidence is also why people too obtuse to understand what's wrong with their position sometimes succeed in convincing others. As Bertram Russell said, "The trouble with the world is that the stupid are cocksure and the intelligent are full of doubt."

That's not the kind of confidence you want to project. That type of confidence is fragile and brittle. And it's too often revealed as false— ideally sooner rather than later—when it's buffeted by reality. The confidence you need to project comes from having made your proposal the best it can possibly be, from understanding the downside and having made peace with it, from adding as much water to the glasses of the stakeholders as you can.

And it comes from laying your cards on the table, granting the people you're dealing with their legitimate points when they have doubts, so they can make a completely informed decision. And knowing that if they do, in most cases they will and they should go along with your testimony.

That's real confidence. The operative word being *real.*

ALL THE FACTS

Tell the truth, be the expert witness. Grant people their legitimate points. If a new program you're explaining to your employees has drawbacks, point them out. They'll discover them anyway. Explain why those drawbacks are there, and why the program is in the company's best interest and in their best interest, despite those drawbacks.

> **TIP:** If you can't make a case with the truth, maybe you should reexamine what you're proposing.

> **TIP:** If what you're proposing doesn't work for one or more of the people you're trying to convince, say so. If there are no extenuating circumstances and you can't sell it honestly, don't sell it. Keep your credibility and preserve the relationship for another day rather than jumping on any short-term gain.

A friend of mine who works for a corporate conglomerate keeps an engraved quote from William S. Burroughs on his desk instead of a name plate. It reads, "Paranoia is just having all the facts." If your employees have to slice through a glossy patina of lies to get at the facts—the truth behind what you're telling them—paranoia is what you're going to generate in your company. And it's what you deserve.

DEFENSIVENESS

Obviously successful expert witnesses don't get defensive in the face of skepticism, objections, criticism, or opposition. Why should they? Their stance is that they are doing their best to be an instrument of objective truth, granting the other side their legitimate points.

Defensiveness comes from insecurity, what's sometimes called, "imposter's syndrome." Realize that almost everyone feels like they're faking it, especially when they get a promotion or they're thrust into an unfamiliar situation. Thus the expression, "Fake it till you make it." Develop your expertise: your general expertise—like the credit expert I mentioned earlier—or just the specific expertise you need to advance a particular proposal.

> **TIP:** Nothing gives a greater feeling of security than the knowledge that you know more about what you're proposing than anyone else in the room.

One of the best examples of the confidence and sense of security engendered by expertise comes from football player Deion Sanders. On the field Sanders sometimes offers advice and coaching to the very people he's competing against.

After one game, Ram receiver Isaac Bruce said, "Instead of giving me a hard time, [Sanders is] kind of coaching me. He's saying, 'Look, you need to stay low when coming out of your cuts, so I won't be able to tell where you're going.'"

Of course, the coaching didn't prevent Sanders from holding Bruce without a reception that day. Reporting all this in *Sports Illustrated,* John Bradley wrote, "To offer advice to your own teammates is one thing; to give it to the player you are trying to stop reveals a self-confidence that is downright spooky."

I think I'd rather be taunted by the competition.

SOMETIMES, VIRGINIA, THERE ISN'T A SANTA CLAUS

TACTIC: With enough confidence, you can even try the *Miracle on 34th Street* maneuver.

Jack was the head of a small high-tech scientific instrument company. One of his best clients, Amalgamated Bio Tech, wanted to place a very substantial order: between 10 and 14 of the company's latest machines. The machines really weren't designed for the specific application the customer had in mind. They would have done the job, but marginally. Still, the head of Amalgamated had great faith in Jack's company. She pressured Jack to go ahead with the deal. And she called two of Jack's partners, and they pressured Jack as well. After all, their machines were what the customer wanted.

Jack flew out to Amalgamated and actually demonstrated why the competition's less expensive machine would meet this particular need better than his machines could. "We're not in business to provide you with equipment you won't be 100 percent happy with," he insisted. The competition got a very nice sale without having to lift a finger.

Of course that was the last time Amalgamated ever bought anything from Jack's competition. They buy more from Jack's company than they ever did before. But what's really boosted sales is that in the last few years the woman that runs Amalgamated has become extremely influential in industry groups. Her recommendations have turned what Jack's partners once called "the order Jack was too good to sell," into what Jack calls "the most profitable deal I never made."

That's the *Miracle on 34th Street* tactic. You become Santa Claus, sending the customer to Gimbels' even though you're with Macy's— because that's best for the customer. I know it worked for Kris Kringle in the movie and it's worked for Jack's company and countless others, but I can't guarantee the results you might get. I know a middle manager who talked his superiors out of offering him a lucrative promotion because he knew he wasn't properly qualified for the job. I wish I could say he's first on the short list for the next promotion he is qualified for, but I can't. Refusing the position hurt his career, though probably not as much as taking the job he knew he wasn't qualified for would have.

Still, obviously, few things build credibility like doing what's best for someone else rather than grabbing something that appears to be in your own short-term interest. The only thing that could ever stop me from doing business with the mechanic who told me all I needed was a $7 part when I took the car to him for a new transmission was his retirement.

A great salesperson can earn so much trust from a customer that the customer would never want to take the risk of buying from anyone else.

What would it do for your career if you were trusted that much by the people you work with?

CHAPTER 13

Fail toward Success

I consider myself to be a reasonably intelligent person. I've had some great successes. When I think about the stupid mistakes I make on a daily basis, I'm just thankful that I'm not a surgeon. And the thought of being operated on by a fallible human being like myself is great incentive either to stay healthy or to investigate the mysteries of Christian Science or perhaps even psychic healing.

The leading tenet of medicine is, "First, do no harm." That's not a mission statement that inspires customer confidence. Are they going to cut me open and then do their damnedest just to break even—to just get me closed up again without making everything worse?

Failure happens—regularly, and to the best and the brightest of us. "The brain is a wonderful organ," Robert Frost said. "It starts working the moment you get up in the morning and does not stop until you get to the office." I work at home, so mine often stops earlier.

We are all experts on failure. At least we're all more expert than we'd like to be. Failure is a particularly significant issue for those of us who have to motivate salespeople. They face rejection and failure with every call they make. A salesperson who can't deal properly with failure is a salesperson who can't do her job. If I can't help her, I can't do mine.

A PROCESS, NOT AN EVENT

For many people, the key to dealing with failure is realizing that while failure is an event, success is not. Success, like sales, is a process.

You're not a surgeon; go ahead, do harm.

TIP: Fail.

TIP: Embrace failure.

TIP: Failure is good for you.

"Being in a successful company is easy," Bill Gates says. "But when you're failing you're forced to be creative, and to dig deep and think. In failing companies you always have to question assumptions. I want some people around who have been through that process."

"Adversity reveals genius," the Roman poet Horace wrote, "and prosperity conceals it." Does that mean you might even be better off failing than succeeding? That failure may even be a more successful long-term strategy than success?

Dead Roman gurus and living technology wizards to the contrary, let's not get too carried away here. Still, studies have shown that entrepreneurs who succeed the first time out are no more likely than anyone else to succeed if they try to repeat their success with a second start-up. That's in spite of their business contacts and the advantages they have in financing. On the other hand, entrepreneurs who failed before finding success were far more likely to succeed in their next venture.

In other words, if Mr. Gates left Microsoft, he'd have no greater chance of building another successful company than you or I would. Gail Borden, discoverer of the freeze-dried patient, inventor of the incredible sinking wagon, the dehydrated meat biscuit, and condensed milk, would be more likely to succeed than any of us.

Nothing succeeds like failure.

Salespeople all hate to hear the word No. Every instinct and every bit of their training is geared toward making sure they hear it as infrequently as possible. That's what sales is all about.

But here's a great truth: The most successful salesperson is the one who hears the most *No*es.

The more *No*es—the more rejections, the more failures—that the salesperson gets in any individual call and the more of those calls he makes, the more successful he will be. The leading sales rep in a company is always the person who has heard the most *No*es. To do that, he not only has to be hardworking and persistent, he has to be extremely good at what he does. Because the better he is—the more interest he creates, the more rapport he builds—the longer the prospect will listen and the more patience the prospect will have for his efforts. Thus the more *No*es he gets to hear. He's got to be hardworking. He's got to be persistent. And he's got to be good. In the end, of course, this is the rep who will also hear the most *Yes*es.

Even outside of sales, the most successful people are frequently those who've heard the most *No*es.

TIP: Start collecting your *No*es as soon as possible.

HOT DOORKNOBS

There's a condition that afflicts salespeople known as "hot doorknobs." A rep with hot doorknobs is one who's afraid to turn the knob and open the door. She's afraid to make the call and be rejected, afraid of failure.

She's afraid to start collecting *No*es.

Hot doorknobs has probably kept more people from becoming salespeople than any other aspect of the job. It's a dreaded affliction that can plague even the most experienced reps. Unfortunately, it's hardly exclusive to sales. It's just as prevalent, if less obvious, in every other field. How many of us would rather do anything, find any excuse, rather than attempt to do something that might not succeed?

If you never try, you never fail, right?

One of the most successful young executives I've ever known walked away from an unlimited future because he was terrified of not being able to live up to the astonishing record he'd established. He was terrified of being shown to be not quite as good as everyone had come to believe he was. It was like a rookie entering the major leagues, hitting .432 with 74 home runs, winning the MVP, and then retiring. Because he was afraid that the rest of his career would tarnish his achievement.

It probably would have. In baseball terms, that young executive probably never would have hit over .360 or .370 again. When they put up his plaque in the Business Hall of Fame in Mishawaka, Indiana, it probably would have noted that he barely averaged 65 home runs a year. Or maybe he wouldn't have had a Hall of Fame career. Maybe his career never would have been much more than outstanding, or remarkable, or good, or OK. Or even fair or poor.

At least he would have had a career.

Unfortunately, he was more concerned with maintaining his image than succeeding. He gave up what he wanted to do—which means he failed—because he was afraid of failure.

Too many of us do the same, if not quite so blatantly. And often without even having the achievement. Too frequently we're afraid of tarnishing what amounts to a lack of achievement.

> **TIP:** Discover whatever you're most afraid of failing at and, as soon as possible, go out and fail at it.

Unless it's skydiving or tightrope walking or surgery or some such (in which case please ignore the last tip), you will find that:

1. It didn't kill you,
   and
2. it didn't kill you.
   And,
3. after you do it, after you've already failed, most of the time there's no longer much to be afraid of.

> **TIP:** If it's not something you can actually rush right out and fail at, envision failure. Is it any worse than not trying or trying in a half-hearted way, hoping you can save face if it doesn't work, and virtually guaranteeing you'll fail?

Fail.

Every one of those people whose opinions you're concerned about has failed at one thing or another. Some of them are afraid to try to fill their own glass because they're afraid that if they failed, you'd have a lower opinion of them.

FEAR OF TUMMY TUCKS

Fear of failure is a lot like fear of tummy tucks. Or butt lifts, breast implants, or hair transplants.

I, for example, had a hair transplant. This is, admittedly, a vain and probably dumb thing to have had done. I'm hardly good looking enough to be the kind of guy you'd consider vain about his appearance. But when faced with the prospect of being bald, guess what? To the surprise of virtually everyone who knew me, myself included, it turned out I was as vain as the next guy. Maybe vainer; the next guy didn't bother to have chunks of his scalp sliced out and crammed into little holes elsewhere on his head.

But that's not the point. The point is that once you have a hair transplant—or, I suppose, a tummy tuck or butt lift—virtually everyone you mention it to will confide that they've considered some form of cosmetic surgery for themselves. A great many of them will tell you they wished they had the courage to go ahead and do it.

We're far more alike than we are different.

Don't have the hair transplant. I can't comment on the butt lift. But as for failure, go ahead and fail. Some people will envy your courage. Will others think less of you? Probably. Let them. Do you really value the opinion of anyone who'd prefer that you never tried rather than risk failure? Besides, that type of bozo will think a lot more of you once you eventually succeed.

And if you never succeed? I've always liked what Teddy Roosevelt said:

> It is not the critic who counts, not the man who points out how the strong man stumbles or where the doer of deeds could have done them better. The credit belongs to the man who is actually in the arena, whose face is marred by dust and sweat and blood, who strives valiantly, who errs and comes up short again and again because there is no effort without error and shortcomings, who knows the great devotion, who spends himself in a worthy cause, who at the best knows in the end the high achievement of triumph and who at worst, if he fails while daring greatly, knows his place shall never be with those timid and cold souls who know neither victory nor defeat.

> **TIP:** Never worry about any "cold and timid soul." Unless it's your own. As George Bernard Shaw said, "A life spent in making mistakes is not only more honorable but more useful than a life spent doing nothing."

Consider your past. What do you regret more, the times you've failed or the times you never tried? What would you prefer to look back on in the future?

THE SALES REP'S VIEW

When you see success as a process, you see "failure" in a different light. You see it the way a great salesperson might see it, as a small victory, a step on the path to ultimate success. If the customer didn't buy today, the salesperson may still have moved the sales process along, building rapport, transmitting valuable product information, gaining trust. Next time the prospect may well buy. Or the time after that or the time after that. The biggest and most rewarding sales usually take the longest. Good salespeople understand that.

Or maybe the call was a total washout. The prospect showed he'd never be a customer. That's also a step in the process, the rep has removed some of the hay from the haystack, making the needle easier to find.

> **TIP:** Try. And even when you fail, do your best to move the process of success along, even if the only progress is eliminating one possible path to your goal.

We've all heard that a journey of a thousand miles starts with a single step. Sometimes it's a step in the wrong direction. Discovering that it's the wrong direction is a success, not a failure.

Gail Borden's dehydrated meat biscuits were either a ludicrous failure or a step on the path to condensed milk. Here's a little maxim that may never catch on in the boardroom: *You can't develop condensed milk without dehydrating a few meat biscuits.* (I don't think I need to worry about copyright protection on that one.)

I always tell people that they should be like scientists, who can be as excited by failure as they are by success—because to them failure is success. David Kelley is CEO of IDEO Product Development and a Stanford professor. Paraphrasing K. Eric Drexler, Kelley insists, "Enlightened trial and error outperforms the planning of flawless intellects."

Since none of us have flawless intellects, this is good news for the human race. Seek out new experiences and learn from every one of them.

A great salesperson learns from every single call, good or bad. Shaky presentations are analyzed and perfected for next time. There's always a more effective way to answer an objection, a better way to overcome the prospect's uncertainty and close the sale. If a great salesperson has one of those frustrating, "If only I'd said . . ." experiences, where he works out the perfect response driving down the street 15 minutes after leaving the call, he doesn't carry the frustration forward. He simply screams, smashes his fist into the steering wheel a few times, and learns. Because the exact same situation is going to recur. Maybe not that day. Maybe not for several weeks. But he has the opportunity to be ready.

PRACTICE FOR SUCCESS

The rest of all know that we should learn from experience, that there's always something to learn in every experience. The gurus have been telling us that as long as there have been gurus. Most of us believe it. But we don't encounter the exact same situations over and over again in the same the way a salesperson does when making sales calls. If we come up with a perfect, tardy, "If only I said . . ." phrase, we'll probably never get the chance to use it. It's easier for us to focus on the frustrations of the specific situation—more difficult to see the lessons in it.

> **TIP:** Few situations in life are unique. Our own behavior almost never is. Just as in sales, apparent failure should help you make things go smoother next time. No matter what the outcome, good, bad, or indifferent, always take a moment to ask yourself how you could have improved your performance.

"I'm like a lawyer," one new CEO confided. "I don't manage, I practice management. And the more I practice, the better I get. Life is about education and about growth. Fifteen years ago I was a rotten manager.

I had no experience, no training, no decent role models. How could I be anything but rotten? Ten years ago I was an average manager. Five years ago I was good, and now I've reached very good. Five years from now I fully expect to be great.

"So you don't believe that everything you needed to know you learned in kindergarten?" I asked.

"I once had an division manager working for me who actually said that. All I could think was, I certainly hope you learned everything you needed to know in kindergarten, because it's obvious you haven't picked up squat since then."

Familiarity breeds success. At least it should. A master craftsman is someone who has already made every possible mistake.

In *The Survivor Personality,* Al Seibert, Ph.D. writes, "The people who are most resilient [when things go wrong] have a learning reaction, not a victim reaction, to bad events. It's distressing, they don't like it, but the question is, Do they have a learning/coping reaction or a victim/blaming reaction?"

TIP: Learn.

TIP: Cope.

TIP: Avoid saying things like "learning/coping" and "victim/blaming."

MAKE NEW AND BETTER MISTAKES

My mother is a devout Catholic. She used to tell me whenever something went badly wrong that I should "offer it up to God." The idea was that "offering up" frustration here on Earth would get you credit toward salvation. By that reasoning, with everything I had screwed up by the time I was eight, I figured I already had enough credit for Heaven. From that point on, any additional failure would be a waste unless I could find some way to benefit from it.

Failure is too good to waste. Benefit from it. Make new and better mistakes.

Few of us are good at anything the first time we try it. So why are we so hard on ourselves when we fail? Maybe you did blow it, and maybe you'll blow it the second time. Like a salesperson who doesn't close the sale, you can still make each attempt as successful as possible, moving the process of success along, even if it's nothing more than building rapport and gaining trust with those around you, positioning yourself for your next chance.

TIP: If nothing else, failure is the perfect opportunity to demonstrate to those around you how well you handle adversity.

TIP: Failure is also the perfect opportunity to demonstrate to yourself how well you handle adversity.

It can also be a great motivator. One of my most recent clients is an Internet entrepreneur who's been through some tough times. "The more I fail," he insists, "the more I want to succeed. And the harder—and hopefully smarter—I try. To make certain that I do."

I've been an in-line skater for the last four or five years. I like to learn new moves, but since I'm not 14 any more, my main concern is not to fall down. I'd rather not master a move and keep my limbs intact. Teenagers, children, and toddlers who have been skating much less time than I have, can do leaps and spins and pirouettes that I can't imagine even trying. Because they don't care about falling. They fall all the time.

You can't master the move if you aren't willing to fall. The corollary to that is, if you're willing to take any fall, you can master anything.

If the fall doesn't kill you.

A PERFECT CONFESSION

TIP: Beware of *negative nostalgia.*

Sometimes our failures do us harm. Worse, sometimes they harm others. This is especially true with those failures we consider ethical lapses. It's not my job to punish you. And it's not your job to punish you, no matter how much you may feel you deserve it. Punishing yourself will accomplish nothing. I don't care if you really are Attila the Hun. I don't care if you're Adolf Hitler. I don't care if you're Satan.

Did I state that strongly enough?

I don't care what you've done in the past. I only care about what you are now and what you will be in the future. Stop trying to change yesterday. Like my good Catholic mother making a perfect confession, absolve yourself of the past. Free yourself of it or risk being either paralyzed or corrupted by it. If you honestly feel that the damage you caused merits some form of restitution, make it. Then learn your lessons and move on. Beating yourself up over the past—negative nostalgia—is like any other form of nostalgia: it's not going to improve tomorrow, and it can divert your attention and keep you from taking advantage of what's going on around you today.

THE FREEDOM TO FAIL

> **TACTIC:** Grant yourself and your people the freedom to make mistakes. If you get paralyzed by fear of failure, tell yourself that anything worth doing is worth doing wrong. That's frequently how you learn to do it right. Applaud mistakes made when taking risks, as long as they are well-considered risks.

We claim to value risk taking. Yet most companies venerate risk takers when they succeed and punish them when they fail. We live in a society that tries to insulate itself completely from risk.

KENNEDY VERSUS NIXON

When you do fail, when you make a mistake, keep your head—unless you can think of a lot of situations that were actually improved by panic. And own up to your mistake—to yourself and to any others involved. Anyone who doesn't realize that's the best course of action hasn't been paying much attention to politics for the last 40 years. The

Bay of Pigs was a massive fiasco. Privately, Kennedy was convinced he'd been deceived by the CIA. But publicly, he immediately took full responsibility. He was president, so it certainly *was* his responsibility. He looked more presidential, not less for accepting that. Contrast his response with Nixon trying to pin the Watergate cover-up on one subordinate after another, Bush insisting he was out of the Iran/Contra loop no matter how many meetings he might have attended, and Clinton's tortured exercises in legalistic hair-splitting.

> **TIP:** When in doubt, tell the truth.

If you can't admit your mistakes to yourself, you're never going to learn from them, and you're going to keep repeating them. When you admit mistakes to others who might be affected, you're showing confidence. It's astonishing how well the phrase, "Boy, I screwed that up; let me take care of it," works—if you don't have to use it too often.

When Alfred P. Sloan ran General Motors, he used to say that a manager who is right half the time is doing very well indeed. Managers, coworkers, employees, salespeople, customer service reps, or anyone else for that matter who pretends to be right all the time is simply revealing her insecurity. She's seldom fooling anyone anyway.

Taking responsibility can be difficult. It's not just politicians who have an easier time saying "Mistakes were made" than "I made a mistake." As if the mistakes were some sort of unavoidable act of nature.

A corporation that had recently become a Wall Street darling had to announce that they'd miscalculated their earnings for the previous quarter. The stock price plummeted. The next day I was called in for a little damage control. The volatile chief financial officer was hardly the most popular person in the company, and I walked into his outer office just in time to catch his matronly secretary facing out the window with her sweater pulled up around her shoulders. At first, I thought she was flashing her fellow workers as they arrived in the employee parking lot below. Then she turned toward me in surprise. Before she could pull the sweater back down, I caught a quick glimpse of the tee shirt she was wearing underneath. It read: "Mistakes have been made. Others will be blamed."

A few minutes later, I discovered that she'd done an excellent job of anticipating her boss's strategy. As Fran Liebowitz said, "It's not whether you win or lose, it's how you lay the blame." His failure to accept the blame was the main reason he later lost his job.

Still, it's certainly not necessary to admit your mistakes to anyone who isn't affected by them. Many of the mistakes we make are not really anybody else's business. Even so, bringing them up can be useful. Years ago, when I was selling advertising, I used to make it a point to find a problem in the spec ad I'd had created for the customer, the ad I was trying to sell to him. That way, I got him involved in coming up with a solution. And the very lack of perfection made my enthusiasm for the rest of the ad more believable. The fact that I'd pointed out the flaw added to my credibility and my expertise, demonstrated my attention to detail, and showed that I was still working to improve the ad.

Hall of Fame football coach Bear Bryant used to remark that to hold a team together:

There's just three things I'd ever say:

- If anything goes bad, I did it.
- If anything goes semi-good, then we did it.
- If anything goes real good, then you did it.

That's all it takes to get people to win football games for you.

THE POWER OF NEGATIVE VISUALIZATION

TACTIC: Tap into the power of negative visualization. Before undertaking a course of action, visualize what might go wrong. Then figure out how you're going to deal with it if it does.

Some Pollyannas will insist that this is the worst thing you can possibly do. You need to visualize success, they'll tell you. They'll say that visualizing problems is a prescription for disaster.

Not being prepared is a prescription for disaster. That's why pilots spend hours on flight simulators, struggling with every possible difficulty that could arise.

Dear Pollyanna:

You'll be delighted to learn that the surgeon who's about to perform your heart bypass was trained using positive visualization exclusively. He's never even considered the possibility that anything might go wrong.

Sincerely,
Barry Maher

Visualizing success without taking potential problems into account is more magical thinking than serious preparation. By increasing your preparedness and helping you to feel ready for every foreseeable eventuality, negative visualization increases your confidence and your performance. After you've completed your preparation, you can and should visualize success—and you'll have a much greater likelihood of actually achieving it.

At Sun Microsystems, president and COO Ed Zander holds weekly, "whack-o-meter" sessions to try to figure out how competitors could try to whack Sun. "It helps us think strategically," Zander says. When a competitor does act, Zander and his team are often ready for it and react quickly.

THE BEST PREPARATION

Salespeople prep thoroughly before every call, anticipating the difficulties they might encounter. You want to do the same in preparing for each step in the process of your success. Still, no one can anticipate every eventuality; and some salespeople paralyze themselves with overpreparation, forgetting that the best preparation for making sales calls is . . . making sales calls.

As Napoleon, one of the greatest strategists of all time, noted, "The torment of precautions often exceeds the dangers to be avoided." Which doesn't mean that Napoleon ever marched into a battle unprepared.

METAPHORIC TIP: If you spend all your time tinkering with your engine, someday you might find you're too old to take the car for a drive.

Prepare as well as possible, then seize every opportunity. Gain experience. Practice, learn, prepare some more, and advance yourself in the process of success.

> **TACTIC:** Evaluate your progress by the day, the week, the month, the year. That way, improvements aren't just short term, and you can see the big picture.

> **TIP:** Revel in the process—in the adventure and the exploration. Revel in matching yourself and your talents against the challenges.

By *challenges,* I mean challenges. The Pollyannas have co-opted that word and turned it into a euphemism for cataclysm, impossibility, and screw job. As in, "We do have a challenge for you here, Marsha. We're cutting your staff and doubling your workload. And you're going to be required to produce twice the results in half the time. Oh, and this water—make it wine." I like to see if we can get the word back so it means *challenges.* As in "Life is a challenge. Revel in it."

Revel in the challenges.

As I said, this hour—any hour—can be the hour that transforms your life. You simply have to choose to make it so. That doesn't mean you won't stumble. You will. And, from it, you'll learn how to stumble less frequently in the future.

PERFECTION, AND WHY NOT?

The good news is you're never going to be perfect.

I doubt if you'd want to be. If you were perfect, if you never made mistakes, if you never failed, you'd have no challenges, no triumph— because there'd be nothing to triumph over. Remember the young executive I mentioned earlier who quit because he was afraid of tarnishing his success? Here's the opposite scenario. One of the best salespeople I ever knew actually stopped selling because he became too good at it.

"It was like I knew what would happen before it happened," he said. "I knew what I was going to say and how they were going to respond. I knew how I'd answer that response, and how they'd reply to my answer. I knew what I'd propose, and how they'd react. I knew that we'd negotiate and that I'd end up with a sale—and it would be about two-thirds or three-fourths of my original proposal. I was so bored I'd stopped listening to what I was saying. I'd let calls get out of control just to see how far I could let them go and still recover."

Once this rep actually told a woman he was pitching that one of his secondary products was garbage. A few minutes later, he sold her that very product as an add-on at the end of the sale.

Where's the joy in perfection? Fail toward success.

ALLOWING FOR GRAVITY

TACTIC: Allow for gravity.

If you aim at a target a long way off, you have to take gravity into consideration. You aim above the target.

Aim above your goal. Tell people the higher goal is the one you want to reach. Never even mention the lower one. This is a basic sales strategy, closely linked to the "change the scale" strategy we'll be discussing later. You go into Harry's Haberdashery thinking you'd like to buy a $300 suit. Harry sells you on the benefits of the $900 suit. It's a far better suit with double stitching and superior fabric, and it makes you look like Michael Douglas. Still, $900 is too much money for you and though you'd like it, you end up settling on a $600 suit that has a number of the same qualities that Harry sold you on, and makes you look like Anthony Hopkins. If he'd tried to sell you that $600 suit in the first place, you probably would have settled on a $400 suit that makes you look like your Uncle Ralph.

If your boss thinks you're shooting for CEO and knows you're readying yourself for that, how can she not promote you to assistant plant manager? If the powers that be know you're preparing yourself to be regional director, they might not promote you that far, at least not yet. But they might make you area manager. If you'd simply prepared yourself to be area manager, you could have been just one of several with the same qualifications. They may well have picked someone else.

If CEO is your goal, the sooner you start thinking of yourself as a future CEO, the sooner your superiors will too. That's the career path you want to be on, and it's never too soon to get on it. Ultimately, if you aim for CEO and fail, you may end up as a vice president. Aim for store manager and even when you succeed you'll be way below the vice president who failed to make CEO.

It's another way of failing toward success.

THE LINCOLN MODEL

When gurus talk about dealing with failure they frequently point to Lincoln. Lincoln lost his job in 1832, and that same year he was defeated for the state legislature. His business failed in 1833. But in 1834, he made it to the legislature. The woman he loved died in 1835, and he went into a depression that was virtually a nervous breakdown. In 1838, he was defeated for the office of speaker of the state legislature. In 1843, he lost the nomination for Congress. In 1846, he was elected to Congress, but in 1848 he failed to be renominated. The next year he was rejected in his bid to be a land officer. He was defeated for the Senate in 1854. Two years later, he was defeated for his party's nomination for the vice presidency of the United States. And he was defeated again for the Senate in 1858.

The triumph of the story, of course, is that Lincoln was elected 16th President of the United States in 1860. The gurus usually fail to mention that right after he was elected, the South seceded from the union, and the country was torn apart by the bloodiest and bitterest war we would ever know. The fact that it also devastated Lincoln's health didn't really matter, I suppose, since he was assassinated as soon as it ended.

That's what his perseverance got him. It got us perhaps our greatest hero, but neither the great man nor his family knew happiness. And I have my doubts about Lincoln as a model for overcoming failure. Would any of the gurus who invoke him or any of the rest of us switch places with him or with a modern Lincoln?

Be careful of what you aspire to: you just might get it.

Obviously, we can never foresee all the results of our actions. And if Lincoln had known the results of his, he may have chosen the same path without hesitation. Still, if you're failing toward success, be as sure as you can that the success you're failing toward is the success you really desire.

CHAPTER | **14**

Making the Skeleton Dance—Bragging about the Negatives

"If you cannot get rid of the family skeleton, you may as well make it dance."

— GEORGE BERNARD SHAW

It's 3:30 on a hot Friday afternoon. The room is stuffy, and we've drawn the blinds against the direct sunlight so it's dark, almost cave-like. The three people I'm with have been conducting job interviews since 9:00 AM, and I've been kibitzing, consulting on a way to improve a hiring process that has left the company with a 37 percent yearly turn-over rate.

Our sixth interviewee of the day steps into the room. He introduces himself to us as Clyde Thompson. He's African-American and well-groomed, but like me he's got a nonstandard body that can make a $3,000 Armani suit look like it came off the rack in K-mart. His hair and mustache are gray; he appears to be in his mid-50s. We've already got three strong candidates and only two openings. And in two days of in-terviewing, the area manager has shown an unshakable predilection for "vigorous and energetic"—meaning young—candidates, and appears to be threatened by anyone her own age. Her two subordinates take their cues from her.

As I look over my copy of Thompson's application, I mentally reduce his chances from minuscule to nonexistent. I glance at my watch. I've got an early flight. I wonder how long it will take my com-patriots to blow poor Thompson off.

"So why should we hire you, Mr. Thompson?" the area manager asks, starting with the question she usually finishes with.

Thompson smiles.

"I'm 53 years old," he says without hesitation. "I'm black. I've been unemployed for almost five months, ever since my last company went belly-up. I've got no experience in your industry. If you take a look at my application you'll see that there's a checkmark next to the yes on that question about whether or not I've ever been convicted of a felony. I've applied for any number of other jobs and no one else will hire me." He looks at us each in turn while he's slowly ticking off these points on his fingers, as confidently as if he were explaining his Harvard MBA, his Olympic gold medals, and his seven years as CEO of General Motors. "So let me tell you why I'm the best possible candidate you're ever going to find for this position."

And that's exactly what he proceeds to do—demonstrating the poise and assurance and experience he'd gained in those 53 years.

"If you hire me, I can't afford *not* to succeed!" he tells us with passion and conviction. "I don't have the option of being able to move on to greener pastures—or even brown pastures—when the job gets too grueling. I'm 100 percent committed. As locked into this position as I was locked into that jail cell 35 years ago. And if you'll notice that's where I earned most of the credits for my college degree. I never wanted a Master's, so I've made sure I've never had to go back. But what I learned in that place—the formal and the informal training—has a lot to do with why I've been so successful at every job I've had since then."

Clyde Thompson walked into the interview room with about as much chance of getting that job as he had of being elected Miss Congeniality in Atlantic City the following September. Then he provided us with all the reasons why we might not want to hire him: all the ones that we probably would have brought up on our own once he was out of the room, and a few more we might never have come up with.

When he did leave, however, the discussion barely touched on any of those negative points. Since Clyde had put them all on the table, it was as if we'd already dealt with them. Not that I talked much, mostly I just sat and listened—with growing amusement. Clyde had turned his unemployability into his greatest strength. And the fact that the other leading candidates were so good that they could quit and get hired anywhere else had actually become a liability for them. Everybody in the room was convinced that Clyde would never add to that 37 percent turnover rate. Not if there was anything he could possibly do to prevent it.

The area manager selected Clyde Thompson as her number-one choice. Her two subordinates immediately made the selection unanimous. The following Monday, they offered Clyde the job. He surprised everyone by asking for 24 hours to think it over, then called back the next morning to thank them and turn them down.

"Unemployable" Clyde Thompson had received a much better offer.

CARRYING NEGATIVE BAGGAGE

Maybe you've never been to prison. Maybe you aren't yet middle-aged, and maybe you've never even been unemployed or anything like unemployable. But we've all walked into rooms like Clyde Thompson walked into that day. We often face situations where we're going to be judged: perhaps by a boss or a potential employer, or by our coworkers or those who work for us. We present ourselves for different types of judgment to any number of people on a daily basis.

We've all been in Clyde Thompson's position, having to face evaluation while knowing that we were carrying negative baggage. It might not have been anything as extreme as a prison record, or even anything we were ashamed of. It could be any type of negative, any of the many we've already discussed.

Sometimes we're just uncomfortable with something we've done or something we haven't done. Or it could be the circumstances that surround the situation: the raise we aren't going to be able to give an outstanding employee; the rotten results we have to explain to the boss. Or it might be something about us personally: a flawed résumé or a gap in experience or deficiency in skill. Maybe it's even a problem with our physical appearance, or a lack of grace and style. Or a sense of inferiority, if we don't believe we're as smart, as well educated, or as rich as those we're facing.

In this country we frequently add not rich enough, not beautiful enough, not good enough—even not famous enough—onto any other negatives we're carrying.

For an astonishingly large and varied number of reasons, many of us nurture feelings of inferiority. That's the cliché: "nurture feelings of inferiority."

TIP: There may be a lot of things you want to be doing with your feelings of inferiority. Nurturing them should not be one of those things.

We've talked a lot about filling the glass and making peace with the negatives in your career and your business life. The true test of how well you've succeeded in making peace with a negative and how successfully you've been able to add water to the glass often comes when you have to present that negative to the judgment of others.

That's what this chapter is about. Are you as cool, confident, and comfortable with your negatives as Clyde Thompson was? You might not be a salesperson, but presenting your negatives to others is a selling situation. And that governs how you're likely to react.

HIDING COWS

The worst case scenario is that you'll find yourself acting like one of those characters I call "hidden cow" sales reps. You've probably met one or two hidden cow reps in your time. If there's a rotting cow in the well that supplies the drinking water of the country estate they're trying to sell you, they'll do their best to keep that annoying fact hidden. If you mention the nasty smell that you've noticed, they'll tell you they don't smell a thing. If you persist, they'll do something clever to change the subject or distract you. This is known as the "Hey, look, there's Elvis!" stratagem.

Hiding the rotting cow can get the sale. That's why so many inferior salespeople—and non-salespeople—seize upon it when they're desperate. And why the truly lame use it religiously, often shamelessly, in business and even in their personal lives:

- "Congresswoman, I wouldn't even worry about it. With the kind of controls we've got in place there's no way this weapons system is going to go over budget."
- "Dairy Queen? If I had a McJob like that, would I apply for an apartment that was this expensive? No, I have no idea who those seven people are in that car outside. I told you I have no roommates."
- "Of course I have a villa in the south of France. Do you honestly think I'd make something like that up just to impress a woman in a bar?"

You've probably never been quite that blatant, but who among us has never concealed an uncomfortable fact that someone else had a right to know: an assignment that might have been forgotten rather than never assigned; new information that indicates our pet project might just be a dog; an "innocent" lunch date with a coworker that didn't really bear mentioning to our spouse; an oil leak in the used car we sold to the new shipping clerk?

We've all hidden the occasional cow in the water well. And some of us have stashed away some pretty good-sized herds.

I'm not talking about the little white lies, what some people call "social lubrication":

- "Yes, Linda, that new hair color looks lovely on you. And it will certainly . . . ah . . . brighten up the outer office. How long did you say it would last?" Or,
- "It's a wonderful painting, boss. Be sure to thank your wife for me. She's really updated daVinci, hasn't she? Imagine including Jimmy Swaggert and Oral Roberts as apostles at the last supper. And is that Sally Jessy Raphael as Christ?"

No, I'm not talking about white lies; I'm talking about information that you'd feel you deserved to know if the situation were reversed.

COWS FLOAT

The problem with hidden cows is that they have an annoying way of floating to the surface. Usually sooner rather than later.

> **TIP:** At the first good whiff of the rotting cow, anyone who doesn't smell it loses all credibility.

Salespeople who lose credibility lose the sale. But for those who aren't in sales, the stakes are far higher. If you lose credibility, you've lost the possibility of trust: not the trust of a single prospect that you might never see again, but the trust of a boss, a coworker, a subordinate, maybe even a friend or someone else who's likely to be a key player in your life.

Salespeople hate to lose prospects, but it's much easier to lose a good prospect than a good friend. The dollars and cents penalty for not making a sale pales in comparison to the financial—and nonfinancial—cost of having a boss who doubts your word. It's difficult to relax and enjoy life when the people around you are sniffing the air suspiciously.

> **TIP:** Never try to hide a rotting cow. Not even a little one.

Work at avoiding it. Think about the times you may have done it in the past and how you could have handled the situation differently. None of us currently on the planet is approaching perfection, but the cleaner the air we breathe—and the well water we drink—the better we're all likely to feel.

Fortunately, most of the time, most of us are smart enough to avoid behaving like hidden-cow reps.

Unfortunately, we act like mealy-mouthers instead.

MEALY-MOUTHERS

To mealy-mouthers, potential negatives are terrifying obstacles, which they proceed to stumble over blatantly enough to guarantee that those negatives become the focal point of anyone within earshot.

Initially, they might try to slip the negative in unnoticed:

"Nothing really back in there. That's where the old barn used to be. Over in that far corner you've got your septic tank. Over in that direction, as you can see, that's your well. There is a dead cow down there at the moment. Back in that other corner is the perfect place for that garden you've been talking about. In this soil, you can grow tomatoes the size of softballs. Why last year Mrs. Cathcart down the road . . . What? No, I said *cow*. A dead cow. But anyway when you taste those tomatoes . . . What?"

Then they'll probably try to minimize it:

"Really? That concerns you? Not to worry. You do have *one* dead cow in the well. But it is just the one. A lot of times in these parts, you'll find five, six, seven, maybe even eight cows in your water well. Believe me, no matter what you might hear, it's no big deal. Especially not one little cow. One cow in all that water, you'll never even notice it. A lot of people might not even bother to have a single cow removed. And, of course, a cow is organic. And if at some point you do feel like you want to get it out of the well, we're not talking big bucks here, not at all. Especially when you amortize it over the effective life of your property and, blah, blah, blah, blah, blah. . . ."

Mealy-mouthers will spend so much time and energy trying to reduce the rotting cow to insignificance that by the time they've finished you swear you can smell it on the drapes and in the carpeting. You walk away from the deal with the sour taste of contaminated well water in your mouth even though you never took a sip.

We've all done it. Just for fun—if you happen to think self-flagellation is fun—take a few moments right now to think about the times when you might have done a bit of mealy-mouthing of your own. Did you try to slip that last client complaint past your boss with a little verbal misdirection? Are your explanations for your department's shortfalls last quarter reminiscent of a medieval argument for the number of angels that can dance on the head of a pin? Though you're listed with the payroll department as having seven exemptions, have you got 32 reasons and 23 convoluted excuses for failing to pay *any* child support?

Do these questions or ones like them make you uncomfortable?

Forget about feeling bad. If you're failing toward success, you want to use those past mistakes as stepping-stones—not rocks for a self-inflicted stoning. Of course, that doesn't mean the check for the overdue child support shouldn't be in the mail today.

> **TIP:** If you find yourself mealy-mouthing—not hiding a fact's existence but not dealing with it directly either—that's a sure sign you haven't found a way to come to terms honestly with something you consider to be a negative. And if you haven't made peace with it yourself, you certainly can't hope to convince anyone else to make peace with it.

Mealy-mouthing seldom fools anyone, at least anyone who doesn't want to be fooled. And when it does, the result for the poor mealy-mouthing manager, CEO, engineer, accountant, doctor, lawyer, or Indian chief is dissonance and stress. Exactly what happens to the mealy-mouthing salesperson. Which is hardly surprising, since that's what he's become at that point: a mealy-mouthing salesperson who's managed to wheedle someone into trusting him and then used that trust to sell that individual a bill of goods.

When mealy-mouthing works, you're always left wondering if you hurt the person who believed you and how badly you hurt her. The bigger your mealy-mouthing success—the more that person trusted you—the more you'll worry and the worse you're going to feel. That is, if you allow yourself to feel, if you don't simply become as cynical as any common, garden-variety huckster.

BRAGGING ABOUT THE NEGATIVES

Fortunately, there's another way to present your negatives when you walk into one of those rooms of judgment. Use Clyde Thompson as your model, and handle those negatives like a truly great salesperson.

Great salespeople never try to hide potential negatives, and they certainly don't stumble through them. Great salespeople use potential negatives as selling points. They even brag about them.

"Do you know the best feature of this country estate? The best feature is that there's a rotting cow in your drinking water!"

"Excuse me?

"There's a dead cow in the well. Which is the only reason this place wasn't snapped up a long time ago, and at a considerably higher price. I've got a guy lined up who'll take care the removal and clean up for $525. And you can thank your lucky stars for a nearsighted bovine and an owner that simply didn't want to deal with the problem. I got him to take $5,000 off the listing price. That's the best deal you'll ever get on beef."

In this particular case, the $5,000 discount is how the sales agent added water to the glass, so he could make peace with the negative in the first place.

CRISIS OR OPPORTUNITY?

In 1912, the printer was all set to run three million copies of Teddy Roosevelt's nomination speech, complete with photographs of Roosevelt and his VP candidate, the immortal Hiram Johnson. Then the chairman of the campaign committee discovered that no one had obtained permission from the photographer who had taken the pictures. Legal penalties for the copyright violation could be as much as $3 million.

The printing plates were made. Changing the photos would be extremely expensive. But no one knew what the photographer might demand for the rights. It was even possible that, heaven forbid, the man was a Democrat. There were a number of them afoot in those days, and they were an unpredictable lot. The photographer might even deny the Republicans the pictures altogether.

The chairman sent off a quick telegram: "Planning to issue three million copies of Roosevelt speech with pictures of Roosevelt and Johnson on the cover. Great publicity opportunity for photographers. What will you pay us to use your photographs?"

"Appreciate the opportunity," the photographer replied, "but can only pay $250."

The chairman accepted without dickering. He probably could have held out for $350 or $400.

THE KRISPIE CRISIS

Four months after the introduction of Kellogg's Rice Krispies Treats—and the expense of all that new product marketing—the company ran out of stock. Plenty of advertising but very little product. People wanted it but couldn't find it.

So turning crisis into opportunity (did you know that in Chinese the word for *crisis* is the same as the word for *no Krispie Treats?*) and bragging about the negative, Kellogg ran apologies in major papers across the country asking consumers for patience. The headline read: "OK. Who took the last one?" The ad explained how hard the company was working to keep up with the incredible demand for Rice Krispies Treats.

It would have been difficult to have planned it any better.

LOUD AND PROUD:
THE ULTIMATE SALES TRICK

TIP: If you can brag about a negative, you've made peace with it. Often the secret to making peace is to find a way that you *can* honestly brag about it. Having a skeleton in the closet is a lot more fun when you can make it dance.

Now obviously, this isn't a call to swamp everyone around you in as much negative information as you can possibly unload on them about yourself, your situation, your vision, and your proposals. What you reveal or don't reveal and to whom you reveal it or don't reveal it is up to you. Again, this is not about ethics. This is about maintaining your own sense of integrity—about being the person you want to be—so you can be as successful, on your own terms, as possible. If you're honestly comfortable keeping a piece of information to yourself, if that creates no dissonance for you and your glass remains full, that's between you and you.

But if you believe the person you're dealing with has a right to know about a potential problem—or if, right or no right, they're likely to discover it anyway—give it loud and give it proud. Confidence sells.

"Will that other design firm do the project cheaper for you, Ellen? Absolutely. Much cheaper. But do you really think they would charge less if they could charge more? They're no humanitarian operation. They want to make as large a profit as possible just like anyone else. They charge less because that's all they can get anybody to pay for their work. We charge more because we think we're worth more. And here's why all our clients agree and are more than willing to ante up the extra investment . . ."

Or,

"No, boss, I can't possibly finish that report by Tuesday. I could rush it but then that's what we'll have—a rush job. That's not the kind of job you need me to do. If we want to get that appropriation, it's going to take more research and it's going to take more time. But the result is going to be worth it."

Bragging about the negative—making the skeleton dance—means getting the issue out on table where you can deal with it. Explain why the negative exists or why it doesn't matter or why it's actually a positive. Why leave it hidden for someone to stumble upon later, when you have no control at all over the situation?

The unspoken message is, *Yes, this potential problem exists, just like you suspected. I'd never try to kid you about that. But obviously, it doesn't bother me to let you know about it. I'm sure you're still going to go along with me. And here's why.*

TIP: Truth is the ultimate sales trick. Nothing disarms a potential doubting Thomas like honesty.

The skeleton protocol shows you how to make your negatives braggable, in a wide variety of situations. The tactics are closely related to those we've discussed earlier in the book.

THE SKELETON PROTOCOL

1. Own up to the specific negative. Be honest with yourself. It may be something you yourself are concerned about or it may be an objection others have raised or seem likely to raise. Understand the potential downside: to yourself and to the others involved.
2. List as many positives as you can come up with about the negative, for yourself or for others.
3. Ask yourself if the negative exists because of a potential positive. "The report will be late because it's going to take me longer to write one that's sure to get the appropriation." Without the negative (the delay) there is no positive (the certainty of receiving the money).
4. Ask yourself if the negative actually is a potential positive. Clyde Thompson's unemployability could be shown to make him a more dedicated and more committed and therefore more desirable—employee. Thus the negative (unemployability) becomes a positive. Or at least it's integral to a positive (a more desirable employee).
5. Ask yourself if the very existence of the negative is evidence of a positive. "Our professional fees are much higher than the competition's. And why are our clients willing to pay the extra money? Because we deliver superior results." The positive (superior results) can be deduced from the negative (higher fees).
6. Ask yourself if you can brag about the situation on balance, negative and all. "Yes, boss, I'm probably the worst shooter of any guard in the league. But I deserve $7.6 million a year because I never turn the ball over, and I'm one of the best playmakers you'll ever find. Bottom line: The team will score a lot more points with me than without me." Even if there's nothing positive to say about being a terrible shooter, on balance the picture

is extremely positive. (Whether it's extreme enough for $7.6 million is not my call.)

When a woman complained to Frank Lloyd Wright that the roof of the building he'd designed was leaking on her desk, he simply replied, "Why don't you move the desk?" To him, on balance, the building was worth any negatives that others might perceive it to have. Of course it wasn't dripping on him.

7. Ask yourself what you can bring to the situation so you can brag about it with complete honesty. "I know my people have let you down in the past. And with the transition we're going through, until we get them all properly trained I can't promise they won't let you down again. But I'm going to oversee the restructuring personally—step by step by step. And let me remind you how successful my track record is. And why I can guarantee we're going to finish on time and below budget." You become the difference between a negative and a positive situation.

8. If none of the above works, the negative simply isn't braggable. You need to add water to the glass. Talk the estate owner into reducing the price or just get the damn cow out of the well.

Now here's my brag. By the time you finish this book, you should be able to make your assets every bit as impressive as those of a middle-aged, unemployed, ex-con like Clyde Thompson.

CHAPTER | **15**

Change the Scale
to Make the Sale

Thirty thousand dollars is a fortune for a Hyundai but it's dirt cheap for a Rolls-Royce. If you're buying dishwashing detergent, five gallons is a huge amount—unless you were originally considering (or the sales rep got you considering) a 200-gallon drum.

One thing we've all learned in the last hundred years is that everything is relative. Great salespeople turn big numbers into tiny numbers by demonstrating value—the Rolls-Royce could be a much better deal than a Hyundai—and by changing the scale.

A congresswoman once asked me how she could "explain away" a piece of legislation's $5 billion price tag. She was looking for a way to mealy-mouth it past a prominent senator.

I shook my head. "The senator isn't an idiot, Congresswoman, he just plays one on TV. You aren't going to slip that much money past him unnoticed. This is a guy who makes his staff kick in for the office coffee. What you've got to do is change the scale."

"How do you change the scale on $5 billion? That's an awful lot of coffee."

"Five billion dollars!?! That's peanuts for a program like this! Why last year alone, China spent $17 billion on the problem. Seventeen billion!" When changing the scale, it's sometimes necessary to use exclamation points.

"They did?"

"That's one way to change the scale," I said. "When you're explaining all the wonders of the program—before you ever get to the issue of price—you dangle a really big number in front of the senator, the biggest number you've got. Then you finish going over all the benefits."

"It will do a lot for his constituents."

"Stress the even more magnificent things it will do for the senator himself and his reelection campaign. After that, you move for the commitment. Then simply be quiet. Let him ask about the price tag."

"And if he doesn't ask?"

"If he doesn't ask, he doesn't want it badly enough yet. You have to make him want it."

"Okay, so he asks. And I say, 'It's a lot less than you might think.'"

"You could. But I'd say just the opposite: 'Senator, it's a lot. It's one huge pile of money!' Then I'd pause while he's soaking up that image and imagining this incredibly high price tag, hopefully something much larger than it actually is. You get him wanting the program, but anticipating the worst. If he's thinking it's going to be $10 billion, $5 billion is a bargain."

"Changing the scale."

"Exactly. From that point, your stance is, 'Yes, it's $5 billion. And it's worth every single penny of it—and then some.' And you reiterate the reasons why it's a $5 billion bargain, using the same passion and honesty you bowled me over with last week."

You put the negative in perspective. You change the scale.

My problems are monumental because they're so close to me. Yours are farther away from me and therefore smaller. But we can change the scale to put our own problems in perspective.

I may be struggling to get by financially. But did you know that just $1,000 a month would put me in the top 1 percent of the world's population in terms of income? An even smaller percentage have enough to eat every night and a car and a home with a phone and central heating and cable TV.

If you're 65 and filled with regret over the chances you've let slip by, imagine being 85 and how much you'd give to be 65 again with another 20 years of opportunity.

That's changing the scale.

DREAMS AND NIGHTMARES

For the most part, Tim Hennessy likes his job on the production line, but sometimes it can become tedious. "That's when I have my lunch out in the sunshine on the back patio," he says. "I watch the migrants bent over and picking, planting, or tending the strawberries. Whatever they do, they're always bent over. I know that once in a while they look up and gaze over at us and *dream* of having a job like mine in this factory. Of making the kind of money I do, with the kind of benefits I have. Of being cool in the summer and warm and dry when it rains. Of being clean; they never even get to wash up for lunch. I've got a dream job—and I never want to forget that."

Too many of us who have spent our lives as professionals don't really understand what real, backbreaking work is. And how little it pays. And what it is to be truly stuck in a life, knowing that you're never likely to be able to do any better, never likely to be able to earn any more.

Just as death focuses the mind wonderfully, so—I can assure you—does standing up to your knees in overflowing sewage, holding an electric drain rooter with a badly frayed cord. It was at just that point in my life when I suddenly realized at a gut level why my father had worked so hard to send me and my brothers and sisters to college.

> **TIP:** You may well have someone else's dream job. That doesn't mean it's your dream job, or that you shouldn't try for your dream. It does mean that maybe it's not nearly as awful as you sometimes think.

"But my life *is* a nightmare," a woman once confided after one of my workshops. "How do you change the scale on a nightmare?"

It's not my place to minimize her problems or anyone else's. I'll be the first to admit that the vast majority of the people in this country and on this planet have worse problems than I do. I always thought that was one of the contradictions those of us who do motivational speaking need to recognize.

I once stood in the back of the room as a particularly perky motivator addressed an awards dinner for construction workers. A middle-aged man stood stiffly beside me, apparently too uncomfortable to remain seated. As he listened, he massaged his hands. They were misshapen and arthritic. They'd been scrubbed clean, almost raw, yet were permanently stained with imbedded grit.

"Why shouldn't she be upbeat," he muttered, nodding in the direction of the speaker. On the screen beside her, her PowerPoint presentation morphed into number 11 of her trademarked *26 Secrets of Success.* "Who wouldn't be upbeat if they could make the kind of money she makes by just flying in here, talking for an hour, scattering a little sunshine then picking up a fat check and flying back home? Let her try working 60 hours a week hot-mopping asphalt on a roof in 98 degree heat. Then she can come back here and preach to me about hard work and persistence and positive attitude. What has she ever done, aside from telling other people how to live? Twenty-six secrets of success? What success has she ever had besides selling people on those 26 secrets?"

He paused and took a moment to look me over, apparently realizing for the first time that I wasn't a construction worker. Then he asked, "What do you do?"

"Motivational speaker," I said. "I'm on next."

"I can hardly wait," he grumbled. Then he moved off to stand by somebody else.

Weiler's law says that nothing is impossible for the person who doesn't have to do it himself. It's not my place to minimize the problems you might have to live with or overcome. And it's certainly not my place to minimize any nightmares you might have to face. It's not my place. But it might be yours.

How do you change the scale on a nightmare?

After all, life can be brutal. Helen Keller, who should know a lot more about life's difficulties than you or me (at least certainly an infinite amount more than me, and I would be willing to guess a rather large amount more than you as well), said that "although the world is full of suffering, it is also full of the overcoming of it."

> **TIP:** It's not my place to minimize your suffering. It's *yours.* Particularly if it doesn't quiet reach the level that Helen Keller had to overcome.

And there are a great many of us who don't ever do any real suffering at all, though we sometimes think we do.

TURNING TRAGEDY INTO TRIUMPH
AND TRIUMPH INTO TRAGEDY

Your personal sense of scale defines your triumphs and your tragedies, and everything in between. That's never more true than with victimization. Kacey McCallister is a young boy who lost both legs in an accident, one above the hip, one six inches below it. He plays baseball and basketball, at 2 feet 7 inches tall. He was interviewed by Bob Baum of the Associated Press.

"I realize," Kacey said, "there was nothing I could do to change it unless they come out with something that can grow legs. I just go with what I have."

His family stays in touch with the truck driver who accidentally hit Kacey while the boy was crossing the street. "I think what [the driver] has gone through is much, much worse than what we have gone through," Kacey's mother says.

On the other hand . . .

At a convention for a multilevel marketing company, one of their top distributors addresses the group. Whatever you may think of multilevel marketers, this is a man who's worked hard and overcome great odds. He's become a remarkable financial success; he probably makes over a quarter of a million dollars a year. Tonight he tells his story.

He'd been a copier salesman, a milk truck driver, a bus driver. He'd been fired; he'd failed in business. When he started with the multilevel company, all his friends and relatives ridiculed him. He'd invited them all to his first home meeting, then he waited—and waited—and none of them showed up. He never forgot that night and he'd used that hurt and anger to propel him to success.

He smiles though, as he tells of the day he invited them all down to see him off as he and his wife took their first award-winners' cruise. He talks of the feeling as the ship pulled off, of sipping champagne and looking down at the dock as the whistle blew and the streamers flew by. And of his moment of triumph as he gazed down on those who had scoffed at him—presumably all his friends and relatives—and gave them the finger.

Who can fault someone for wanting to prove to himself and to others that he's better than any of them imagined—and using that desire to motivate himself to get wherever it is he wanted to go? It just seems to me that sailing off on a luxury liner away from a lifetime's worth of friends and family is not the most triumphant image I can imagine. Or if it is a triumph, it's one on a much, much smaller scale than a 2-foot, 7-inch–tall boy playing basketball.

> **TIP:** Granting forgiveness when you've been wronged is one way to change the scale completely. It can turn a tragedy into a triumph. Failing to grant forgiveness can turn triumph into tragedy.

FORGIVENESS AND SURVIVAL

Eighty percent of Americans believe that forgiveness takes the help of God. It doesn't. Robert Enright, professor of psychology and founder of the Forgiveness Center explains, "The essence of forgiveness is always the same. You've been hurt by someone. You choose to give up the resentment to which you are entitled. You offer benevolence and mercy to someone who does not deserve it." To someone who, at least in your eyes, does not deserve it. And it makes *you* feel better.

> **TIP:** You forgive for your own sake, more than the sake of the person you're forgiving. That person may not care in the slightest if you forgive her or not; she may not even believe she did anything wrong; she may even persist in what she's doing. You forgive her because it makes you feel better. If living well is the best revenge, forgiveness is one way to help you live well.

"Forgiveness and reconciliation aren't necessarily the same thing," says Enright. "You don't have to cave in to the other person. But you can break the cycle . . . if you are willing to forgive."

> **TACTIC:** Sometimes forgiveness can be about reconciliation. It can be a gift you give to someone, knowing that you've also done things that others considered wrong, remembering times when you were forgiven and how good that felt.

TACTIC: Another way to change the scale when you think
you've been wronged doesn't necessarily involve either
forgiveness or reconciliation: it's simply to see yourself as a
survivor rather than a victim.

"I never focus on what they did to me," says a woman who'd been fired for something the company later acknowledged—in confidential, internal memos—that she couldn't have done. "I focus on how I made it through. I'd rather draw strength contemplating my achievement than waste my time making myself furious about their shortcomings."

She leaves that to her attorneys. Jesus might not have handled it quite this way. But Attila would have been a hell of a lot worse.

CHANGING THE SCALE ON INTIMIDATION

Sometimes we need to change the scale we're using to measure those around us. Too often too many of us are intimidated by our boss or our boss's boss or our boss's boss's boss. Why?

Why are we intimidated by any prominent person? We all understand that no matter how intelligent or rich or powerful or good looking or famous we ourselves are, we have a full assortment of insecurities and fears, of weaknesses and regrets. But we sometimes have trouble believing that the same is true of others—especially those who are more intelligent, powerful, rich, good looking, etc., than we are.

You and I have difficulty discerning the difference in intelligence between a collie and a dalmatian. I've always thought a being that came to Earth from some other planet would have difficulty distinguishing what appear to us to be vast differences between us. And in that most prized and prideful characteristic of humanity—intelligence—someone from a planet circling Alpha Centuri might have trouble telling the difference between an Einstein and a village idiot. On the Alpha Centurian's scale, the distinction could be tiny.

Certainly on any absolute scale of all there is to know, none of us knows much.

"I used to be intimidated by prominent people," an extremely successful high-tech entrepreneur says. "Until I met one of our most respected television icons. Not only did he obviously put his pants on one leg at a time, he'd forgotten to pull up his fly. He was very gracious, but nothing else he could have done would have set me so completely at ease. We're all human—and clay feet are endemic to the breed."

> **TIP:** Neither Pierce Brosnan's nor Julia Roberts' good looks make them better than you—just better looking.

> **TIP:** Warren Buffett's billions don't make him better. Nor does Bill Gates's money, fame, and power.

Mother Teresa *was* probably better than you. And better than me. So is that guy who donated a kidney to help a complete stranger. But both you and I are far more likely to be intimidated by wealth, fame, or looks than we are by those who are actually better people than we are.

Why are we more intimidated by human beings who are successful (successful by standards we often insist we don't hold) than we are by those who are successful as human beings?

If you want a value check, consider this: A man becomes rich. Maybe he even stole the money. Or maybe he won the lottery. Maybe the lottery machine at the 7-11 selected the winning numbers, so he didn't even accomplish that on his own. Still, all of a sudden everyone starts treating this guy better. That may be understandable. We'd all like to get a piece of those winnings, even if it's just a tiny piece. So maybe we're sucking up to him. Not commendable perhaps, but understandable.

What's less understandable is that we also start thinking of this guy as a more valuable, more worthwhile person. We respect him more. We ask his opinion and his advice, and we actually pay attention to it. We're flattered and honored to be in his company.

We have a higher regard for people with money. And that's true even if they simply made their money the old fashioned way: by inheriting it. It's even more true if they're old money, which might well mean that no one in their family has done much of anything constructive—anything of any social value—for generations.

> **TIP:** Sometimes changing the scale involves a value check.

DELIBERATE INTIMIDATION

Then there are the Marvin Winchells of the world, those who try to intimidate deliberately.

"Marvin has to let you know that he's really too important to be dealing with the likes of you," one of Marvin's vendors complained. "He's always late for meetings. He'll keep you cooling your heels while he chats on the phone about his golf game. He's got that huge office. Giant desk. His chair is a leather throne. The two cloth chairs for visitors are smaller and shorter. The topper is, he's actually whittled down their legs. And the front legs are shorter than the back. So you can't get comfortable, and if try to balance anything in your lap, it slides down to the floor."

"An old trick," I offered. "I think psychiatrists used to use it."

"Sure. I've heard of it, but I've never known anyone else who actually went to the trouble to do it. Then he has to act distracted and uninterested in anything you have to say. And shake his head while you're talking as if he's much too smart to believe a word of it. And, of course, nothing you do is ever right—or ever likely to be."

"And at the slightest excuse," I offered, "the screaming starts. And the demands."

He chuckled, "You know Marvin."

"I was in sales. Every sales rep knows a Marvin."

He nodded. "Saying Marvin is high maintenance is like saying cancer is annoying. With all the aggravation and all the hand-holding required, I was spending more in antacid than we were making on the account. So one day I get a call."

"From Marvin."

"Don't be silly. Marvin's much too big a deal to call me directly. I get a call from Marvin's secretary. She says, 'Please hold for Mr. Winchell, please.' This is typical Marvin. Then he'd leave you hanging there for 20 minutes. Only I'd had enough. So I say, *'The only thing I'll hold for Mr. Winchell is his trophy wife. And I can't do that right now cause I'm busy canceling his last order—his very last order.'*"

Why should anyone feel intimidated by someone like Marvin, someone with such massive insecurities that he feels he needs to go to such lengths to gain an edge? This is a person you should feel sorry for. What could be more pathetic than the image of this guy down on his knees in his best, overpriced, dressed-for-success suit, shaving down those chair legs?

> **TIP:** Never be intimidated by someone who thinks his best shot is winning through intimidation.

He's usually just telling you that he's in competition with the world and that—without the intimidation—he doesn't believe he can win. And he's usually right. He tries to blow himself up like a balloon—hoping for larger than life. When it doesn't work, when the balloon pops, well, you'll never see a greater change of scale—a greater loss of stature—in any human being.

Any good salesperson would love to run across a Marvin Winchell. An unethical one could take him for everything, including the defective office furniture.

SCALE

Think of the most stressful thing likely to happen to you at work this week or this month. Then imagine that right before it happens, you find out that the person you love most has only an extremely limited amount of time to live. How stressful is that big meeting with the finance department likely to be? What are the chances you're even going to bother to show up for something that inconsequential?

> **TIP:** The person you love most does have only an extremely limited amount of time to live.

You too.

It's been estimated—a phrase that usually means *my best guess is*—that 99.9973 percent of our seemingly traumatic problems pale into insignificance in the face of life's largest and most profound negatives: the marriage that's falling apart, the child that's slipping into schizophrenia, the stomach cancer.

It's all about scale.

A FEW ISSUES OF SCALE

First issue. Two hundred million years ago, a sustained volcanic explosion centered in Florida split apart the ancient supercontinent, creating the Atlantic Ocean and destroying much of life on Earth. You or I may be having a bad day, but nothing that happened to either of us today was likely to be quite that bad. Chances are excellent that whatever I'm currently bothering myself about is unlikely to have quite that impact 200 million years from now. Or 200 years. Or next week.

Second issue. In *Out of the Night: A Biologist's View of the Future,* Nobel Prize winner H.J. Muller asked his readers to imagine the history of life on this planet as a rope reaching from Boston to the center of the desk in J.P. Morgan's Wall Street office. That's about 220 miles representing three or four billion years. The rope starts with the first primeval protoplasm—in the Massachusetts statehouse by the Boston Common. (I used to hang out around there when I was a kid, and I can attest that it's still brimming with primeval protoplasm.)

Genes multiply, differentiate, or mutate. The creatures along the rope in Massachusetts and Rhode Island and Connecticut aren't impressive. No actual four-footed land animals emerge until we're well inside the New York City limits. In Harlem, the first mammals and birds show up. The last dinosaur is at 42nd Street. Monkeys develop near Macy's. We're already inside Morgan's building before we get Neanderthals. According to Muller, "Man the wise," *Homo sapiens,* "leaves his first remains within the private office, only seven and a half feet from the desk." Three feet later, the initial signs of civilization appear.

"On the desk, one foot from the center, stands old King Tut. Five and a half inches from the center we mark the fall of Rome and the beginnings of the Dark Ages. Only one and a half inches from the present end of the cord comes the discovery of America and the promulgation of the Copernican theory [that the Earth revolves around the sun not vice versa]—through which man opens his eyes to the vastness of the world in which he lives and his relative insignificance." Then, a half inch from the end, "The first faint reverberations of the Industrial Revolution. . . . A quarter of an inch from the end, Darwin speaks, and man awakes to the transitory character of his shape and his institutions."

Muller wrote this a while ago but the scale is basically the same today. All of our history has happened in the last foot of a 220-mile chain of life. That's 1/1,161,600 of the rope, .0000008 of life on the planet.

And, we don't even want to talk about—nor are we really capable of conceptualizing—how insignificant that planet is in the scale of the universe.

Now let me tell you about this *huge* problem I'm having with the plant manager in Boise.

Third issue. Playwright Tom Stoppard said, "Eternity's a terrible thought. I mean, where's it going to end?" If you've been wondering about that, astronomers tell us the sun will become a red giant and exterminate all life on earth in the year 4,000,001,999. They aren't saying what month.

Fourth issue. Imagine starting out at something the size of Great Britain and moving down to something the size of a house, then to the size of a person, the size of an atom and finally to the size of the nucleus of an atom. Theoretically—meaning according to PBS—the space between that nucleus and the other subatomic particulars is filled with bubbles of quantum foam. The size of each of those bubbles is in the same proportion to that nucleus as the nucleus is to Great Britain itself.

Fifth issue. Several times in this book, I've pointed out that we're all more alike than we are different. How alike are we? Well, 99.9 percent of all our genetic makeup is identical.

Identical.

TINY FACTS

We all know that we can be truly horrendous to each other. But I like to measure those horrors against a couple of tiny facts.

Imagine you are driving. You're wearing your seat belt. The person you like least in the entire world is sitting next to you, not wearing a belt. Suddenly, a beer truck runs a red light, and you have to slam on the brakes.

You will simultaneously throw out an arm to protect that person you dislike so much.

Now, imagine you're walking down the sidewalk. An older woman is directly in front of you. Suddenly she hits on an unseen patch of black ice. Her legs go out from under her and she's about to crack her head. You're very likely to leap forward and fling yourself between that vulnerable skull and the sidewalk—without considering how you may bruise yourself or how it may ruin your expensive new outfit.

"Well, if I had time to think about it, I'd never do it," someone once said to me cynically. "At least not for that guy I hate."

That's just the point. You don't have to think. These responses aren't thought out. They're programmed in. We have evolved as social creatures, as a community, no matter how imperfect it might be. There is something in us that wants and needs to protect each other. I find that extremely encouraging—in spite of all the other tendencies we have.

PROGRESS

We are making progress. Again, you have to put it in perspective. We still commit horrors against each other. The technology we have today gives us the potential for bigger and better horrors than ever before. But at least today we are horrified by those horrors. In Attila's day, that kind of behavior was simply accepted.

We no longer eat each other. Some of today's self-help experts may offer the occasional outlandish recommendation, but there was a time when our gurus advised sacrificing babies to get rain.

Progress happens. You have to place our present sensibilities—as uncivilized as they may sometimes seem—in a larger scale of time. Not that many years ago, you could buy yourself someone condemned to death and have him drawn and quartered to entertain your friends. In another popular form of family entertainment, two blind men would be pushed into tiny pens, given clubs and forced to beat each other to unconsciousness or death. Maybe TV and the World Wrestling Federation aren't so bad after all.

TRAGEDY VERSUS STATISTICS

Changing the scale should be about gaining perspective, getting a better look at reality, not obscuring it. Too frequently using an inappropriate scale can hide the reality behind a situation. Mass murderer Joseph Stalin knew this well. "When one man dies, it is a tragedy," Stalin said. "When thousands die, it is statistics."

An estimated 136,986 individuals died the day Stalin died. Most of them better than he was—more successful at being human beings. Numbers don't die. Numbers don't go hungry, numbers don't suffer. Individuals do. One by one.

Numbers are meaningless unless put into a scale, a context. Is $30,000 a lot of money? For a Hyundai or a Rolls-Royce? In a book called *Filling the Glass,* I couldn't possibly omit the next story. In 1990, Congressman Jim Rogan was a deputy district attorney assigned to prosecute a highly publicized local trial. A man had tossed down ten beers then climbed into his car and killed two women and two children.

After all the evidence had been presented and both the prosecution and the defense had made their cases, the time came for Rogan to give his final summation. Slowly, he rose from his chair. He picked up his briefcase, and without saying a word, walked over to the jury box. He opened the briefcase. He took out a glass and a can of beer. He put the glass on the rail of the jury box. Then he opened the can and filled the glass. He took out a second can and a second glass and did the same thing. Then a third. He kept pouring until ten full glasses and ten empty cans lined the rail.

He looked at the accused. He looked at the survivors of the crash. He looked at the jury. Then he snapped his fingers and sat down. Without ever uttering a syllable.

The jury returned a guilty verdict in less than 45 minutes.

In *What They Don't Teach You at Harvard Business School,* Mark McCormack relates one of my favorite examples of changing the scale. It happened when Robert McNamara was president of Ford Motor Company in the 1950s. The company's finance people were insisting that Ford needed to close yet another plant in order to cut costs. At a meeting of top executives, no one wanted another closure yet nobody wanted to stand up to the numbers men.

Finally, one senior executive asked, "Why don't we close down all the plants and then we'll really start to save money."

That remark and the perspective that came with it turned the meeting around. The plant remained open.

STRESS

The stress that seems to surround us these days can also be treated as a problem of scale. Experts say that reacting to events as stressful is learned behavior. We can unlearn it and learn new ways to react. Of course none of these experts ever worked for your boss. Still, it's really not the outside event that's stressing you out. You and your body are stressing you out. You're allowing the outside event to trigger that reaction.

TACTIC: Ask yourself: Does this really have to be a stressful situation? Do you gain anything from allowing it to generate stress?

TACTIC: Consciously work at lowering the stress levels for the people you work with, changing the scale of the ambient stress in the office. You'll be surprised how quickly that can lower your own stress level as well.

TACTIC: Sometimes simply backing off from a situation helps change the scale and lower your stress. Take meditation breaks. Get out of the office for lunch. If it helps, play hooky occasionally—even if it's just leaving an hour early on a Friday afternoon for a movie date with your spouse. Take your vacations; they'll make you more successful not less.

Workers at one Japanese firm take a hula break every day.

Paul Sheehan is an architect and the CFO of the Dyer Sheehan Group, Inc., a leading investment real estate brokerage in Ventura, California. He's also a former professional musician. Paul handles stress as well as anyone I know. When he does need a break, he shuts off his

202 | FILLING THE GLASS

phone and closes his office door—a sure sign he's not to be disturbed. Then he picks up his guitar.

"I might spend 15 or 20 minutes concentrating intently on whatever song I'm writing," he says. "And depressurizing. For those few moments, work becomes the farthest thing from my mind."

TACTIC: Take a one-minute vacation several times during the day. Close your eyes and imagine yourself on the beach in Bermuda or skiing down a slope in San Moritz. Like the beer commercial says, "It's a whole new latitude." And you know as well as I how often a solution to an intractable problem pops up once you stop hassling about it and let it percolate around in your unconscious for a while.

TACTIC: Seeing your situation through the eyes of others can't help but put it in a completely different perspective. That's why support and peer-coaching groups can be so effective. And of course they also allow you to tap into a far broader range of experience than you could possibly gather on your own. Just being able to vent in a truly safe environment—preferably outside the company—can often deflate an overblown problem.

TACTIC: In your off hours, if you happen to have any, find something interesting enough to keep you from obsessing about your job. This can be tough, especially when you consider that one of the main causes of lack of sexual interest in both men and women is preoccupation with work. Like Pandas, humans often have difficulty breeding in captivity.

If sex—or at least sex with your spouse—can't get your mind off your job, find something that will. Learn to dance or play a musical instrument, exercise, play in a softball or bowling league, take adult ed courses, take a day trip, have a night on the town, collect matchbook covers—or manhole covers for that matter—or just do something you've never done.

If you've got to obsess away from the job, do it about something other than work. Back in the early 1970s, a good friend of mine got deeply into the "Paul McCartney is dead" hoopla.

"I decided to worry about that," he said, "so I won't have to worry about anything more important."

If all else fails, worry about Paul McCartney. I mean, could *Silly Love Songs* really have been written by the same man who wrote *Yesterday?* If he's not Billy Shears, who is? What is really going on here, and isn't it just possible that Brian Epstein and John Lennon were eliminated because they knew too much? And how does Marilyn Monroe fit into all this?

TIP: If you don't have any off hours, get some.

I'll be talking more about using your off hours in the next chapter. For right now, let me just note that changing the scale to keep from obsessing about work benefits your company as well as yourself. Did you know that, according to one study, employee headaches alone cost businesses $17 billion a year?

In *Modern Madness: The Hidden Link Between Work and Emotional Conflict,* Douglas LaBier writes, "Stress causes or worsens an estimated 70 to 90 percent of all illness, and costs industry about $75 billion yearly, by spawning hypertension, heart attacks, depression, anxiety, and other problems." A United Nations report, *Job Stress: The 20th Century Epidemic,* estimates the cost of occupational stress in the United States at $200 billion a year.

Two hundred billion dollars. That's a big number.

At least it is on most scales.

CHAPTER 16

Never Settle for Success

I almost didn't get to write this book.

Let me tell you my story. You may have been waiting for that. What business self-help book would be complete without the author's rags-to-riches story? Only mine doesn't start out exactly in rags. My father, as I've mentioned, was a Boston attorney, educated at Harvard Law. With seven kids in the family, we were hardly wealthy, but I don't get to start this tale in the streets of Harlem or the hills of Appalachia. The closest I got to deprivation was the four years I spent waiting for the weather to clear in South Bend, Indiana, at the University of Notre Dame.

Obviously, this kind of background was a massive handicap for an aspiring guru. But through pluck and overconfidence and just a touch of stupidity, I managed to overcome it; and by the time I was 30 I was as broke as any grade-school dropout. No, I wasn't in bankruptcy and I wasn't addicted to drugs and my wife hadn't left me. And yes, I had already had some pretty fair success. But hardly as much as I would have liked.

Certainly if I'd known I was going to be an author and a professional motivator, I would have found a way to sink far more deeply into the depths of abject despair. But I was still relatively young, and given all the advantages I'd started with, this was really the biggest failure I could muster at the time. I *was* broke. And it shook my confidence and it ticked me off. Badly. Especially since it seemed that virtually everyone else I knew was already a great success.

I decided that I was going to do one simple thing. I was going to see what I could accomplish if I found a decent sales job and did it as well as I possibly could do it. No matter how tired I might be on any given day. No matter how much I might feel like slowing down because I was ahead of quota or slacking off because I was behind.

Because like a lot of us, I knew I was better than what I appeared to be—which was a 30-year-old failure—but I honestly didn't know how good I could be. Because, in spite of the things I had accomplished, I'd never really done anything—not one single thing—as well as I could possibly do it. Not one single thing. In my entire life. So this was my way of measuring myself. This was to be my yardstick.

I had a strong résumé, so I managed to talk my way into a Fortune 100 sales organization. I wasn't even sure if I was good enough to be able to keep the job, much less to really succeed at it. They sent me to the home office for five weeks of classroom training. When I returned, my manager threw me out in the field by myself. He was far too busy politicking for promotion to have time for any actual sales managing. After two or three days of stumbling around, I'd sold virtually nothing.

I thought about quitting. I'd barely given it a try but I thought very seriously about quitting. Not because the work was tough. It wasn't. Not because I wasn't making any money. I was still on guarantee—being compensated as if I were making quota.

I almost quit because I was doing my absolute best, and I couldn't face the prospect of failing.

It's always easier to quit and walk away than it is to test yourself, to give your best and run the risk of proving to yourself that those nagging doubts about yourself—those three-in-the-morning doubts that we all have—might just be right. I was frightened of proving that I didn't have the potential I'd always believed—and I'd always needed to believe—that I had. I'd never used it. Not really. But I needed to believe I had it.

Fortunately, I managed to hold my fragile ego together and focus on my short-term goals. My very short-term goals: simply doing the best job I possibly could in the next call. And then in the one after that. Pretty soon I popped a small sale. Two calls later, I popped a big one. Then another.

It was like a revelation. I could play with the big boys, and I could succeed. Then I had to know: Just how far could I possibly go? Just how much could I succeed? And not incidentally, because I *was* broke and because in sales, money is the way you keep score, how much could I make?

The next week I made about $6,000. Not a bad week today, and a great week back in the early 1980s, especially for a guy whose bank account was in negative figures. I finished the year as the number-one rep in the company, out of about 900. I stayed number one from that point on—in spite of being in a business where reps didn't build up a territory, where we all started from scratch every year. I was making more money than anyone in the company with the single exception of the guy who was running the company.

Obviously, I worked hard. And, at first, I put in a lot of extra hours. Then something surprising happened. I was able to reduce those hours without reducing the results. Eventually I was working no more—and in some cases I was working less—than reps who were making a third of what I was making.

And I'd almost quit. Three days into a job that changed my life, I'd almost quit. And I never would have known how good I could be if I really gave it my all. Right now, I'd probably be working for some second-rate company making $35,000 or $40,000 a year. And none of the opportunities that have opened up for me since then would have ever materialized.

Instead of writing this book, I'd probably be searching through somebody else's book, looking for some secret to success.

Never settle for success.

A GOAL WITHOUT A NUMBER

To me, never settling for success is really several different strategies. First, as applied to your career, it means that your ultimate goal has no number attached to it. Your ultimate goal and your short-term, medium-term, and long-term goals all become essentially the same: to simply see how well you can perform if you perform as well as you possibly can; to utilize every ounce of talent you can muster in every applicable situation, each day, each week, each month. And after each significant interaction, and each day, each week, and each month, you evaluate yourself to fine-tune your course.

So you don't slack off when you're surpassing goals, so you don't give up when you're falling far behind.

"In college, I was a B and C student," a successful senior manager says, "until one semester I got irritated by a couple of the professors and busted my butt to become an A and B student. From that point on— once I realized what I could do—I was an A student. Likewise as a manager, I was always just a bit above average. Then I got passed over for a promotion I should have received. They gave it to a guy I could outmanage from a coma. So I busted my butt to give them numbers they couldn't ignore. I became one of the top managers in the region. But after that—after I realized I could do it—I became *the* top manager."

He also experienced the same time phenomenon I had. "I work more intensely now," he says. "But after the initial learning curve, it doesn't take that much more time to be the best than it took to be average."

We all know we can do more. We all know we can do better. But too frequently we settle for less. "There is more in us than we know," Kurt Hahn, the founder of Outward Bound, said. "If we can be made to see it, perhaps, for the rest of our lives, we will be unwilling to settle for less."

Never settling for success is about being unwilling to settle for less.

TIP: Great leadership is about showing your people that there is more in them than they know—so they'll be unwilling to settle for less.

Great leadership is also about helping your people to overcome the fear of failure, the fear of giving their best, yet not being the best— perhaps not even being all that good—and proving to themselves, to you their boss, and to those around them that they do not have the potential they all want to believe they have.

TIP: You can't help your people overcome their fear of failure unless you first overcome your own. If you're afraid of failure, your people will be afraid.

Pollyanna positive thinkers will tell you that you can do whatever you think you can, that you have no limits. That can work, until you run headfirst into one of those limits, and crash and burn.

You have limits. I have limits. We are human beings, we are limited, we are fallible. That's reality. Pat little bromides that try to convince us otherwise, notwithstanding.

Here's my pat little bromide: You can do far more than you think you can. You have limits, but they're expanding limits. And running up against them can be great practice for expanding them in the future. In all likelihood you've never pushed those limits anywhere near as far as they can be pushed. Most of the time, we're stopped by the limits we impose on ourselves long before we'd ever be stopped by the limits imposed by reality.

I don't know what your potential is. In all likelihood, neither do you. Maybe it's time you should try to find out. With the possible exception of daytime TV, potential is the most useless thing on the planet—if it remains only potential.

By any standard, one of the most successful people this country ever produced was Benjamin Franklin. Every night before sleeping—and not just on those rare nights when he was sleeping alone (because he was very successful at that, too)—Franklin would review his entire day. He'd evaluate everything he'd done and try to puzzle out how he could have done it better. Philosopher, scientist, inventor, diplomat, revolutionary, publisher, cabinet member, Franklin's bad days were probably more successful than most of our best ones. Because success was never good enough for Ben Franklin. "Success," he said, "has ruined many a man."

The truly successful, in any field, never settle for success.

TAKE A RUN AT YOUR POTENTIAL

Never settling for success is often a great way of filling the glass. If you're not getting the recognition or the respect or the advancement or the pay you want out of life, try filling the glass with your own efforts: take a run at the limits of your own potential and see what it gets you.

Are your efforts toward your goals shortchanging your company? That's unfortunate.

Are your efforts shortchanging yourself?

That's tragic.

Can you fail? Absolutely. That's the challenge of it. That's the fun of it. That's where the growth is and the opportunity. Why would you bother to play a game you knew you could never lose? But people with a lot less going for them are succeeding at something you'd like to succeed at every day. Other people with more going for them are sitting on their hands and letting their lives pass them by, letting things happen to them instead of going out and happening to things.

A successful CEO called a friend right after agreeing to head a new company in an entirely different industry. "I took this job because it was something I never in my wildest dreams envisioned I could do," he said. "Between you and me, it scares the hell out of me. Sure, confidence is important. But I take confidence in the fact that none of us—no matter how confident we might seem—are completely confident when confronting an unknown situation. That's the challenge. And the fear. And the fun. At the very least it'll be an interesting ride. I won't be bored."

When Andrea Jung become the first woman to head Avon, one of only four women running a Fortune 500 company, she echoed those sentiments. "Am I overwhelmed, a little bit scared? Absolutely. Do I think it's a good feeling? Yes."

KAROSHI

The Japanese have a word for death by overwork: *karoshi*. A recent survey said 40 percent of all Japanese workers fear that they will actually work themselves to death.

Karoshi is not my idea of success. Never settling for success is not a prescription for becoming an obsessive or a workaholic. That type of single-mindedness is more likely to lead to burnout than peak performance. Never settling for success simply means that you commit to maximum effort within the hours of your life that you've allotted for pursuing a particular pursuit. And you do that in spite of the 1,001 excruciatingly attractive reasons, excuses, distractions, and temptations that you can find for doing less.

TIP: *Focus* is a good buzzword. *Multitasking* is a bad one. Computers multitask, and usually lose efficiency when they do. When people do it, it's usually not multitasking at all; it's usually that older cliché: spreading yourself too thin.

TIP: During working hours, consider working.

TIP: During nonworking hours, consider doing something else.

Now obviously given the realities of life today, there are likely to be times when you're going to have to work during what you would like to be nonworking hours. Sometimes. But you'll never fill the glass unless—at least generally speaking—you can find a way to be as comfortable as possible with the amount of your life you're devoting to the job. Then you make those hours as productive as possible.

"If I worked as much as others," Stephen Wright said, "I would do as little as they." There's more than a grain of truth to that statement.

Fortunately, as a society we're finally beginning to realize that chronic overwork is not a badge of honor; it's a sign that somewhere, something is wrong.

TIP: If you don't have something in your life more worthy of bragging about, find something.

TIP: If you find yourself proudly bragging about your hours or your workload, you're probably putting in more time than you should.

TIP: Intelligent people don't brag about being overworked. They complain about being overworked.

"Working hard has always been a measure of success in the office," says Alie Hochchild, author of *The Time Bind.* "Now we've internalized it. So instead of the boss harassing you to work more, we do it to ourselves."

The better the manager, the less time it takes him to do his job. A good worker takes care of her health and her sanity, and is as productive as possible during the hours she is working. An astute company values its people and doesn't abuse them or any other asset.

Yet on consulting assignments, I keep hearing remarks like, "Around here, if you don't show your face early mornings, late nights, and weekends, you're not considered committed." I've seen low-level managers cowering in their cubicles, pretending to be busy, afraid to leave the office before their boss leaves—no matter how late it gets, no matter how little they're accomplishing. If they do leave first, it's commented on the next day, either by the boss or by their peers.

I remember an executive who made a great show of carrying home armloads of work every night. Sometimes he had so much he had to make two trips to the car. After I got to know him, he admitted he never worked on any of it. He just lugged it home at night, then lugged it back the next day.

"Don't laugh," he said, patting the pile he was gathering for that night. "I'm considered one of the hardest workers in the office. And it's always a lot easier to influence the guy I'm working for with reputation than with achievement, believe me."

ACTIVITY VERSUS PRODUCTIVITY

The idea—for those of us who sometimes forget—is to get the job done as well and as efficiently as possible. I'm always in favor of letting your results do the talking, and of measuring subordinates by the results they achieve. When I was an employee I wanted to be so good at what I did that I didn't have to worry about trying to impress anybody any other way. That saved me a lot of wasted energy—energy that probably helped improve my productivity.

In sales, you can never confuse activity with productivity. No matter how many hours someone puts in, no matter how much he appears to be working, the only measurement that really matters is the results.

TIP: In business, the only measurement that really matters is the results.

The refreshing news nowadays is that among all the people bragging about their long hours, we're also beginning to hear a few executives boasting that they're good enough at what they do to be able to leave at a decent hour, to get more done, and have time to get home and refresh themselves so they can put in another efficient day's work the next day.

> **TIP:** Never let your company, your boss, your boss's boss, or anyone else make you feel guilty that you're not a workaholic.

Workaholics are people with problems. Do you feel guilty that you're not obsessed by sex (okay, would you feel guilty if you weren't)? Or by chocolate? Do you feel guilty that you don't want to spend your entire life playing golf, loafing, reading, or watching TV? Or that you're not addicted to alcohol or narcotics? Why should you feel guilty that you're too well rounded an individual to want to spend your entire life working?

Barbara Gorski is a self-admitted workaholic who's written on workaholics in her doctoral thesis. "I use work to cope, to achieve self-esteem, to find meaning in my life," she reports. If that's you, and that makes you happy, great. But there are at least 60 Workaholics Anonymous chapters around the country, suggesting some of us might like to see the spouse or the kids from time to time.

Writer Ted Janusz believes that we sometimes focus on work to the neglect of what we supposedly consider to be the more important things in life because work "can be quantified in ways that other parts of life often can't." At work we know we have to make our numbers and we know what the numbers are; evaluations tend to be straightforward and feedback is often immediate. "So when trying to decide between watching your child in a school play or staying late to complete a report that could determine a raise or promotion, which would you chose?"

Which is really the best use of your time?

GETTING THE CAMEL THROUGH THE NEEDLE

Never settling for success also means never settling for mere material success. As Benjamin Franklin would have been the first to point out, lasting satisfaction in life is not for sale.

We all know that you can't buy your way to happiness. Every guru and every religion teaches that—often right before they pass the collection plate. But we all keep trying. There's certainly nothing wrong with achieving financial security. But is that all you really want?

"Security is mostly a superstition. It does not exist in nature . . . Life is either a daring adventure or nothing."

That's a great quote. Helen Keller said it. But I don't think you have to go through what she did to appreciate life as a daring adventure; it shouldn't even be an advantage.

Recent studies are proving that those who make affluence their focus in life experience an unusually high degree of anxiety and depression, as well as more behavioral problems and even more physical problems than the population in general. Dr. Richard Ryan, professor of psychology at University of Rochester, calls this "the dark side of the American dream," adding that our culture seems to be built on the very factors that are detrimental to our mental well-being. "The more we seek satisfaction in material goods, the less we find them there," says Ryan. And the satisfactions we do find are very fleeting.

Ted Turner's father was a man who achieved his main goal in life—becoming a millionaire—and felt there was nothing left for him to do. Turner believes that was at least part of the reason he killed himself at age 53.

The problem of course is not affluence. There's nothing wrong with being rich; I would never say there was. First of all, I'd like to be rich myself. Second, nobody would pay the slightest bit of attention if I did say it. For good, bad, or indifferent, we live in a world where "Jesus CEO" has taken precedence over the Jesus who said that it was easier for a camel to pass through the eye of a needle than for a rich man to enter the kingdom of Heaven. I don't know that that's necessarily a bad development. I've never found poverty to be, in itself, particularly ennobling. In any case, my job is to help people get what they want, not to try to convince them to want what I think they should.

Still, as far as I can see, affluence itself isn't the problem; I wish the whole world were affluent. The problem seems to come in what Dr. Ryan calls "living a life where affluence is your focus."

Someone once said that life is like juggling in your bare feet. You've got five balls in the air: work, family, health, friends, and spirit. Work's a rubber ball. Drop it and it will bounce back. (I don't think this guy ever worked for some of the companies I've worked for, but you get the idea.) The other four balls are made of glass. Drop them and you'll be walking around on broken glass for the rest of your life. And you're probably not going to be doing a lot of dancing.

> **TIP:** You're asking much more of your career than it's likely to be able to supply if you can't find satisfaction in any other aspect of life.

CHAPTER 17

Enjoy

Now we're going to talk about sex.

That's called an interest-creating remark. Which is a good way to start off any sales presentation. And I'm about to try to sell you a concept. It's the simplest and most self-evident concept in the book. It shouldn't take any selling at all, yet it always seems to be the hardest sell. And the concept is?

Enjoy.

It's really a part of never settling for success, but if you like, you can consider this a bonus strategy: number eleven of the ten filling-the-glass strategies.

To try to sell you this concept, I'm going to talk about sex. At least I'm going to talk a bit about sex and a lot about selling. Which is probably because I know a lot more about selling than I know about sex.

The first thing I tell salespeople—the most important thing I ever tell salespeople—is that selling is like sex: if you're not having fun, you're not doing it right. The converse is also true: if you're not doing it right, you're probably not having any fun.

I would suspect the same is true about your job. And your career. And your life.

Have fun with your job. The last thing I tell myself before I start work every morning is just that, "Have fun—enjoy." If you've read this far, you realize that I write for my own entertainment as well as yours.

Having fun and enjoying your job is one of the best ways of filling the glass. If you can't enjoy your job, you've got a leaky glass that's going to be very difficult to fill. You may need to consider finding something else to do with your life.

Don't save sex for your old age. Don't save enjoyment. Or fun. Or happiness. Not if you can possibly help it.

LAUGHTER

What do you do when you're making a presentation or having a discussion and everything goes wrong, when you fumble or stumble, when you can't find the numbers you need to refer to, when the numbers you do find are wrong?

Try laughter. Try making a joke out of it, using self-deprecating humor. It shows confidence. It shows that you're amazed things went wrong. It makes what could be a problem fun for the people you're dealing with.

Humor sells. In one study of humor in negotiation, "buyers" who made their final offer with a smile and a quip, "Well, my final offer is x dollars and I'll throw in my pet frog," were able to make the buy at a lower price. Sellers who laughed out loud were even more likely to grant concessions than those who didn't. Imagine if the joke had actually been funny.

Salespeople use humor to get attention, to build rapport, to break down resistance, to make a point more memorable: to get people to listen and to enjoy listening. Professional speakers do the same. The old dictum is true: When you use humor, you don't have to yell. Always makes sure the humor is appropriate, of course; and always use it with care. Some people will throw up barriers if you appear to be getting overly friendly too fast.

"If you would rule the world quietly," Emerson said, "you must keep it amused." You can rule the office the same way. In *The Light Touch,* Malcolm L. Kushner notes that humor "can relieve tension, enhance relationships, and motivate people, if it's used correctly. In today's competitive environment . . . humor can provide the winning edge."

Business is like sex. It's not supposed to be painful.

Kushner tells a story of Adelle Roberts, a police officer called to the scene of a domestic disturbance. As she approached the house, a TV came flying out a window. She knocked loudly to be heard over the yelling.

"Who is it?" an angry male voice snarled.

"TV repairman," Roberts replied.

The man burst into laughter, and opened the door. She probably wouldn't have gotten quite that response if she'd said, "Police."

Humor's effectiveness in diffusing anger and breaking down resistance can be particularly important in today's work environment. In one study, 49 percent of the respondents said they're usually at least a little angry on the job. *Forty-nine percent* say they are *usually* angry.

I've known salespeople who have been threatened with guns. Some of them deserved it. Though that's carrying sales resistance to an extreme.

TIP: Nobody is going to shoot you while they're laughing.

TIP: Long after people have forgotten what was said, they'll remember how they felt about the person who said it.

Self-deprecating humor is also a great way for executives and managers to put themselves on the same level as their subordinates. It shows they can take a joke, that they too put their pants or their pantyhose on one leg at a time.

When Jack Kennedy wanted to defuse the issue of his family's wealth, he told everyone he'd just gotten a telegram from his father. "Dear Jack," he read, "Don't buy one more vote than necessary. I'll be damned if I'll pay for a landslide."

A new manager was obligated to post a lengthy list of rules right after being promoted to the position: hardly the best rapport builder. He posted the list all right, but he signed it at the bottom, "A. Hitler, Gruppenfuehrer." His superior snatched it off the wall as, "inappropriate." Perhaps. But by then everyone had already seen it.

"We'd read the rules," one worker reports. "We figured the *Gruppenfuehrer* was going to enforce them. We knew the iron fist was there, and we appreciated that he'd stuck it in a velvet glove and used it to poke a little fun at himself. Otherwise we'd have seen it as a new guy coming in and throwing his weight around."

Another midlevel manager had a grumpy-looking doll with a tape recorder inside that he'd programmed to say, "Get your mangy butts back on the job and stop wasting the company's time." The doll would deliver the message whenever the manager decided it was needed. People took the hint, and nobody was offended.

As humor expert Kushner says, "Learn to take your work seriously without taking yourself so seriously. No matter how serious your work or topic, it's always safe to poke fun at yourself." Still, don't overdo the self-deprecation. You don't want to end up looking like a neurotic, bumbling cartoon character. I once had a boss who was constantly making fun of himself. Everybody liked him. Few respected him.

Apparently, laughter even makes you healthier: reducing stress, stimulating the immune system, speeding recovery, lessening pain, increasing alertness, improving memory. According to one researcher, it's even exercise. One hundred laughs is the equivalent of ten minutes on a rowing machine. And you don't get blisters on your butt from laughing. At least not usually.

In India, laughter guru Dr. Madam Kataria holds sessions where people simply get together and laugh. No jokes, just laughter and "laughter exercises," whatever they are. I assume the doctor charges for this. (And I thought motivational speakers had a great gig.)

EXISTENTIAL SEX

It's been said that virtue is its own reward. Perhaps. Enjoyment certainly is. But it can also be good business, and good management. You're in business for the long haul. If you can make the journey even more enjoyable than the destination—for yourself and your people— you're going to have a better trip. The more odious the journey, the more difficult it's going to be for the destination to be wonderful enough to make the trip worth the effort. And the more likely you and everyone with you are to be disappointed once the goal is finally reached.

Business can be like sex. And sex is the most existential thing in the entire universe: getting there is *all* the fun.

Enjoy. Have fun. I know this is work we're talking about here and they don't pay you all that money because it's easy. But that doesn't mean it can't be fun. The business gurus of Zimbabwe used to say, "If you can walk, you can dance. If you can talk, you can sing."

Dance. Sing.

Sure, you're anxious to reach your long-term goals. But if you can't appreciate what you already have, what makes you think you'll appreciate whatever it is you're working so hard to get? Don't put off sex until your old age.

Work at making your job enjoyable. Imagine how great your life would be if you got as much enjoyment from your job as you do from your favorite hobby. Imagine what your people could accomplish if you could help them have that type of enjoyment, if you could give them as much motivation for the job as they have their greatest passions in life.

Can you do that? Probably not. This isn't Oz, this is the planet Earth. How much fun can anyone have stripping the hair and fat from dead hogs? But the closer you move in that direction—even if it's only a step or two—the greater the benefits for you, your people, and your company.

WALK THE ELEPHANT

If you're trying to make the job fun for your people, watch out for simply foisting your own concept of fun on them. One supervisor created dissention by scattering candy dishes around an office where most of the employees were trying to diet. She had Muzak pumped in, and everyone hated the music she selected. Then she decided to fill the office with motivational banners, and insisted that everyone contribute a saying. This, at least, was fun for one person. The last time I was there, his inspirational message still hung proudly by the main entrance: "Walk the elephant and pitch to the giraffe."

You may not find that inspirational. You may even find it confusing, if you don't recognize it as the answer to the ancient philosophical question: "What do you do with an elephant with three balls?"

You walk the elephant and pitch to the giraffe. Let that be an inspiration to us all.

MORE LINCOLN

We've already talked about what Lincoln went through both before and after he became president: from political defeats to debilitating bouts of depression, to civil war. He also endured the death of an adored child, and a wife who made Glenn Close's character in *Fatal Attraction* look like Harriet Nelson. Yet with all that, Lincoln concluded that people are just about as happy as they make up their minds to be.

> **TIP:** Make up your mind to be happy, to have fun, to enjoy. See what happens.

Obviously there are an infinite number of tactics that can add to your enjoyment of life—that can increase your happiness. The only question is, why don't more people seem to be using any of them? You know far better than I what it takes to make your life more enjoyable. But here are a few tactics that those I've worked with have found to be particularly effective.

> **TACTIC:** It's been said a thousand times, but let me start out by saying it again. Cultivate your relationships with family and friends. James M. Citrin, coauthor of *Lessons from the Top*, says, "True success is not a trade-off between one's professional life and family life. Contrary to conventional wisdom . . . there is a causal relationship between a strong family life and the greatest levels of professional accomplishment." And friendships in your business or your personal life don't just happen. They need to be cultivated. Cultivate them.

Psychologists insist that if you want to pursue happiness, caring and loving relationships should be a priority. I think that means before money. Strong relationships also increase your resiliency: your ability to deal with adversity. In this country, though, many of us have trouble accepting that. The myth of the rugged individual pulling himself up by his bootstraps is too strong.

> **TIP:** Stand up. Reach down and grab your own bootstraps. Pull. See how far you get by yourself. It's like trying to lift yourself by the nose.

CEOs trying to create family-friendly companies are learning to practice what they preach. And not just to save their own families. Vance Brown, CEO of Goldmine Software, says, "I call it 'the balance effect.' With employee capital our most important asset, we need employees to live balanced lives. To protect that capital, if for no other reason. But you can't talk it and not live it. Employees see right through that. You've got to be the role model."

As Vance and I talked, his two-year-old was drawing on the office white board. The real treat for the boy would come when he discovered that the drawing would print out. And that he could take it with him when he and Dad left for home in a few minutes.

Mike Goodrich, CEO of the engineering and construction firm BE&K, once had a client meeting run late. It was Halloween and Goodrich had promised to go trick-or-treating with one of his kids. He left the meeting. Not a bad standard to set for employees concerned about balancing their home and work life.

> **TACTIC:** Even when you have to travel, you don't always have to travel alone. There may be times when you can take your spouse or even your whole family with you on business trips. About 25 million business trips a year include a child. Your spouse and the kids take in the sights while you're working, and it becomes a minivacation for the family. Maybe that's the best use for those frequent flier miles you've been building up. And if you stay over a Saturday, the company saves money.

> **TACTIC:** Even when they aren't customers, treat the strangers you deal with as people—even those you encounter by phone or through e-mail. People are more fun to deal with than faceless functionaries. It's amazing how much this improves the immediate results you get from these individuals, and how much the relationships you develop can ultimately help you in business. What's even more amazing is how much they can add to your life.

> **TACTIC:** Salespeople are goal-oriented, not time-oriented. If you focus on the clock, time drags and little is accomplished. On the other hand, you know how time compresses when it's extremely limited and you've got a goal to achieve. And that's

true no matter how arduous the task. Think of taking the college boards. You might have had two hours for a section but those two hours were gone long before they should have been. And you still had more to do.

Time *is* extremely limited. You do have a goal to achieve. Focus on what you're trying to accomplish and get the most out of each passing moment.

TACTIC: Do something nice for yourself during the work week, something outside of the same old rut, even if it's nothing more than going out to a movie. If you're living for the weekend, the weekend is seldom wonderful enough to justify your expectations, leaving you let down and depressed on Sunday night and suicidal on Monday mornings.

TACTIC: If you're lugging around regrets about something you didn't do in the past, ask yourself, *Is it really too late?* If it's that move you didn't make on the head cheerleader or star quarter-back 20 years ago in high school, the answer is probably yes. For a lot of other things though, where you might be telling yourself it's too late or you're too old . . . you aren't and you know you aren't. Not if you really want to do it. If not now, when?

Never? Fine. But that's a choice you're making. Just like the choice you made earlier, the one you now regret.

Imagine you're 20 years older than you are today, or 10 years older. What are you likely to regret that you didn't do today? How much would you give at that point to regain the opportunities that you have right now but aren't using?

SOMETHING YOU ALREADY KNOW

TACTIC: Exercise your body.

You'll have more energy and accomplish more during work, and you'll feel better at the end of the day. Do it regularly, at least three times a week, and your body will crave it, telling you when you need it. You'll even find yourself looking forward to it. Avoid the trap of trying to do too much too soon. If you can't do anything else, just take a brisk walk. You'll feel the tension flowing out of you.

At the University of Wisconsin, researchers on depression found that sufferers who jogged showed more improvement than those who underwent psychotherapy. Of course I've heard of other studies that showed that doing nothing for mental problems works just as well as psychotherapy. But that still means that jogging works better than doing nothing. According to Jim Fixx in *The Complete Book of Running,* a factory in the old Soviet Union reduced its annual sick days from 436 to 42 after instituting a running program for all its employees. (And yes, Jim Fixx did run himself into a heart attack. In setting up an exercise program, I'd rely on my doctor's advice before anything I read in some self-help book.)

Your body needs exercise, just as it needs food and water—just as your brain needs stimulation. If you don't give it what it needs, if you don't maintain it as you should, it's not likely to work as well as it should for as long as it should. You aren't going to feel as well as you could, and if you don't feel as well as you could, you aren't going to be as happy or as productive as you could be.

Of course you already know that. But here's something else you know: Knowing something is worthless if you don't act on it.

SHOE MUSEUMS AND BOY SCOUTS

TACTIC: Exercise your mind. Keep learning. Learn about whatever interests you. Pick up a little basic background in a few things that you never thought would interest you at all or that you never thought you could absorb. Read. Personally, whatever else I might read, I make it a point to read every article in every single issue of *Smithsonian* magazine every month because it exposes me to such an encyclopedic variety of topics. A few are as boring as an afternoon in a shoe museum. Many are fascinating, and most of the rest—like the recent article on the shoe museum—are far more interesting than you'd ever expect.

TACTIC: Remember the way the Boy Scouts used to do one good deed a day? Try it. Try to make a small difference in one person's life every day with a bit of sincere praise or encouragement. It'll make you feel better. It certainly beats sitting around thinking of how rude and inconsiderate everyone seems to be nowadays. Not everyone is inconsiderate. You're not. At least not always.

THE WONG WAY

TACTIC: If your job is keeping you from activities you used to enjoy, make a point of doing at least one of those things every week. Or make a list of things you've wanted to do but haven't gotten around to doing. Then start getting around to them.

TACTIC: Consider earning more time off.

More and more people are deciding that they don't need the cheese badly enough to put up with the rat race. Albert Wong left the turmoil of AST Research, the multi-billion-dollar computer company he'd co-founded. He took a year off to relax, spend time with his kids, and cook. Today he owns a much smaller company and—one would hope—leads a less stressful, more satisfying life.

Perhaps filling the glass for you might mean cutting back on expenses, so you can cut back on work, or afford to work at a less lucrative job and enjoy more time off. As I noted in the previous chapter, too many of us are working more and more hours. In a recent survey, the Family and Work Institute found that in the last 20 years, the time spent on the average full-time job has risen from 43.6 to 47.1 hours per week. That's an extra month of 8-hour days a year.

More of us are also working more jobs. Vacation time and sick time are down. And some of those vacations aren't exactly getaways. One emergency rescue team located hikers stranded in the wilderness who'd remembered to bring their laptop computer but had forgotten to bring adequate food and water.

The nonstop busy-ness from the office is taking over our home lives as well. As Alie Hochchild notes in *The Time Bind,* the day-planner mentality runs 24 hours a day, seven days a week, filling up our lives and the lives of our children—with social obligations, play dates, and riding lessons—in 15-minute increments. Relaxation time is almost accidental.

It's not even relaxation anymore, it's considered *downtime,* the implication being that the proper, efficient use of our time is work. *Downtime* is a term for machinery: sometimes necessary, ideally as brief as possible, something that any efficient operation wants to minimize.

And to think that the generation that's invented phrases like *downtime* and *multitasking* is the same one that used to worry about becoming cogs in the machinery of business.

There are sociologists who scoff at this so-called decline of leisure, and tell us that the reason we feel we have less time is that we waste so much of it watching TV or surfing the Internet. That may be the case. Certainly it would be great to have the time that most of us—myself included—waste. But what's your experience? Do you feel you're working more than ever? Or working more jobs and repeating the old joke that you've just heard that the economy created another 200,000 jobs, and that you've got 3 of them?

You might think about what you're working for. And whether you might be happier simplifying your life and cutting your spending. In *Choose to Live Peacefully,* Susan Smith Jones, Ph.D., writes that simplification is to your life what rejuvenation is to your body. She adds, "You don't have to continually go faster simply because everyone else is doing so."

As Thoreau said, "The man is richest whose pleasures are the cheapest." He seemed to be having a pretty good time in that shack at Walden Pond. Though as I remember he spent a year there, not a lifetime.

Mary Ann Halpin and her husband Joe Croyle used to run a photo studio in downtown Los Angeles, working ten hours a day, six days a week. Even so, the overhead was so high, it was a constant struggle to pay the rent. Nowadays they work out of their home, four days a week, and spend the rest of their time relaxing and enjoying life.

"People are always saying to me, 'You're so lucky,'" Halpin told home-office experts Paul and Sarah Edwards. "But it has nothing to do with luck. It's figuring out what you value, what makes you happy, and what brings you peace, and then slowing down your life enough . . . to make the changes you need."

What you choose to spend your money on is your own business. But perhaps you should evaluate potential purchases in terms of the hours out of your life it takes to get them. Because that's what everything you buy actually costs: hours out of your life. According to *Money* magazine, in average wages, in 1916 it took 3,162 hours of work to earn a refrigerator. Today it takes 68. Refrigerators have gotten a lot cheaper. Of course a year of public college tuition has gone from 160 hours in 1966 to 260; and a year at a private college has increased from 537 hours to 1,295.

TACTIC: Figure out what you net for an hour's work. Then figure out how many hours that new blouse or suit or SUV would cost you. If you get that much enjoyment out of it, great. If not, maybe you'd rather have the hours instead. And maybe you can find a way to get those hours back, either now or a few years down the road. Thanks to the wonder of compounding, a penny saved can soon be a lot more than a penny earned. What's the secret of *The Millionaire Next Door?* According to the authors of that book, it's lifestyle. Not self-denial, just not wasting money any more than you should waste time.

The average family has gotten smaller in the last 50 years, but the average new home has doubled in size. And it's filled with a lot more stuff.

TIP: We keep hearing that time is money. Time is far more than money. "It's more valuable than platinum and more perishable than a sunset," is the flowery way a former professor of mine used to put it. But the money we spend is—in a very real sense—time. And that money, as Emerson noted, is often far too expensive.

In our society, luxuries quickly turn themselves into necessities, wants into needs. We rail against materialism to our children at the same time that we teach them that shopping—buying for the sake of buying—is a hobby, a leisure pursuit. In a recent study, 71 percent of Americans saw TV as a necessity in their lives, 40 percent thought microwaves were, over 25 percent listed VCRs, answering machines, TV remote controls, computers, and basic cable TV. About one in six said a second TV was a necessity. These people were serious. The more affluent among us of course are the most needy, most likely to have the most clutter crammed into the necessity level of their hierarchy of needs. For example, 56 percent of those making over $50,000 per year believed they couldn't survive without credit cards.

A much better self-help book than this one was the source of that observation that it's easier for a camel to pass through the eye of a needle than for a rich person to enter the kingdom of Heaven. Of course, it didn't say it couldn't be done. We're an extremely wealthy country. Still, maybe too many of us spend too much of our time trying to cram some really big camels through some very small needles.

Oscar winner Rod Steiger told *Modern Maturity* that to him success means having control over the time in his life. "A shoemaker who owns his own shop and gets up one morning and says, 'I'm not working'— that's a successful guy."

AN ATTITUDE OF GRATITUDE

TACTIC: Do more than one good deed a day.

Ben Cohen of Ben & Jerry's Ice Cream quit as CEO to spend more time working for charity and pursuing his interests in the arts. Like so many others, networking expert Jacque Daniel does charitable work in her spare time. "I always want to have what I call an 'attitude of gratitude,'" she says. "Helping others helps get me away from my own problems. Sometimes when I'm away the problem solves itself. Even when it doesn't, at least I'm in a better mood to try again."

Nonprofit groups are desperate for people with business skills. And you'll never find a more satisfying way to use them. Bill Shore is the founder of Share Our Strength, a group that takes a businesslike, profit-minded approach to altruism. To Shore, helping others is the best way to help yourself and to help build a better world. And using your skills to help nonprofit groups create wealth may be the best way to help others.

"Creating wealth is fun," says Shore. "But you can have that fun and fulfill your need to give back at the same time. It's so simple."

Some nonprofit groups offer service vacations. You get a low-cost vacation, a chance to travel and, at the same time, an opportunity to help others and be part of something worthwhile.

Pat Bakar of Atlanta always wanted to join the Peace Corps. She took her vacation working for Global Citizens Network and helped build a health center in Kenya. For 15 years, Bill Sheppard's vacation trips had him creating and repairing trails with the Sierra Club. Then he retired. At least, he retired from work. He still takes the vacations. Other "vacationers" work with groups like Habitat for Humanity or provide labor at archeological digs.

Then there are those who fill the glass by filling the chalice. Nowadays, more than half of those entering seminaries to become ministers, priests, or rabbis are over 35. Ted Schmitt was senior vice president of the Home Entertainment division of Universal Studios when some rough times caused him to reevaluate his long-term goals.

"I didn't think that I had the ability *not* to be selfish, not to worry about money and things, but those things aren't important," he told *Parade* magazine. "Now I have no aspirations to do anything but to be a good priest."

David Miller's story appeared in the same article. Miller wrote 500 business associates explaining his reasons for leaving banking and going to Princeton Theological Seminary to study religion. He thought he might get a few replies. He got over 200, every one of them positive. Beyond that, he said, "I was struck by the number of people who were really hurting. Seeing that sort of validated what I did."

Others are bringing their religion or at least their spirituality into the workplace. According to one recent survey, when employees work for organizations they consider spiritual, they report that they're less fearful, less likely to compromise their values, and better able to fully commit to their work. Some respondents believed spirituality could be the ultimate competitive advantage. Others thought spirituality at work could be beneficial as long as it wasn't used to promote a particular religion.

Obviously, that's the problem. I can remember the complaints—from believers and nonbelievers alike—when a corporate vice president pulled out the Bible and tried to preach his sales force into higher sales.

Business Week reports there's been a 29 percent increase in religious discrimination charges since 1992; the more receptive that businesses are to prayer meetings or study groups or religious seminars, the more likely they are to experience conflicts.

And as *Business Week* noted, how do you handle "the maintenance man who insisted he was the Messiah, the administrative assistant who routinely dropped to her knees outside of people's cubicles to speak in tongues, and the male witch who insisted on having Halloween off?"

One woman sued her former boss, a police chief who, she says, believed he was on a mission from God to save as many people from damnation as possible. She claimed he objected to her living with a female roommate, and accused her of watching pornography with men, having sex with members of her own family, and sacrificing animals to the devil. She said he told her that if she didn't straighten out she'd be better off simply killing herself. The chief denied the charges. The woman settled the case for over $100,000.

THE ACADEMY OF LEISURE SCIENCES

TACTIC: Enjoy every minute of free time you do have.

Did you know that there's an Academy of Leisure Sciences? (And, no, they don't meet in a bowling alley.) According to the academy, we are losing the skills we need to get the most out of our time off. We spend too much time with passive entertainment—TV, videos, movies, activities that provide immediate gratification but no challenge.

"You could argue that understimulation provokes anxiety," says Dr. Geoffrey Godbey, professor of leisure studies at Penn State. When I mentioned Dr. Godbey's position at a recent workshop, someone wanted to know if there was a Chair of Leisure Studies at Penn State—and if it was a La-Z-Boy. Cheap humor aside, research suggests that activities requiring higher levels of physical and intellectual energy yield higher satisfaction. Which means that you might feel like just watching the tube when you get home from work, but you'll probably get more out of playing with the kids, or learning the bassoon, or building a model railroad.

The average American spends a third of his or her free time watching TV. Socializing and reading are a very distant second and third. These same people report that they'd like to see more of their friends and they'd like to read more but they just don't have the time.

There's even a theory that we tend to regard the characters on our favorite TV shows as our friends. And that too many of these "friends" are too happy and too affluent, increasing the dissatisfaction we feel with our own lives. I'm not sure watching shows about poor, unhappy people would make us feel better: though that might explain the popularity of the *Jerry Springer Show.*

Interestingly, research indicates that the longer a person watches television, the less he or she enjoys it, but the more difficult it becomes to turn it off.

> **TACTIC:** Use your leisure time to complement your job—to round out your life with elements that might otherwise be missing.

If you're a brain surgeon and have to spend all day in the strictest mental concentration, you might find rejuvenation in a strenuous physical workout or even in something as mindless as washing the car. On the other hand, if you work at a car wash, exhausting your body and boring the hell out of your mind, try taking up a hobby that requires intense concentration—though perhaps not brain surgery.

"I work alone," a magazine writer says. "I often feel isolated. My only hobby was long-distance running, which made things worse. I would have taken up group sex if I wasn't so much of a hypochondriac, but I finally settled on joining a tennis club. You meet almost as many people and the locker rooms are cleaner."

A salesman I know has a daughter with a birth defect. He thought he could help fill his glass by aiding the charity that had done so much for his family and for others in the same situation.

"I figured my selling skills made me the perfect fund-raiser," he said. "But after hearing No after No all day long, getting turned down by potential donors in the evening was just too much. So I switched to the distribution end of the charity. I'm not asking, I'm giving. Everyone's thrilled to talk to me—and that's not always the case during the day, believe me." Now he can hardly wait to get started in the evening. It's enhanced his life, his attitude, and his selling career.

TIME FRAGMENTS

TACTIC: Use "useless" time. One of the reasons we feel we have less free time is that much of it comes in small, apparently useless time fragments: the 20 minutes you spend waiting for someone or waiting for something to happen; the 7 minutes after you finish getting ready for work, but before you need to leave.

Salespeople often find their days full of time fragments: with gaps between appointments, calls ending early, and cancellations. They become expert one-minute managers. Every minute of work they complete during a fragment is a minute of work they won't have to do later.

Don't squander pieces of your life, no matter how small. If you can't work or simply prefer not to, read. Do relaxation exercises. Take one of those one-minute vacations I mentioned earlier. Does waiting in line or just waiting for anything stress you out? Why not use the time to consciously relax or to change the scale and gain perspective on your life? Or use it to enjoy the day; to examine the people or the architecture around you; to work on your posture; to practice deep breathing; to try to figure out what happened to Jimmy Hoffa or Amelia Earhart; anything.

TIP: Use waiting time to decrease your aggravation, not to increase it.

TACTIC: Managing your time successfully doesn't mean cramming as much as you can possibly cram into every minute, every hour, and every day. It means using your time to do the things that get you closer to the goals you want to reach.

ONE FINAL TACTIC

TACTIC: Know who you are. And that's aside from being CEO of Amalgamated Amalgates. If your self-worth is dependent on your work, you are heading for a fall, sooner or—at the very least—later, when retirement comes. There's more to you than what you do for a living. Or at least there should be.

You aren't your job, no matter how successful or how unsuccessful you are at that job. We all know some big career successes who are very unsuccessful people. And some who are very unhappy. None of us should be surprised that there are some very successful and very happy people—great friends, loving spouses, wonderful role models for their children—who have never cashed a big paycheck.

"His picture hangs on every wall," one self-described peon said of the company's chairman of the board. "His name is invoked in reverential tones. But aside from making himself very rich, what does he really do for the world? Besides making it safe for one more set of unnecessary, environmentally devastating, energy wasting products."

"He's helping to perpetuate a lot of jobs," I answered. "Yours included."

"He is. But judging by the happiness the people around here seem to be getting from those jobs, they may not be eulogizing him at his funeral for that."

> **TIP:** Maybe you're already better off than you would be if you were successful—by the standard definition of success. Especially if that's not really your definition.

A friend once said of his very successful partner, "He gave up his life in the single-minded pursuit of wealth. And once he got there he found that wealth was all he had. Which means he obsesses about losing it. Since he never had a life, he has no idea of what to do with his money, even if he had time to enjoy it, which he doesn't because he's so accustomed to the treadmill he can't even imagine getting off. Of course, the beautiful thing about the pursuit of money is that it's never enough. So he keeps on chasing it, simply because he has no idea of what else to do with his life."

I like money as much as anyone—more than many. And a big title impresses. (It especially impresses small minds, those we're least interested in impressing.) But never forget, this is business: *quid pro quo.* You always have to measure the value of what you're getting against the value of what you're giving up.

CHAPTER 18

Odd and Appropriate

I'd like to close the book with one more example—and a rather unusual one—of adding water to a customer's glass. It's an odd but appropriate way to conclude what I hope is an odd but appropriate book.

A few years ago, a sales and marketing expert came up with what he considered a first-rate idea. With so many unhappy, lonely people in the world, he thought he could give them a little comfort and make money at the same time by offering them personalized, written advice on their problems. After all, Ann Landers and Dear Abby can't get to everybody.

Since so many people have problems that are similar, he figured he could train employees to write a quick paragraph or two of personalization—probably a lot less once he built up a database of problems and good solid advice—and fill up the rest of the letter with appropriate boilerplate. He placed a trial ad in a leading tabloid. The problems came pouring in.

He read four letters. And immediately killed the project.

"I realized I was dealing with living, breathing people," he says, "not a marketing opportunity. I realized the answers I'd provide would have an effect on their lives. They all had such heavy burdens compared to anything I'd ever gone through. Their problems went far beyond the scope of any boilerplate, beyond the scope of any quick, pat answer. I was completely unqualified to tamper in their lives. I ended up returning their money, and absorbing the price of the ads."

But he did a little more than that. With each refund he sent along a personal, handwritten response. This is one of those letters:

Dear Lennie:

Thank you for writing. Sorry to hear of your situation. Sometimes we simply have to endure until we finally get the life we deserve. And you've endured. I'm returning your $9.95 because I want you to have the money. From your letter, it sounds like you need it more than I do, and I want the best for you. I also want *you* to want the best for you.

I know you feel small and alone, but you're not alone. You're a human being, which means that you're related to all of us—a relative—a part of us all. Biologically—in your genes—all your ancestors going back to the beginning of time are a part of you. They struggled and slaved so that you, their descendant, would someday walk this planet. It's taken billions of years to create the universe of possibilities that's within you.

If you undervalue yourself—if you sell yourself short—you're undervaluing all of us, and all of those who came before you.

But even beyond that, you are, as an individual human, a miraculous being, more alike than unlike the greatest men and women who ever lived. More alike than unlike Jesus and Einstein and Lincoln and Mozart and van Gogh—with many of their greatest qualities lying somewhere inside you. With thoughts and feelings and desires. And—most miraculous of all—the divinity within you that we call free will: the ability to control those feelings and desires, and therefore to control your own destiny, to actually control what you are today and what you will be tomorrow.

Your responsibility is to use that free will to make the most of that creation of your ancestors and our society, to be the crown of creation. And to make the most of every instant of the life that so many, including yourself, have participated in creating.

Always the best,
Barry Maher

FINAL TIP: You wouldn't settle for half empty. Never settle for half full. Fill the glass.